Moments in the Sun

For Zoe, who got a foul ball at her first game,
and Donna, who got hers at the altar,
and in memory of Dad and Mary—*Mark*

For Denise, Ethan and Shaina
the authors of my life;
and for Dad,
who taught me there are lessons in life
you can't learn from sports, but not many—*Mike*

MOMENTS IN THE SUN

Baseball's Briefly Famous

by MARK MCGUIRE
and
MICHAEL SEAN GORMLEY

McFarland & Company, Inc., Publishers
Jefferson, North Carolina, and London

Pictured on the front cover: Ron Necciai
(PHOTOGRAPH COURTESY OF RON NECCIAI)

British Library Cataloguing-in-Publication data are available

Library of Congress Cataloguing-in-Publication Data

McGuire, Mark, 1963–
    Moments in the sun : baseball's briefly famous / by Mark McGuire
and Michael Sean Gormley.
       p.   c.m.
    Includes index.
    ISBN 0-7864-0549-X (sewn softcover : 50# alk. paper) ∞
    1. Baseball players—United States—Biography. I. Gormley,
Michael Sean, 1960– . II. Title.
GV865.A1M376   1999
796.357'092—dc21
   [B]   99-11100
                                               CIP

Manufactured in the United States of America

McFarland & Company, Inc., Publishers
  Box 611, Jefferson, North Carolina 28640

ACKNOWLEDGMENTS

We have many people to thank for making this book possible. Special appreciation goes out to subjects of this book who helped us: Joe Bauman, Odell Barbary, Bert Shepard, Mike Benjamin, Ron Necciai, Carl Scheib, Ron Blomberg, Brian Doyle, Dave Bresnahan, and Al Weis.

We would also like to thank Edward Waitkus, Jr., Lou Chapman, Jack Lang, Bruce Kimm, Joe Pignatano, Peter Flynn, Dean Chance, Veda Ponikvar, W. P. Kinsella, Bill Moose, Bob McDonald, William Loushine, Jay Feldman, Shirley Povich, Neal Bandlow, Ian Shearn, Mike Fitzpatrick, Stanley Cohen, Bob Bluthardt, Jay Black, Leslie Juchna, Marc Okkonen, Terry Pluto, and Frank Sullivan.

To everyone at the Society for American Baseball Research, especially Richard Puff, and for the proofreading of coworkers Paul Gibbons and Marc Bona, thanks.

The National Baseball Hall of Fame and Museum was cooperative with every request, and we would particularly like to cite Scot Mondore, Patty Gracey, Greg Harris, Jeff Idelson, and Pat Kelly. We haven't forgotten the others at the Hall: You were all great. Thanks.

TABLE OF CONTENTS

SPOTLIGHT ON THE SERIES

AROUND THE HORN

Introduction

There are many people in baseball whose contributions have been buried by the parade of successors. They were not the Ruths or Mayses or Aarons or DiMaggios, giants of the game whose careers are as spectacular as any individual play they made. Regardless, many of these lesser players, umpires, and others have small yet intrinsic roles in the storyline of baseball's history. They are not individual chapters in the sport but are still stirring passages.

They are the game's footnotes.

Some were well known in their day, featured on the sports pages—and sometimes the front pages. They accomplished feats and misdeeds so notable in this unpredictable game that they deserve to be remembered, instead of being relegated to the "Oh, yeah" bin (as in, "Oh, yeah, wasn't he the guy…"). This book is about just some of them.

Some you may never have heard of, like the Appalachian League pitcher who threw a no-hitter while striking out 27 in 1952. Or the original strikebreakers, the team that took the field May 18, 1912, for the Detroit Tigers in place of the wildcatting regulars. Then there was the utility infielder who hit .161 for his brief career but led his team to a title as a rookie by hitting .438 in the World Series. Another helped his team win a World Series and secured his place in history solely because he liked a good shine on his shoes.

Many baseball fans today would be pressed to recall the name Bert Shepard. But for a nation in the midst of the Second World War, he was morale personified. Shepard, a veteran fighter pilot with 34 missions to his credit, pitched for the Washington Senators in a 1945 game despite having lost a leg after being shot down over Germany the year before. Because of its novelty and the inspiration it brought to wounded veterans, the story was recounted extensively in newspapers and sports magazines.

Shepard pitched that one game, then faded away as the game's stars returned home from war in 1946, but the Californian said he was not sad to see his moment go by. "That never bothers you," he said almost a half-century later. "That's part of the story, part of life."

Professional baseball players are inherently famous. Ordinary folks seek their scribbled signatures on pieces of paper, cheer (or boo) the announcement of their names, and covet their cardboard likenesses. Still, the vast

1

majority of ballplayers go through their careers in historical anonymity. Seasons, games, innings, plays, and pitches are compressed into composites. They are vaguely recalled but not truly remembered; their childhood dreams were first realized, then boiled down into trivia.

Their dreams start like they do for all baseball fans—in a backyard, an open field, or a city street where three manholes constituted a four-bagger. A baseball, jackrabbit, tennis ball, or Spaldeen, it didn't matter; any one of them could make you a Koufax or Gibson or Maddux. A broomstick stolen from Ma's closet and sawed off just right made a bat so perfect it was worth the grief when she found the disembodied bristles. Day after day the pennant or World Series was won or lost in games so perfect only the mind could construct them. *Newsday* columnist Stan Isaacs got it right: "The greatest baseball arena is in our heads."

Eventually, these dreams fade with reality. For most of us, any glory we hope to achieve on a diamond will be in some softball beer league. Yet while opportunity passes, fantasy remains.

"There's sort of a universal wish among us all to be the great American sports hero," George Plimpton remarked to a Dallas newspaper. "[James] Thurber once said that 95 percent of the male population puts themselves to sleep striking out the lineup of the New York Yankees. It's the great daydream, an idea that you never quite give up. Always, somewhere in the back of your mind, you believe Casey Stengel will give you a call."

Even for many who make it as far as the minors, stardom in the majors is as unattainable a dream as the one most of us had playing back in the neighborhood. For all the millions who have ever felt raised stitching in their hand, for the hundreds of thousands who were good enough to be deemed prospects, only 14,000 ever made the majors over the past 110-plus years. For those who make it that far, the chance of superstardom is slim: Only about 1 of every 85 players to make the majors makes the Hall of Fame.

More often, fame is fleeting. Bernie Carbo hit a dramatic three-run home run in the eighth inning to tie Game Six of the 1975 World Series, but his feat was practically buried within an hour or so by an even more momentous homer by Red Sox teammate Carlton Fisk. Though the game is spread over nine months from spring training to the Fall Classic, baseball can turn quickly on an individual. Roger Peckinpaugh, the fine Washington Senators shortstop, was the American League MVP in 1925, but a few weeks after the regular season all glory was gone and his name was cursed in Washington after he committed eight errors in that season's World Series.

Heroes and goats and everyday players of the day are sometimes immortalized but are more often lost in the passing of their generation. Take a man named Smith. He was a pitcher. He is dead. And he's forgotten.

Smith started one game for Baltimore of the Union League in 1884, going nine innings while giving up one earned run on fifteen hits. He walked three, struck out five, went one for four at the plate, and had one putout and seven assists in flawless play in the field.

That day was the man's career.

What happened to Smith? Was he just not good enough? Too old? Needed back on the farm? C'mon, a righty or a lefty?

There is nothing more to the story, other than questions. The box score line from one game is the sole artifact *The Baseball Encyclopedia* could resurrect from this player's short career. No age. No hometown. Time has even erased the man's first name. Smith is just another of baseball's long line of forgotten players.

Some players remain in the forefront of sports legend decades after their feats or misdeeds. For years in New York, making a mistake could be called "pulling a Merkle," in dishonor of Fred Merkle, whose failure to touch second base cost the New York Giants the National League pennant in 1908. Although Merkle was a fine major league player for 14 years and was absolved of any guilt by teammates, "Merkle's Boner" was added to the lexicon of baseball, and of America.

There was considerable debate between the authors over whether to include Don Larsen in this book. His World Series perfect game in 1956 is one of the all-time benchmarks in sport, much more than a footnote. In the end we decided that Larsen, a pitcher who once went 3-21 in a season and had a career losing record, was the perfect example of the probability of the improbable in baseball. He's in here.

Many of the subjects were interviewed for this book. Others involved in or witness to the events were also contacted. Newspapers of the day, periodicals, films, broadcasts, and books were also utilized. During research it was discovered that in some cases, especially those involving old-time players, discrepancies arose between source materials regarding statistics or other information. In most cases, the authors chose to go with the most consistent figures cited. *The Baseball Encyclopedia* was used to break deadlocks. In other words: Stat freaks, we tried. But this is a book about more than numbers.

Bo Belinsky sums up fame grasped and lost. Like Sandy Koufax, he was a Los Angeles lefty brimming with potential. On May 5, 1962, he pitched a no-hitter for the Angels (then sharing L.A. with the Dodgers) against the powerful Baltimore Orioles. He seemed to be only warming up.

Belinsky threw hard but partied harder. Strikingly handsome, Belinsky was the hottest party guest or date, hanging out with Ann-Margret, Tina Louise, and other movie stars on the Hollywood scene. Eventually his nights on the town affected his days on the mound. Bo finished his career with a monumentally disappointing 28-51 record. But he offered no apologies for squandering his potential.

"I don't feel sorry for myself," he said. "I knew sooner or later I had to pay the piper. You can't beat the piper, babe; I never thought I could.

"But I'll tell you who I do feel sorry for—all those guys who never heard the music."

These are for the guys who did hear the music, if only for one dance.

Mark McGuire
Michael Sean Gormley

The Rookies

BERT SHEPARD

Undersecretary of War Robert Patterson called for a contingent of released POWs under care at Walter Reed Hospital in early 1945 to meet him at his Washington, D.C., office. He wanted to know how American prisoners were being treated by the Germans—stories that could be fed into the wartime propaganda machine.

At one point in the meeting, a question went around the room: What do you want to do after the war? A wounded Army Air Force pilot from Clinton, Indiana, surprised the cabinet member.

"I want to play baseball," Lt. Bert Shepard said.

Patterson chose not to patronize the pilot and told him flat out: "But you can't do that."

"Oh, yes I can," Shepard countered. "I did it before the war, and I'm going to do it after the war."

Maybe out of sympathy, maybe recognizing the tremendous symbol this man could be, Patterson placed a call to Clark Griffith, the owner of the Washington Senators. I have a soldier here: Would you give him a tryout at spring training? Griffith agreed.

That spring of 1945, Shepard packed and left for his first major league training camp. A mediocre minor league player, it's doubtful he would have made the majors if Undersecretary Patterson hadn't placed that call.

It's certain Lieutenant Shepard wouldn't have made the majors if he hadn't had his leg blown off.

"I would have been 25, 26 years old [at the end of the war]. I would have stayed in [the service] as a test pilot," he said years later. "If it hadn't been for me getting my leg shot off, I never would have made the majors. I never would have known Joe DiMaggio or Ted Williams, or have met Connie Mack and Ty Cobb." Or, as he said 46 years later: "I'm sure glad it happened to me instead of somebody else.... I was able to handle it."

Bert Shepard is an easy entry to pass over in *The Baseball Encyclopedia*. In fact, the tome and major league baseball have had his formal name incorrectly listed as Robert Earl "Bert" Shepard for years. (To this day Shepard doesn't know where the Robert Earl came from. He's just Bert. It fits.) His major league career consisted of one game, 5⅓ innings of mop-up relief work in a lopsided game in August 1945.

7

But Shepard's unparalleled comeback rallied the hopes of wounded World War II veterans everywhere. If there was any doubt in Shepard's determination and status of folk hero, it was erased the moment he walked assuredly in from the bullpen to face his first batter.

Then he struck him out.

Before the war, the Hoosier had talent. No control, but talent. The left-hander had a decent fastball and a lively curve. And, for a pitcher, he also could swing a bat. Still, he earned the tag of minor league journeyman. From 1939 to 1941, he bounced among six teams with an overall pitching record of 6-8. Even though his career batting average was a meager .213, he had thoughts of switching to first base or the outfield.

Then came World War II. Although President Franklin Roosevelt, in his famous 1942 "Green Light Letter," determined "it would be best for the country to keep baseball going," ballplayers were susceptible to the draft. Many, like Bob Feller and Hank Greenberg, enlisted. In all, about 500 major leaguers would enter service by the end of the war, as well as 3,500 to 4,000 minor leaguers. On May 2, 1942, Shepard became one of the thousands, enlisting in the Army Air Force. Soon he would fly P-38 fighter planes for the 8th Air Force out of England.

Lieutenant Shepard was in the 55th Fighter Group. A little more than two years after signing up he was a veteran of 33 missions, not to mention the

Bert Shepard ready for a World War II mission (courtesy of Bert Shepard).

manager and star pitcher of the air wing's baseball team. May 21, 1944, was one of the best of days for the 55th. It was Opening Day.

But first for Shepard was his 34th mission. No problem; the game was at 2 P.M. Hop in the plane, fly over the North Sea, drop a little ordnance on Berlin, and be back in time for batting practice. Shepard, who had flown in the first daytime bombing raid over Berlin 17 days before, reached his target safely and was heading home flying low at 300 mph through flak-filled skies.

Shepard was about 70 miles outside Berlin, over the town of Ludwigslust, when the first round pierced the plane. He looked down at his leg, or what was left of it. Another round hit, catching him in the chin. That second blast was too much: he passed out and fell forward with such force that he crushed his skull on the gunsight, a wound that would require a two-inch piece of metal over his right eye. He crashed into the countryside.

Shepard was going to miss this Opening Day. He still doesn't know who won the game.

A mob of German farmers armed with pitchforks and hoes descended upon the crash site, determined to exact revenge on the wounded pilot. Just then, a Luftwaffe doctor arrived on the scene. He pulled his Luger, dispersed the crowd, and got Shepard medical attention. The man who saved Lieutenant Shepard's life would be a mystery.

German doctors did an admirable job in the operating room but had to amputate his right leg just below the knee. (Shepard maintains he got better medical care as a prisoner than he did later in the States.) While they knew his wounds would heal, these doctors were concerned how the pilot would react when he awoke and discovered his leg gone. They did not know Shepard was a ballplayer. They did not know Shepard was a driven man. And they did not know that Shepard would soon plan his comeback.

Sixteen hours after the crash, Shepard finally came to. He looked at where his leg used to be, then at the enemy doctors.

Then he smiled.

"Thank you for saving my life," he said.

The pilot was sent to Stalag IX-C in Meiningen, Germany. Rather than wait idly for his release and return to the States, Shepard began his rehabilitation. Another prisoner, a Canadian named Dan Errey, fashioned a crude but serviceable artificial leg. Using a cricket ball, Shepard started throwing again, beginning his comeback not on a ballfield, but behind barbed wire.

But there is more to being a pitcher than pitching. Shepard employed other prisoners to help him learn how to field bunts on an artificial leg. He was mindful of Monty Stratton, the Chicago White Sox pitcher in the 1930s who lost his leg in a hunting accident. Stratton still could pitch and might have climbed back to the majors had he figured out a way to come off the mound and field bunts. He never did, and he never made it. A "B" movie on his life remains more memorable than his career.

A month after being released from the POW camp in a prisoner exchange in early 1945, Shepard was prepared to sign with the Senators. But before joining Washington, Shepard worked out in Atlantic City, New Jersey, with the New York Yankees before a crowd of 3,000, including some disabled vets. Griffith was furious, accusing the Bronx Bombers of kidnapping the rookie.

The irony has Shepard giggling 50 years later: two clubs fighting over a 6-8 career minor leaguer with one leg.

Shepard went on to report to the Senators in Maryland. Griffith had his man, touting him as an all–American hero.

"This boy is a symbol of the courage of American youths," Griffith said of the 25-year-old. "The same spirit that carried him into combat with our enemies is with him in baseball. He believes in himself, and we believe in him."

News of Shepard's story spread quickly. Walter Haight wrote in the *Sporting News* in March 1945 that it was "doubtful if any athlete in sports history has become so famous in such a short time as has Lieutenant Shepard." The pitching pilot's saga was drawing reporters from around the country to the Senators' spring training (which was being held in Maryland that year instead of Florida because of wartime restrictions on unnecessary travel). Suddenly, Shepard had a taste of the oppressive glare of superstardom without having to be a superstar first. One of the things that made Shepard so well liked among his new peers was that the attention did not change his down-to-earth persona.

"Being in combat, being in a prison camp, being lucky to be alive, had a settling effect," he said. "I was just so happy to be alive after being unconscious and that terrible crash that nothing bothered me."

Newsreel cameramen set up their tripods to record his every step. They filmed him batting, pitching, and warming up. Someone may have thought of Stratton.

"What about bunts?" a newsman yelled out. "Can you field bunts?"

"I can field a bunt," Shepard said. "Let me know when you're ready."

Cameras were repositioned, then began to whir. Shepard reared back and pitched to Al Evans, who laid a bunt down the third base line. Shepard bounded off the mound, picked up the ball, and fired to Joe Kuhel at first base. The prison camp practice had paid off.

"Atta boy, Shep," Washington manager Ossie Bluege yelled, shaking his head along with several players.

Shepard joined Washington first as a coach, with the promise that he would have a chance to play. On April 1, against a Naval Training Base team, Shepard got called into the game in the eighth inning. The 8,000 servicemen on hand applauded wildly.

The first batter bunted. Just as he had done for cameramen a few weeks before, Shepard dashed off the mound, fielded the ball, and threw the runner out. He also retired the other two batters he faced.

Bert Shepard (courtesy of Bert Shepard).

When the regular season got under way, Shepard's pitching was relegated to batting practice. The pilot was itching to play but instead was riding the bench. May passed into June and July. On July 10, the American League Senators played the National League Brooklyn Dodgers in a war-fund exhibition game. Appropriately, Shepard made his debut.

Shepard pitched four innings, giving up two runs on five singles. Shepard was credited with the win in the 4–3 victory. "The kid looked good against the Dodgers, didn't he?" Bluege said. "Looks like I'll have to put him on the active roster."

But this was just an exhibition, and Shepard had yet to pitch in an actual game. Still he pitched batting practice. One day in Boston, Shepard's artificial leg kept coming loose. Eventually, he grew frustrated with the malfunctioning limb.

"Finally I turn around and kick my leg. My foot and shoe go end over end into center field," Shepard recalled. "The fans are going, 'What the hell is that guy's foot doing in center field—and why are the players laughing?' Ted Williams said it was the funniest thing he ever saw."

On August 4, the Senators again were playing the Boston Red Sox and getting crushed at home in the second game of a doubleheader. The Sox had scored 12 runs in the fourth to take a 14–1 lead and loaded the bases again with two outs. Bluege walked to the mound slowly. Now was as good a time as any. He raised his left arm to the bullpen. The crowd of 13,005 came to its feet as Shepard ambled in to face George Metkovich.

Shepard struck him out. He then breezed through the rest of the game, giving up one run on three hits and striking out two in the last 5⅓ innings. His earned run average: 1.69.

The outing amounted to Shepard's major league career. The following season, 1946, he asked to be optioned to Chattanooga so he could pitch more often and ended up 2-2 for the season. In the off-season of 1945 and 1946, he barnstormed with a group of American League all-stars.

After the 1946 season, he checked into Walter Reed Hospital for a minor adjustment on his leg. Things went wrong, and Shepard would spend the next two years in and out of hospitals. The constant use of crutches made his arm muscles tighten, and he was through as a pitcher.

An antithesis to Shepard's tale is that of Lou Brissie: being a baseball pitcher saved his leg. Brissie was wounded at the Battle of the Bulge in 1944, and doctors in Italy were prepared to amputate his leg. "I'm a baseball player," he pleaded. "I need my leg." The corporal didn't have a bone left in his leg longer than four inches, but a sympathetic surgeon, Dr. Wilbur Brubaker, opted for a delicate surgery that saved the leg. Brissie went on to a respectable 7-year, 44-win career in the majors.

Shepard was done as a major leaguer but not as an athlete. While living in New Jersey in the 1950s, Shepard took up golf. In 1968 and again in 1971, he won the National Amputee golf title. "Oh, what an athlete," said former Yankee shortstop Phil Rizzuto, Shepard's friend and a golfing companion. "He went along like nothing was wrong with him." Frustration with his inability to pivot properly while playing prompted Shepard, a safety engineer, to develop a special prosthesis in 1979. As of 1995 he was still playing golf daily—walking, of course.

His score? "I'm shooting in the low 80s—if money is on the line."

As Shepard's fame waned, something continued to gnaw at him: the doctor who saved his life in Germany. Who was he? How could he find out? Shepard was at a loss.

Then fate once again stepped in. An English businessman, Jamie Brundell, was hunting in Hungary with a 75-year-old doctor from Pandorf, Austria, when discussion turned to World War II. The doctor, Landislaus Loidl, said he once had saved an American pilot's life and wondered what happened to him. With just a name and a date, Brundell began a transatlantic search. In November 1992, the Englishman found Shepard. The doctor and pilot began exchanging letters and had a tearful reunion in Europe in spring 1993.

Shepard's name does not appear in the record books among career leaders in any category, but he was a symbol for America near the end of the war, especially for returning wounded veterans. Maybe more than that one big league game, his final season in organized baseball sums up the man.

In 1949 he was the first baseman and manager of the Class B team in Waterbury, Connecticut. He hit four home runs.

He also stole five bases.

"They thought I couldn't run," he said. "I had an advantage."

Bo Belinsky

He was the man every guy wanted to be back in the days before political correctness. He was a stud who could cut down hitters, pick up "broads," and knock down drinks with anyone, anytime. He was good-looking, witty, irreverent, young, and talented in everything but making curfew.

Bo Belinsky had it all in 1962. Movie star girlfriends. A nasty fastball. All the potential a left-hander could dream of. At 25, he was baseball's king of swing, the game's one-man equivalent of Sinatra's Rat Pack. He owned Los Angeles.

And for one night, he was the best in the game. His talent had finally caught up to his lifestyle. Then the Los Angeles Angel, who was anything but, threw it all away. No one was surprised.

"The guy has a chance of a lifetime," minor league teammate Jim Johnson said in Belinsky's rookie year. "I remember when I had to lend him a quarter so he'd have enough to buy a $2.95 steak, but now he's in a position to make it big and I'm worried to death he'll blow the chance. I mean, broads are okay two, three nights a week—even five nights a week. But seven out of seven?"

Belinsky was always blessed with potential, something that made managers keep coming back to him after all the drunken nights, the missed bedchecks, the apparent indifference to the game.

"The reason we picked him up is because you want to be there when that arm comes back," said Philadelphia manager Gene Mauch, whose Phillies picked up Belinsky in 1965. "He could pitch. He just wouldn't work. I wish I had a thousand guys with his arm and none with his head."

One would think that blowing all that promise on nights of wine and women would haunt a man after the memories of the parties and dates blurred. Not Belinsky.

"It's been a ball," he said shortly after his career ended. "There isn't one regret, not one. I've been there. I've done everything. I've heard the buglers. I've lived enough for two lives.

"Life is to be lived, man. Some guys play baseball and make a few bucks more than me. What do they have when they quit? A big mortgage, a wife, a couple of screaming kids and an ulcer. Me? I got memories."

But not a career. At least not the one he should have had.

14

"My career?" Belinsky told *Sports Illustrated* in 1972, ten years after he burst onto the scene. "It was no big thing."

But it opened doors, opened doors to places that a pool hustler from Trenton never could have entered. Bo Belinsky was a 28-51 pitcher for his eight-year major league stint. It wasn't much of a career, but it was one hell of a party.

Belinsky was off to a 3-0 start his rookie year when he took the mound on May 5, 1962, against the Baltimore Orioles, the team that owned his rights before he was purchased out of the minors by lefty-starved Los Angeles. While Belinsky's minor-league career was checkered, the Angels were impressed with his 13-5 record in the Venezuelan League after the 1961 season.

Belinsky signed with Pittsburgh in 1956 out of semipro ball for a salary that still has him shaking his head in disgust: $185 a month. After bouncing around the minors for six years, Belinsky was able come up with a third pitch, a screwball, down in South America. It made the difference.

Belinsky's reputation arrived in Los Angeles before he did. A flake, he was labeled. A character, he countered. He had already made headlines for holding out for more than a week; he ended up signing for the minimum $6,000 (Belinsky remembers it as $7,500).

But that May night would provide Belinsky with a public relations hook that would last a lifetime: he threw a no-hitter, one hinting at a promise of greatness eventually unkept.

Belinsky's no-hitter came at Chavez Ravine, the home field the Los Angeles Angels shared with the Dodgers. Belinsky struck out nine (then a team record, long before a guy named Nolan Ryan came along), walked four, and hit two. Another Oriole reached on an error in the fourth.

Bo could be just as wild on the mound as he was on the town: he led the league in 1962 with 122 walks. As would mark his career, Belinsky went deep into counts against the Orioles. But on this night he would battle back.

"What I like best about the way Bo did it was his ability to get 'em out with his good hard stuff when he was behind," said Bob Rodgers, his catcher. "The count often was 3-and-1 and sometimes 2-and-0. He kept his screwball down and this set the batters up for his fastball, which really comes in there blazing."

The fourth was Belinsky's most dangerous inning. The error came on a routine grounder to Felix Torres, which loaded the bases for the O's with one out. Belinsky had walked Jim Gentile and Jackie Brandt. Belinsky worked out of the jam by striking out Dave Nicholson and getting Ron Hansen to fly out to center.

In the game there was one fielder's choice and one foul flyout. Nine outs were made in the infield, leaving four outfield putouts. Belinsky retired the last ten men he faced, needing only ten pitches to dispatch the last three.

Bo Belinsky (courtesy of Baseball Hall of Fame Library, Cooperstown, New York).

The ninth started with Brandt striking out. Gus Triandos then grounded to short, leaving Nicholson. The right fielder skied a pop-up in foul ground by third base. Torres, a suspect fielder who wore a batting helmet in the field as a matter of self-preservation for such a play, circled and circled and circled, then fell to his knees. But he made the play, and Belinsky had his no-hitter.

Belinsky became the 107th major leaguer to throw a no-no. He became the first rookie to throw a no-hitter since Bobo Holloman, another flash-in-the-pan, in 1953.

Belinsky took in all the attention with a mixture of bemusement, self-promotion, and nonchalance. "If I had known I was gonna pitch a no-hitter today, I would have gotten a hair cut," he said. Another gem: "My only regret is that I can't sit in the stands and watch myself pitch."

Belinsky also asked the question uttered by many who had reached the pinnacle of their profession: "I wonder what happens next?"

Belinsky may have been born in the Bronx and raised in Trenton, but he was meant to become a star in Los Angeles. "Milwaukee, St. Louis or Cincinnati—it would have been a waste of time to pitch a no-hitter there," he said. He then scoffs in disgust: "You might as well go out and win 20 games." That would be, gasp, a job.

Baseball was fine—it was a rush, although not as much as leaning over the nine ball with a couple hundred bucks riding on the shot. But the real excitement came from "the broads." They were everywhere, and they all wanted to meet the 6-foot-2, 191-pound operator.

True: The Man's Magazine ran a 1962 story with a headline that encapsulated the man: "Bo Belinsky's Dilemma: Baseball or Dames?" It was more like baseball *for* dames.

"We got into New York for the first time this season and Bo's never played there in his life," slugging outfielder Leon Wagner said in 1962. "But there's a whole string of broads waiting for him."

The preoccupation was mutual. "He never says a word while he's pitching," roommate Ed Sadowski said. "But off the field what he likes to talk about more than baseball is 'swinging women.'"

Famed columnist Walter Winchell took Belinsky under his social wing. Belinsky was also often out on the prowl with fellow Angel pitcher Dean Chance, who won the Cy Young Award in 1964 by going 20-9 with a 1.65 ERA. Every night, every city, there was another club to hit, another woman to meet.

His date book looked like a talent agency's roster: Mamie Van Doren, to whom he had been engaged; Connie Stevens; Tina Louise; Ann-Margret. The first to wed him was Jo Collins, a *Playboy* Playmate he met in Hawaii. He would marry twice more; all three marriages ended in divorce.

After a 5-0 start in 1962, Belinsky faded down the stretch, finishing with a 9-10 record for 1962. Belinsky said he was tired: "I had pitched 180 innings of winter ball." Plus, there were a lot of "distractions." Here's one:

On June 13, 1962, Belinsky made his way into the Beverly Hills police blotter. He and Chance found themselves with two girls in Belinsky's red Cadillac convertible at 5 A.M. Belinsky, as he tells it, wanted his girl to leave. She cut herself on the door on the way out, the cops were called (no charges were filed), and Belinsky and the other pitcher found themselves with a $250 fine from the team for blowing curfew.

"When we got caught out at five o'clock in the morning with those crazy broads, Bo took all the blame," Chance said years later. "He said, 'The kid here had nothing to do with it.' That's what I call a friend."

The '63 season was a washout: 13 games, 2 wins, 9 loses, 5.75 ERA. Belinsky was sent down to the minors in an effort to help him relocate his form.

Belinsky's career with the Angels ended in the summer of 1964, after he and *Los Angeles Times* baseball writer Braven Dyer scuffled in Belinsky's Washington, D.C., hotel room. Belinsky was suspended, then shipped to the minors. At the time he had a solid year going: 9-8, 2.68 ERA.

After the 1964 season, Belinsky was shipped to the National League and the Philadelphia Phillies. He pitched with an initially undiagnosed cracked rib and stumbled to a 4-9 record. He was gone after an 0-2 start in 1966, but not before coining one of the best quotes in baseball history, an assessment of Philadelphia fans long famous for ragging the home team: "They would even boo a funeral." An extended version of the quote appeared in 1972: "Philadelphia fans would boo funerals, an Easter egg hunt, a parade of armless war vets, and the Liberty Bell."

Belinsky bounced around a few more years—Houston in 1967, Pittsburgh in 1969, Cincinnati in 1970, with a few stops in the minors along the way. His last failed shot came with St. Louis, which cut him in 1971.

"You could say I no longer heard the Tunes of Glory," he told *Sports Illustrated* a year later. "I never liked baseball that much—at first anyway. I only signed a contract to get out of Trenton. I was hustling pool and hanging around with bad people.

"I quit baseball a number of times over the years, but for one reason or another I always went back. There was no way I could quit. I had learned to love the game by then.

"That's funny, isn't it, Babe? Me, the guy everybody said didn't love the game enough. Ha! I ended up devoting 15 years of my life to baseball. Man, I loved it. I just didn't take it seriously. I mean, Babe, I don't take myself seriously, how could I be expected to take a game seriously? It's a little boys' game. To play it you've got to be a little boy at heart."

By then, Belinsky had an adult problem: he was spiraling deeper into alcohol and substance abuse.

He finally licked his demons in 1976, April 1. "I fooled them all," he said. Today he is the manager of quality control for a Saturn dealership in Nevada. He is single and not planning on wife number four.

EDDIE GAEDEL

Eddie Gaedel approached the plate, much to the delight of the 18,369 fans in Sportsman's Park in St. Louis, a number swelled by the latest promotion. Gaedel was new to the St. Louis Browns in mid–August 1951, and many fans already had noticed what appeared to be a typographical error in their program: "⅛ Gaedel."

Gaedel got into the second game of that August 19 doubleheader against the Detroit Tigers in the bottom of the first inning. "For the Browns, No. ⅛, Eddie Gaedel, batting for Saucier," public address announcer Bernie Ebert said. Out popped Gaedel from the dugout. Gaedel had also popped out between games.

From a cake.

Rookies do the darndest things.

The 26-year-old walked up to the batter's box tentatively, just like any ballplayer coming to bat for the first time in the majors. "Just a little scared," he said afterward. Before he could get dug in, homeplate umpire Ed Hurley called time, took off his mask, and summoned St. Louis manager Zack Taylor.

"Hey Zack, what do you think you're doing?" Hurley asked. "Is this some kind of joke?"

Ever the straight man, Taylor solemnly produced an official American League contract. It showed the Browns had signed Gaedel to play at the salary of $100 a game. Hurley nodded, Detroit manager Red Rolfe howled, and the game went on. Somewhere in the ballpark, Browns owner Bill Veeck smiled.

Gaedel went back to the plate and was ready to hit. He cut a startling figurine in the box: carrying a toy bat and wearing curled-toed elf shoes, Gaedel got into his stance, slightly crouched. As if someone 3-foot-7 and 65 pounds needed to compact his strike zone. By contract and by dress, Gaedel was indeed a Brownie.

Tiger catcher Bob Swift called time and walked to the mound to discuss the situation with pitcher Bob Cain. Gaedel in his stance had a strike zone of all of 1½ inches. They knew no pitcher could put three strikes in that pocket. They didn't know Gaedel had been threatened with summary execution if he even thought of swinging.

Gaedel tiptoed into position, tucking himself in the left-rear corner of the right-hander's batter's box. Gaedel's bat—17 inches, 23 ounces, something

19

like a toothpick for Babe Ruth—couldn't have reached the plate if he had thrown it. Making the scene more ridiculous was Swift getting on his knees before setting a target.

A lifetime 37-44 pitcher, Cain was a slender lefty who could have been remembered most for a double–one-hitter duel he won in 1952 over Bob Feller. Instead, he would be immortalized not for one great game, but for one inescapable walk.

Cain reared back and fired. Ball one. High.

The southpaw tried again. Ball two. The pitcher knew he was licked and started laughing. The next two pitches were half-hearted lobs feet out of the alleged strike zone. Gaedel dropped his bat and jogged to first before being replaced by pinch-runner Jim Delsing. Ever the professional, Gaedel slapped Delsing on the backside as he was replaced.

Veeck, the national pastime's P. T. Barnum, knew some of the lords and scribes of baseball would not look kindly on this one. In fact, Will Harridge, the stodgy American League president, had been trying frantically to get hold of Veeck—preferably by the neck—once he heard of the stunt unfolding. Veeck made sure the word couldn't get through until his Gaedel had his one at-bat.

Veeck was not just a grandstander, but also an astute baseball man, who through trades and acumen built the Cleveland Indian teams that won the A.L. pennant in 1948 and 1954, as well as the "Go-Go" White Sox that brought the American League flag to Chicago in 1959. History might have remembered Veeck most as a pioneer had his efforts gone through to buy and integrate the Philadelphia Phillies in 1944 (three years before the Brooklyn Dodger debut of Jackie Robinson). Instead, Veeck is recalled above all as a showman, an owner who remembered that baseball, glorified as it is in tradition and rite, is still a game. And games are supposed to be fun.

But sending a midget up to the plate? This was beyond even Veeck. As he wrote years later in his autobiography *Veeck—As in Wreck*, his legacy in baseball was sealed once Cain threw that first pitch.

"If I returned to baseball tomorrow, won ten straight pennants and left all the old attendance records moldering in the dust, I would still be remembered, in the end, as the man who sent a midget up to bat."

Bill Veeck the promoter outshines all before or since. While some giveaway nights at minor league parks today might seem hokey by cosmopolitan standards, there wasn't a promotion beneath Veeck. (On the day of Gaedel's game, fans received free cake, ice cream, and beer in honor of the 50th anniversary of the American League and a local radio sponsor, Falstaff Brewery.) Fans could expect to win anything as a door prize. One day it would be a ton of coal, the next a billy goat. Once a fan named Joe Early wrote a letter to the *Cleveland Press*, asking why players got special nights when they didn't need the money. So, of course, Veeck put on a "Good Old Joe Early

Night." The night watchman received a new car, clothes, a watch and appliances, as well as a circus car that backfired and an outhouse. "Anything you do to enhance sales is a promotion," the owner once said. Pure Veeckian.

At least four of Veeck's creations remain on display today. The first is the smiling Chief Wahoo, the Indians' logo. The second is the exploding scoreboard: At Comiskey Park, home-team homers were greeted with bombs and rockets. (Almost every ballpark built in the last 30 years has some sort of pyrotechnic display that would make a traditionalist along the lines of Kenesaw Mountain Landis cringe.) The third staple credited to him was being the first to put players' names on the back of uniforms. The fourth may be the most singular: He's responsible for the ivy that now blankets the brick outfield wall of Wrigley Field.

Veeck the showman held a mock funeral in 1949 at Municipal Stadium the day the Tribe was knocked out of the pennant race. A dirge was played, the flag from the previous year's pennant was lowered and placed into a coffin, and the coffin was eased into a horse-drawn hearse by the pallbearers—manager Lou Boudreau and his coaches. The mortician? Who else but Veeck, suitably dressed for the occasion. He even dabbed his eyes now and then with a handkerchief. Nice touch.

But Veeck, who used to snuff out cigarettes in the hollow of his artificial leg, outdid himself in 1951, the year he bought the St. Louis Browns in midseason. The Browns were and will forever remain one of the most pathetic franchises in sports history. They were pitiful on the field and shunned by heartland fans who sided with the successful co-tenants at Sportsman's Park, the Cardinals. The team's one American League pennant came in 1944, when every major league roster was decimated as a result of World War II. The Browns lost in the World Series that year—agonizingly enough to the Cardinals. In 1954 the Browns gave up and moved to Baltimore, where they became the Orioles and one of the most successful franchises of the past four decades.

The opening line of Veeck's book sums up his time in St. Louis:

"In 1951, in a moment of madness, I became the owner and operator of a collection of old rags and tags known to baseball historians as the St. Louis Browns."

But Veeck was not going to give up on the Browns easily. If he was going to go down, he was going down laughing, and so would the fans. For a change, the snickers wouldn't be directed only at their play on the field.

Negro League legend Satchel Paige was signed at the age of approximately 48 (even Satch wasn't exactly sure) to provide comic relief and actually some dependable pitching. Max Patkin, the Clown Prince of Baseball, was signed as a coach. In addition to baseball, Veeck was presenting high-wire acts, circuses—anything to draw fans and then divert attention from the Browns' play on the field. Sure, the team continued to lose. It was just that Veeck made it enjoyable.

One of his most inspired moments came in a game against the Philadelphia A's that was designated Grandstand Managers Day. The lineup was decided by a fan ballot printed in a local paper. Fans behind the St. Louis dugout (among them was recently retired Connie Mack) were given cards with a large Yes on one side and No on the other. Zack Taylor (who must have been blessed with either an inordinate amount of self-restraint or one hell of a sense of humor) sat on top of the dugout in a rocking chair and in civilian clothes—and slippers. A publicity man held up questions such as "Shall We Warm Up the Pitcher?" and votes were tallied and relayed to third-base coach Johnny Berardino. Of course, the Browns ended a four-game skid, winning 5–3.

These promotions were silly but necessary to keep the Browns near solvency. New ones were conjured daily. But Veeck's ultimate triumph actually stemmed from a conversation years before, when legendary New York Giants manager John McGraw, a friend of Veeck's father, came to dinner. McGraw told them about a hunchback batboy named Eddie Morrow, and how he fought the temptation to send him up to the plate once, just once, to work out a walk. Veeck, only a child at the time, filed the story away.

During the '51 season Veeck put out the word to theatrical agent Marty Caine in Chicago: "I want a midget who's athletic and game for anything." One morning that August, Eddie Gaedel arrived in St. Louis at Veeck's office.

"Eddie, how would you like to be a big-league ballplayer?" Veeck asked. "Eddie, you'll be the only midget in the history of the game. You'll be appearing before thousands of people. Your name will go into the record books for all time. You'll be famous, Eddie. You'll be immortal."

Veeck measured Gaedel's strike zone—1½ inches in a crouch—and offered him $100. Gaedel was not exactly a student of the game. "I know you're supposed to hit the white ball with the bat," he told Veeck. "And then you run somewhere." But a showman himself, Gaedel soon was demonstrating what he thought was a decent swing. Veeck would not entertain any Ruthian delusions the midget might have been having. No swinging. Gaedel was crestfallen.

James Thurber once wrote a short story called "You Can Look It Up." The tale is about a major league manager meeting a midget in a bar and taking him to St. Louis for a big series. The manager inserts the midget into the game in the top of ninth with his team losing, 1–0, but with the bases loaded. His orders are to just get a walk and get the tying run across. Instead, on a 3–0 count, the midget takes a mighty swing and hits a slow dribbler toward third. But the ball gets thrown away into the outfield, and all three runners dash home. Too bad the game ends with the midget still getting thrown out at first, 15 feet from the bag.

Veeck, who had read Thurber's story, wasn't going to let life imitate art. He laid down the law in his typically subtle fashion.

"Eddie, I'm going to be up on the roof with a high-powered rifle watching every move you make," Veeck told him. "If you so much as look as if you're going to swing, I'm going to shoot you dead."

Thus warned, Gaedel still couldn't pass up this opportunity to play. He agreed to the deal and returned to Chicago, with the promise to come back for the August 19 game, when the seventh-place Browns played the eighth-place Tigers. Secrecy was a premium. None of the players were told of the stunt beforehand, and Gaedel's contract wasn't mailed to league offices until the weekend of the game, to make sure no one could squawk until it was too late.

One problem: Where do you find a jersey for a 43-inch-tall major leaguer? The solution was found in the Browns clubhouse, where the 7-year-old son of club vice president Bill DeWitt kept his own uniform. It was commandeered and the legendary fraction was sewn on.

The twinbill drew the largest Browns crowd in five years (some accounts pegged the attendance at 20,299), thanks to the beer promotion. Between games of the doubleheader, several members of the Browns played in a makeshift band (Paige was on drums). A cake was rolled out to the mound, and the public address announcer told the crowd Taylor was getting a real Brownie as a present. (Many expected it to be a popular camera of the day that went by that name.) Out popped Gaedel, dressed for the part. Good joke, the fans thought. That Veeck, he'll try anything.

The sponsors were not amused. They were promised by Veeck he would do something that would get them national attention. This was it?

The mood of the beer people brightened considerably when Gaedel came out of the dugout to pinch-hit, swinging three toy bats. (The man he batted for, Frank Saucier, managed only 13 more career at-bats than Gaedel.) After Hurley waved him into the game, Veeck looked on as Gaedel refused to get into a full crouch as instructed, instead opting for, as Veeck remembered it, "a fair approximation of Joe DiMaggio's classic style." At the plate Gaedel looked like a major leaguer. A very, very small major leaguer. The crowd was rolling, while Veeck was upset. I should have brought that gun, he thought.

Veeck need not have worried: Gaedel could have been standing straight up on his tippy-toes and it was doubtful Cain could have thrown a strike. After four pitches and his triumphant trot to first, Gaedel patted Delsing's butt, shook hands with the first-base coach, and took his time getting back to the dugout as he waved to fans.

"It touched me when Eddie went to bat that day," Cain later said. "At the time, though, it was a complete shock and a surprise to me. I didn't throw extra hard. I was afraid of hitting him. I didn't want to throw one close and he wouldn't be able to get out of the way."

Lucky for Gaedel, Cain was a deeply religious man. There have been more than a few pitchers during the course of major league history who would have figured if the midget was going to get to first anyway, they might as well drill him between the shoulder blades.

The Browns, as was their wont, did not score that inning and dropped both games of the doubleheader, 5–2 and 6–2. Who cared? Everyone went home with a story to tell their grandkids. Everyone was happy.

Except Harridge. The A.L. president was livid, and not only voided Gaedel's contract, but wanted his at-bat stricken from the record. He gave the "detrimental to the game" argument that is trucked out by management types with a scant sense of humor. Veeck countered to Harridge he would then have to void the records of every player in the game. Besides, he argued, what rule is there against midgets? What about Phil Rizzuto? He's only 5-foot-6. Harridge backed off.

And today Gaedel is indeed immortalized in *The Baseball Encyclopedia*, right between Len Gabrielson and Gary Gaetti.

Edward Carl Gaedel, batted right, threw left.

Gaedel never got into another game, but he did bat in an exhibition game that September and miraculously struck out. "You're the worst I ever want to see," Gaedel told the umpire. But Veeck did have him on the field again. The last time was at Comiskey Park, when Gaedel and three other midgets, dressed as Martians, descended from the sky in a helicopter that landed behind second base. The aliens then "captured" the Sox's diminutive middle infield of Nellie Fox and Luis Aparicio, telling the crowd they were there to aid the double-play combo in their struggles against giant Earthlings.

Gaedel, who lived with his mother, made money off of promotional appearances stemming from his official four-pitch career. Between jobs Gaedel also liked to throw a few drinks back, and three weeks after his at-bat, he was arrested in Cincinnati for disorderly conduct. He tried to convince the cop he was a big league player.

One of Veeck's later midget stunts did not go over as well, at least with a Browns manager much more surly than Taylor. Legendary second baseman Rogers Hornsby signed on to manage the team in 1952. During his first spring training, a group of performing midgets came out on the field. Hornsby was furious, screaming at them to get off the field. One who apparently did not move fast enough was thrown over a railing. "We didn't have any midgets around after that," Hornsby wrote in his autobiography. Hornsby was soon gone, too; if there was one thing Veeck couldn't stand, it was a lack of humor.

On June 18, 1961, about a year after his Martian expedition and less than two weeks shy of his 36th birthday, Gaedel died in his hometown of Chicago of injuries suffered in a mugging. The thieves made off with $11. Only one person from the baseball community attended his funeral: Bob Cain, the pitcher whom he made laugh. Cain, a devout Catholic, said he felt obligated. "I'll never forget the little man who affected my life so much," he said.

"But I still wish I could have gotten one strike over to Gaedel," he later added.

The day after Gaedel died several newspapers ran his obituary on their front page. With one at-bat, Veeck had kept his promise: he had made Eddie Gaedel famous and immortal.

JOE CHARBONEAU

He drank beer through his nose, fought bare-fisted in boxcars as a teen, and did his own dental and nasal surgery with a pair of pliers. He was the subject of a punk rock song, the survivor of four stabbings—once with a pen—and used a razor to remove a tattoo after hearing major league clubs frowned on them.

More? He quit baseball in the minors, only to come back and lead his league in hitting the next two years. He was only the third player ever to hit a ball into the left-field third deck at Yankee Stadium—and the first to be sent down to the minors after winning Rookie of the Year.

For one season he was a kid having a blast, awed yet glib, the trappings of a classic character in the making. He was from California, but he was Cleveland. He was an average Joe, but more. Super.

Joe Charboneau brought his massive forearms and live bat to Municipal Stadium in 1980. He would not last, a one-season wonder, his departure hastened by a back injury. But his name is etched in Lake Erie lore. In the town of Bob Feller and Lou Boudreau and Andre Thornton and Albert Belle, a rookie flameout named Super Joe Charboneau still holds a city's imagination years later, one of the few bright spots during the team's darkest period.

"The Indians stunk. Ever since Rocky Colavito left and Willie Mays caught that basket catch, we were the team that was potentially being upgraded," said longtime Indians' backer Frank Sullivan, who organized a fan revolt in the wake of the 1994 labor stoppage. "The diehard baseball fans who were left in Cleveland gravitated to any good performance. Everybody thought this guy was great. He was a piece of good baseball we thought we could hang onto during a dreary period."

Good baseball eventually returned to Cleveland, but Cleveland still hung on to Joe Charboneau.

Charboneau wasn't even supposed to make the Indians in 1980. But after Thornton tore up his knee and left-field replacement Andres Mora didn't hit, Charboneau found himself in the lineup. Writers already knew he was good copy; they found out he was also a great ballplayer.

Using the bats of Cito Gaston, a veteran player cut and forgotten before coming back years later as manager of the Toronto Blue Jays, Charboneau opened the season in Anaheim against the California Angels by hitting a home run in his second at-bat.

After a season-opening 1-5 road trip, the Indians returned to Cleveland for the home opener. In the dark years of Municipal Stadium, more than 60,000 would turn out on Opening Day; about 45,000 would never be seen again until the following April. Opening Day 1980 was no exception, as almost 62,000 turned out on an unusually beautiful day for Cleveland, 65 degrees and sunny. They saw a ballgame, and a legend born.

Charboneau, who entered the game batting a paltry .143, was still roundly cheered as he was announced. Then he walked in his first at-bat, doubled in his second, and homered in his third, on his way to going 3-for-3. The Indian fans gave him a two-minute standing ovation, prompting him to make a curtain call from the dugout. The nameless, characterless, clueless Indians had a hero, maybe their first since, well, Rocky Colavito.

In his book on the Indians, *The Curse of Rocky Colavito: A Loving Look at a Thirty-Year Slump*, noted *Akron Beacon-Journal* sports columnist Terry Pluto devoted an entire chapter to Charboneau. It was Pluto, then a beat writer for the *Cleveland Plain Dealer*, who hung the moniker "Super Joe" on Charboneau in spring training, partly because it was lyrical, partly because he mistakenly thought the character in *Damned Yankees* went by that name (it was "Shoeless Joe" from Hannibal, Mo.).

Pluto admitted in his book that he was looking for good copy in the spring training of 1980. He found all he would need in Charboneau.

Joseph Charboneu was born June 17, 1955, in Belvedere, Illinois, the fifth of seven children. Shortly after the family moved to Santa Clara, California when Joe was young, the father left them. Charboneau and his siblings were raised by their mother, a hospital receptionist. The five brothers shared a bedroom; picnic tables and benches were the living room decor.

Charboneau was the only family member who did not hold a job in his youth, so he could concentrate on baseball. But teens needed pocket change, and Charboneau found his by fighting in illegal bare-knuckles, anything-goes boxing matches down by the railroad tracks. Instead of the ring, the venue was a boxcar.

"I'd fight only when I needed the dough," he said. "I figured it was better than stealing, which I never did." The winner got $25, the loser $15; both had to pay $5 to the promoter. Charboneau said he lost more than he won. He reckoned he broke his nose a half-dozen times.

When he wasn't being hit, Charboneau was hitting. A Philadelphia Phillies scout spotted Charboneau playing for Buchser High School. As is often the case, the scout was at the game to look at another player, Charboneau teammate Steve Bartkowski, who went on to quarterback the Atlanta Falcons. Charboneau was already showing long-ball potential, as weight-lifting was transforming his body into a well-cut figure: 6-foot-2 and a ripped 205 pounds by the time he reached the majors.

Charboneau went on to play at West Valley Junior College, where he hit only .240 as a freshman but displayed enough power for the Minnesota Twins to make him a low draft pick. The next year Charboneau led his league in home runs, and in June 1976 the Phillies drafted him in the second round. Playing in the Western Carolina Leage that year, he hit .298 in limited duty.

The next year Charboneau quit. He was hitting only .172, was not getting any playing time, and was denied his request to be demoted so he could play more. "I was married, not making any money and going nowhere," he told the *Plain Dealer Magazine* in 1980. "I went home."

Charboneau was shocked to find that an envelope from the Phillies that off-season contained not his release, but a contract.

While 1977 was a washout, 1978 was a rebirth. Charboneau, on loan by the Phillies to the Twins Visalia (California) Class A team, started the season 1-for-6 before exploding for eight hits in a doubleheader. He went on to win the league batting title that year with a .350 average.

In 1979, Charboneau kept right on hitting, but not for the Phillies chain. Concerned about his defense, arm, and attitude, Philadelphia had shipped him to Cleveland. Placed at Class AA Chattanooga, he hit a Southern League record .352.

Charboneau was expected to play Triple-A ball in 1980, but the Thornton injury put him into the lineup. While no one foresaw his instant impact, his penchant for the colorful and the bizarre was already on display.

The Indians traveled to Mexico City that spring to play in an exhibition game. There a man approached Charboneau.

"Where are you from?" asked the man, holding a pad and a pen. When Charboneau replied, "California," and reached out to give the man an autograph, he instead found himself stabbed. Only after teammates tackled the assailant did Charboneau realize he had been stabbed with a pen. Charboneau went to the hospital, the man to court. He was convicted and fined the equivalent of $2.27. Charboneau shrugged off the incident with a laugh, stating he had it worse back home by the railroad tracks.

"Heck, I was stabbed three times before with knives in fights. This was only with a ball-point. This guy really flicked his Bic."

Meanwhile, the stories from the minors surfaced, tales of bench-pressing 400-plus pounds and opening beers with his eye socket, fixing a broken nose with pliers, and suturing his own cut. Cleveland is rock 'n' roll, and Charboneau was a rock 'n' roller. The song "Go, Joe Charboneau" became a cult hit in the Cleveland area, and an anthem played before his at-bats.

Charboneau was not only a rocker, but a legitimate ballplayer. On a team that finished a respectable (for Cleveland) 79-81, Charboneau led the club in home runs and RBIs. He hit .289 with 23 home runs and 87 RBIs, splitting 131 games between outfield and designated hitter. The numbers are more impressive considering Charboneau pulled a groin muscle late in the season, restricting him to pinch-hitting in the final weeks.

"The guy is something else," Cleveland manager Dave Garcia said. "No matter how we've used him, he's come through."

Charboneau was a runaway Rookie of the Year winner over Toronto Blue Jay Damaso Garcia, who went on to a solid ll-year career in the majors. Meanwhile, what Charboneau didn't know was that by the time he received the award, his days as a regular player were already over.

In spring training 1981, he ruptured a disc sliding. He played in pain, but his noted power was gone. (Despite his strength, Charboneau never had a good throwing arm because of a high school injury.) He was sent down but was confident he would return and stalled on getting an apartment in Charleston. Eventually, he realized the end could be at hand.

"Well, maybe this is it," Charboneau said, as he cleaned out his Cleveland locker after being sent down. "I've had my year and a half in the big leagues. Maybe that's all I got coming."

That fall a disc in his back was removed, and the next year, down 20 pounds, he was back for spring training. But the back problems persisted, and the power that allowed him to rocket line drives to left was gone. He would undergo another back operation and one to repair tendons in his hand.

The back injury doomed Charboneau. In strike-shortened 1981 he hit only .210 with four homers and eighteen RBIs in 48 games. The following year he lasted only 22 games, hitting .214 with two home runs and nine RBIs.

Charboneau was released by the Indians in June 1983, after going 7-for-35 for Class AA Buffalo. He stayed in the area and worked as a bouncer (he also had a bit role in the Robert Redford movie *The Natural*), and he played in the Pirates chain before he was gone for good by 1985.

Some say the biggest problem with Charboneau's body was his head. Pluto, who coauthored a book on the player after his rookie year, said it was injuries and not attitude that did him in.

"His body fell right apart," Pluto said in an interview, dismissing the head-case theory. "That is why he flamed out as quickly as he did."

Charboneau's career stat lines look meager, just another also-ran who went up and out of the majors quickly and quietly. But as his soulmate Louis Sockalexis did almost three-quarters of a century before, Charboneau left his mark on Cleveland.

"He is sort of a local celebrity," Pluto said. "He is a very, very nice man. He is just a sincere, blue-collar guy, and maybe acted a lot like the guys in the plants and the mills if they suddenly became ballplayers."

After several years he returned to Cleveland. Today Charboneau still runs a baseball school and is active in an area youth center. He is still asked to make appearances. He is remembered.

"He was one of the bigger flash in the pans this town has ever seen. He was kind of a Cleveland guy. He was a good ol' guy," Sullivan said. "People still like him. Most average fans would know his name over the last 10 to 20 years more than any other ball player. He got a lot of play in a time that was terrible."

BOBO HOLLOMAN

Bobo Holloman shared the nickname of another pitcher from his era, Bobo Newsom. Unfortunately, he did not share Newsom's talent.

Bobo Newsom managed to win 200 games in the '30s, '40s and '50s but still finished his career under .500. Bobo Hollomon managed to last only one year in the majors, 1953, posting a 3-7 record with a 5.23 ERA for the sad-sack St. Louis Browns.

Holloman drove managers nuts by his constant pleadings for a chance to get on the mound, and by what he did once he got there.

"He could out-talk me, out-pester me and out-con me," Browns owner Bill Veeck, a con-man in the best of traditions, once wrote of his Bobo. "Unfortunately, he could not out-pitch me."

Brash, Bobo knew he would succeed if he was given just one more chance. Like the somewhat flamboyant and much more successful Newsom, Bobo Holloman was, well, a clown. Unlike Newsom, he wasn't much of a pitcher.

Except for one raw, rainy night.

Alva Lee "Bobo" Holloman had spent seven years in the minors before being called up as a 28-year-old rookie by the Browns. The Thomaston, Georgia native showed up for spring training fat and was marooned in the bullpen (long before relievers were viewed as stars). He begged manager Marty Marion for a chance to start even after getting rocked in his three relief appearances—10 hits, 3 walks, and 5 runs allowed in 5⅓ innings.

Teams had to cut rosters to 25 players by mid–May, and Bobo feared for his job, with good reason. He was back pounding on Marion's door.

"You just gotta give me a chance to start a ball game," Holloman pleaded. "All I ask is just one chance. I'm no good in relief. I can't help the club in relief and I can't help myself. Won't you give me a chance to start just once?"

"But Bo," Marion shot back, "do you happen to know what your earned run average is in the three games you relieved? I think it's around nine runs per game. Do you think that entitles you to start a game?"

Bobo then made an offer Marion couldn't refuse:

"If you let me start a game and then you have to relieve me, I won't annoy you anymore."

31

I won't annoy you anymore. Marion, opting for peace and quiet over sound baseball judgment, gave in and gave the ball to Bobo for a start May 6 against the Philadelphia Athletics. It was a damp and chilly night at Busch Stadium in St. Louis, keeping the usually sparse Browns crowd down to an anemic 2,473. Veeck, realizing only the true diehards and the criminally insane would come out on such a night, authorized an announcement stating fans were entitled to use their rain check stub for another game.

So the huddled masses—well, the huddled few—saw one of the most improbable no-hitters in baseball history for free.

Predictably, the A's rocked the rookie Holloman, hitting several screamers and long drives. And not only was Bobo wild, walking five in the game while striking out only three, but he allowed another hitter to reach base on his own error. All considered, it appeared it was going to be an especially cruel night in the purgatory that was the Browns.

Unpredictably, the Browns played as if Ozzie Smith was at every position. It seemed if a fielder wasn't making a spectacular diving play, he was catching a sizzler hit right at him. When Jim Dyck made a leaping catch against the left-field wall in the second off the bat of Gus Zernial, it was a tip-off that the baseball gods were going to have a little fun in St. Louis this night.

Six-foot-two and down to 207 pounds from a fat 230, the right-hander relied on his breaking stuff—a sinker, a curve, and a killer slider—to perplex the A's. As the game wore on, everyone grew more and more certain something special was going on.

"I knew I had a no-hitter from the fifth inning on, but that didn't faze me," Holloman, who died in 1987, said in an interview 22 years after the game. "When I came off the field after the sixth inning no one wanted to talk to me because they were afraid they might jinx me."

Bobo? Not talk? Don't be ridiculous.

"I don't care if you talk to me or not," Bobo said to his teammates in the dugout. "I know I have a no-hitter going and I'm going to get it whether you talk to me or not, so you might as well talk to me."

Not only was Bobo unconcerned about jinxes, he was also unperturbed by the fact the Browns were being shut out.

"It doesn't even matter if you don't get me any runs, because I'm going to drive in some," Bobo said.

And he did, finishing the game with three RBIs on a pair of singles. They were the only hits of his major league career.

The A's had several chances after Zernial's liner to left. In the fifth inning, Allie Clark hit a foul ball that just missed being a homer by a foot or two. In the sixth, A's catcher Joe Astroth hit a trickler down the third base line that hugged the line before just rolling foul. Still more chances would come in the last two innings.

Bobo Holloman (courtesy of Baseball Hall of Fame Library, Cooperstown, New York).

The Browns were comfortably ahead 6–0 going into the visiting eighth, with only the no-no in doubt. Astroth was up again and hit a shot up the middle. End of no-hitter — until rookie Billy Hunter stabbed the ball behind the second-base bag, spun, and fired to first for the out.

Holloman walked out for the ninth and, as he always did, bent down at the baseline and with his finger carved the initials "N" and "G" — for his wife Nan and son Gary — into the chalk line. Then Bobo, as he always did, got into trouble.

A walk. Then another walk. Two on, none out. Then a double-play ball. Then another walk. Runners on first and third, two out, and big first baseman Eddie Robinson at the plate.

Luck was running out for Hollomon, but he had a few specks left. On an 0–2 count Robinson ripped a screamer to right, but it was a foul ball. The next pitch was hit hard again, high and deep to right. Vic Wertz (whose greatest fame comes from Willie Mays' over-the-head catch of his long fly in the

1954 World Series) went back-back-back-back-back and made the catch for the third out.

It wasn't art, but Bobo Holloman became the first player this century to pitch a no-hitter in his first major league start, winning 6–0. It was also the only no-hitter pitched in 1953.

It was also Holloman's only complete game of his 10 major league starts.

Like so much of the bizarre in the long history of baseball, Bobo's story has a parallel. In 1892 a fellow named Charles Leander "Bumpus" Jones meandered into the Cincinnati clubhouse on the last day of the season. "I'm a pitcher from Xenia, Ohio," Jones said. Manager Charlie Comiskey shrugged: "So you're a pitcher—well go ahead and pitch."

On a damp, chilly day, Bumpus Jones threw a no-hitter in his first start, winning 7–1. He went on to have a meager two-year career with a record of 2-4, and was all but forgotten until Bobo came along.

History almost repeated itself on April 14, 1967, when Red Sox rookie Bill Rohr took the hill at Yankee Stadium in his first major league start. Rohr threw no-hit ball until two outs in the ninth, when Elston Howard (who would be traded to Boston later in the year) singled. It was a magical season for the BoSox, but not for Rohr: he went 2-3 that season, and was 1-0 for Cleveland in 1968 before disappearing from the bigs for good.

Whatever magic Bobo found in his pitching (and the Browns' fielding) was lost quickly, but not before two more near-classic games. In his next start, this time in Philadelphia, Holloman had a no-hitter into the third until a blister on his pitching hand ruptured and he had to leave the game. In his next start in Boston, Holloman again had a no-hitter going into the ninth, until Jimmy Piersall hit a blooper over second for the first Red Sox hit.

And that was all Bobo had to offer. Holloman returned to his pre–no-hitter form, and on July 24 found himself back in the bushes, pitching for Toronto in the International League. He finished the season there with a 5.07 ERA and never earned another shot at the bigs. After bouncing around the minors a few years, Bobo called it quits.

"I kind of regret that I never got to pitch in the majors after that year, but my arm just sort of wore out," Holloman said.

Of the 230-plus no-hitters pitched in the major leagues since 1882, Bobo's may have been the only one resulting from a manager wanting to shut a player up.

"So what happens? He makes such a pest of himself that to get him off my neck, I use him as a starter," Marion said after the game. "Then he makes a bum outta me by proving he was right and I was wrong all the time."

If not all the time, at least for one game.

BOB HAZLE

By the time Hurricane Audrey had finished terrorizing the Louisiana coast in June 1957, hundreds were dead and millions of dollars in property was damaged or destroyed.

There was another hurricane in 1957, across the country to the north, that was not lethal but destructive as hell to National League pitchers. This hurricane struck less than a month after its southern counterpart, unexpectedly and without warning, leaving dashed pennant hopes in its wake.

In Milwaukee, players recalling the devastating storm named the second one Hurricane Hazle. Hurricane Bob Hazle.

Bob Hazle was called up by the Milwaukee Braves late in the 1957 season, after outfielder Billy Bruton went down with a knee injury in a collision with shortstop Felix Mantilla. Hazle's main attribute in the eyes of Milwaukee's brass was that he was a left-handed hitter: the Braves initially considered calling up Hazle's Wichita teammate, Ray Shearer, who was ripping American Association pitching while hitting more than .330, but opted for a southpaw. (Shearer was called up later in the season, going 1-for-2 in what amounted to his two-game career.)

The idea was for Hazle to fill in and not do too much damage to the Braves' pennant chances. Instead, on a team already laden with stars like Hank Aaron, Eddie Mathews, Joe Adcock, Warren Spahn, and Lew Burdette, it was a player who was ready to quit the game that year who delivered the world title.

Hazle was a minor league outfielder with a bum knee and a bleak future, a 26-year-old with a lifetime .279 average in the bushes who was ready to limp away from the game. His major league experience to that point had been six games in 1955 for Cincinnati, where he hit .231.

He was considered a hot prospect at first by the Reds (then called the Redlegs, amid the era of anti-communist fervor), a stocky 5-foot-11½, 190-pounder who batted left, threw right, and had speed. "Packs good power and is gifted with good speed afoot," the Cincinnati scouting report said. But by 1957, a year after he had reaggravated an old knee injury by chasing a fly ball into a fence, Hazle's prospect tag had long since been removed.

"I thought I had had it," he said. "I decided that if I didn't make the majors in '57, I would call it quits and go sell insurance or something. When

35

I got to camp this spring and the knee still bothered me, I was ready to take the first bus back home."

Robert Sidney Hazle was born December 9, 1930, in Laurens, South Carolina, where he became a schoolboy legend. At Woodruff High School, Hazle earned 16 letters—four each in baseball, football, basketball, and tennis. He captained the football, basketball, and baseball teams his senior year, earning all-state honors in each.

Hazle attended Woodruff College in Spartansburg, South Carolina, while being named an all-star in 1949 with the Wattsville semipro team of the Central Carolina League. The next year he turned pro and hit .313 with 70 RBIs for Columbia of the Sally League, where he was also an all-star. He spent the 1951 campaign at Tulsa after being cut from the Cincinnati Reds and spent 1952 in the military.

Except for a brief call-up by the Reds in 1955, Hazle bounced around the minors the next four and a half years. Just before the 1956 season, Hazle was traded along with pitcher Corky Valentine to the Braves for first baseman George Crowe. Hazle was having a solid 1956 season at Wichita (13 homers and .285 average) when he got hurt. With Hazle hurt and Valentine never making the parent club, Braves fans grumbled when Crowe became a solid starter for the Red in 1957; he would end up with 31 home runs and 92 RBIs for the season.

Meanwhile, Hazle struggled through much of the 1957 campaign at Wichita and was hitting as low as .230 as of June 26. He expected the manager to call him into the office any day, announcing he was being shipped down to minor league oblivion. But then his knee got stronger and so did his swing. Over the next month, Hazle hit .364, raising his average to .279 for the year. In late July, he got the call to go to Milwaukee.

Lou Chapman was a sportswriter for the *Milwaukee Sentinel* from 1940 to 1980 and covered the Braves from the time they hit town from Boston in 1953 until 1966, when the team departed for Atlanta. He said Hazle's nickname, applied by teammates cognizant of the killer storm in Louisiana and the 1954 Hurricane Hazel that hit Bob's native South Carolina, was a natural.

"That was easy—he was like a hurricane when he came up," Chapman said almost 40 years later. "They called him a hurricane, and he was hitting like mad. They couldn't get Hazle out. He was hitting .500."

That's right, .500. In his first 15 games Hazle went hitless only twice. He had a four-hit game, 5 three-hit games and 4 two-hit games. "Don't wake me up," Hazle said amid the splurge, "I'm still dreaming."

In game one of a key three-game series against the Cardinals August 9–11, Hazle hit his first major league home run, to go along with three singles and two RBIs. He followed that with three hits and three RBIs in game two. He was 7-for-12 in the series and 7-for-10 in the next three games, against the Reds.

After that series, Hazle was hitting .545 for the season. Two weeks later he was still hitting .507, going 34-for-67.

"I'll suppose he'll cool off," Braves second baseman Red Schoendienst said during the pennant drive, "but right now this kid is Musial, Mantle and Williams all wrapped in one."

Milwaukee, a baseball-mad city to start with, immediately embraced Hazle as an unexpected savior. Every baseball fan and writer had the same question: how the hell was he doing it? Even Hazle didn't have an answer.

"I'm not doin' anything different than I did before," he said that season. "I'm just up there swingin', that's all."

Adding to the mythical quality of the player was his reticence to seek the limelight. Despite his sudden fame, Hazle remained a reserved Southern boy.

"He was a mysterious character," Chapman said. "He disappeared and didn't come back until the next day. He was like the guy in *Damned Yankees*. He sort of seemed to fit into the woodwork. He was pretty much of a loner."

Hazle cooled off in the final days of the race, which was more of a stroll as Fred Haney's Braves beat the Cardinals by eight games. Still, for anyone, let alone a minor-league retread, his numbers were staggering: 41 games, 12 doubles, 7 home runs, and 27 RBIs while scoring 26 runs—many the result of late-inning heroics. Batting average: .403. While it's doubtful that if Hazle had played a full 154-game season he would have been the first since Ted Williams in 1941 to hit .400, his projected numbers in other hitting categories—45 doubles, 26 home runs, 101 RBIs, and 98 runs—could have been within reach.

In the World Series, Hazle was relatively quiet, hitting two singles in 13 plate appearances (.154) while scoring two runs. The Braves didn't miss his heroics, as Aaron hit .393 and Burdette won three games, leading Milwaukee to a 4-3 series win over the New York Yankees.

Sadly, before his 30th birthday, Hazle would be out of baseball.

"But to tell you the truth, once I left the game, I never thought about going back managing, coaching or whatever," he said. "What's done is done. Besides, the way it ended, I left with kind of a bad taste in my mouth for baseball."

That bad taste began to form after Hazle's miracle season. Braves general manager John Quinn came through with a promised bonus, but for only $1,000. Hazle thought the amount was insultingly low and mailed the check back. And despite his exploits, his Braves teammates only voted him a two-thirds World Series' share.

"We were really that cheap?" Mathews said in surprise to author David Lamb many years later. "Damn, that's awful. We couldn't have won without him."

Then came the beanings in 1958, once in spring training and again in St. Louis. "He was never the same," Chapman said. "He never came back after that."

After hitting only .179 for Milwaukee in 20 games, Hazle was traded that season to Detroit. He played 43 games in Motown in 1958, hitting .241. But Hazle had differences with manager Bill Norman; the next season he was exiled to the minors, never to return to the bigs. He retired after the 1960 season at the age of 29, convinced he still had major league talent.

"Everything went wrong, and that was the end of it," he said. "I told my wife it was time to wrap it up."

"Please appreciate, I'm not griping. I had my shot. It's just that in the majors you have that vinegar, that intensity, that gives you strength, and in the minors I couldn't get that pep back. Oh well ..."

Hazle went on to sell tombstones and later liquor in his native South Carolina. In 1987 the *Los Angeles Times* did a front-page feature story on him (unfortunately spelling his name "Hazel"), more for the fact that he was a traveling whiskey salesman and the newspaper was doing a series on the working class. Even 30 years after his momentous half-season, Hazle still hadn't figured out how he did it.

"I wasn't doing anything different," he repeated. "It was just that everything was working for me. I didn't want to wake up. Gosh, that was a good life."

Hazle, who had had a previous heart attack, died in 1992 in Columbia, South Carolina. To Milwaukee fans, Hazle was still remembered and revered as much as anyone from that magical year of 1957.

"There was only one Hazle," Chapman said. "There was only one Hurricane."

CARL SCHEIB

With World War II depleting the ranks of eligible ballplayers from both the major and minor leagues, clubs became desperate for any sort of talent they could enlist.

One target was the 4-Fs, deemed physically unfit for service but still serviceable to professional sport. The second pool was those too old for the military draft, faded veterans back for one more go-around. The third was going after those too young for the military. After all, isn't baseball a kid's game?

A 17-year-old named Tommy Brown played shortstop for his hometown Brooklyn Dodgers in 1944 and again in 1945. Another 17-year-old infielder, Eddie Yost, played seven games for the Washington Senators in 1944; he came back in 1946 and went on to an 18-year career. The most noteworthy of the teens was Joe Nuxhall, who became the youngest major leaguer ever when he pitched for the Cincinnati Reds in 1944 at the age of 15. He pitched only one game, two-thirds of an inning actually, giving up two hits, five walks, a wild pitch, and five earned runs. Nuxhall was then pulled, leaving him with a horrific 67.50 earned run average for the game and season. It took Nuxhall seven years to return to the majors, but he then went on to a successful 135-117 career.

There was another teen, younger than Yost and Brown and not much older than Nuxhall, who not only played in the majors but stuck. For some reason he has been forgotten: even in Bill Gilbert's fine book on baseball in World War II, *They Also Served: Baseball and the Home Front, 1941–45*, this player gets no mention.

It took a war, a widowed grocery store clerk, and a tryout in the rain, but Carl Scheib made it to the majors in 1943 by age 16, the youngest American Leaguer ever. As a boy in tiny Gratz, Pennsylvania, Scheib was as big a fan of the game as you could find, although his love came from playing, not watching. The World Series on radio was about it for him. He didn't even have a favorite team.

"I played baseball every minute I could, but we didn't have the time to follow the big leagues," he said. "I was ignorant of the big leagues."

But he could play. Everyone in town knew that.

Hannah Clark was a clerk in Smeltz' Grocery in Gratz, population 800. Clark had never seen a major league game, but she knew baseball, just as she knew a well-behaved young man when she saw one. Scheib was such a teen, who never lit a cigarette or stole an apple. She knew he was a ballplayer, but the shy youngster didn't want to brag.

Gratz High School (not be confused with Simon Gratz High in Philadelphia) had about 30 students. Scheib's size and pitching prowess made him stand out. "I was big and strong and could throw hard," the right-hander remembered more than a half-century later. "I had already developed a curve. I was pretty well grown, 180-something pounds."

Clark was a fan of Philadelphia Athletics legend Connie Mack. "Such a grand gentleman," she called him, "the man I would want to send my son to, if I had one." News reports in 1942 abounded about teams, including the A's, having wartime difficulty finding players; she thought of 15-year-old Carl Scheib. How could she tell Mack about the young fireballer?

Al Grossman, a traveling salesman, was a regular at her store. The widowed grocery clerk mentioned the radio report about Mack's talent troubles and referred to young Scheib's talent. Grossman decided to write Mack.

If Mack knew anything, it was the history of the game; after all, he was the history of the game. Mack knew the story of a traveling cigar salesman who wrote to Clark Griffith about another strapping farm boy pitcher. That pitcher, Walter Johnson, turned out to be all right. Sight unseen, Mack invited Scheib to Philadelphia for a look-see, and on June 23 Carl and his father Oliver were off. "At the time it seemed like around the world," Scheib remembered, "but it was only 120 miles."

Scheib's heart sank as he and his dad pulled up to Shibe Park (both the stadium and the pitcher are pronounced like "tribe"). Beneath the rain drops was a sign outside: "Game Off." He trudged inside, thinking the tryout was also canceled. But the rain let up, and Mack still wanted him to pitch out in the bullpen for him.

"I was so countryfied," Scheib said. "When I went to Shibe Park, I didn't even have a glove or spikes."

Mack watched him pitch for about 10 minutes, then draped his arm across the boy's shoulders. "I like your stuff very much," he told the pitcher, "but I think you should go back to high school another year."

Dad thought that was fine. Son did not. He was determined to make it back in 1943. And he did, reporting after school ended in June 1943. Scheib was put on salary as a batting practice pitcher. In late August, Scheib got into his first game, albeit an exhibition against the League Island Marines in Philadelphia. He pitched the final four innings, allowing no hits while striking out seven.

Scheib was very much a boy in a man's world, a world where any rookie, teenager or not, was not going to get help from a veteran clinging to a job.

"In those days those teammates didn't tell you much," Scheib said.

"Coaches? They didn't work with you. They just went out to third base and directed traffic. It was hard to get used to.

"I was intimidated. I was a bashful, shy kid coming out of the sticks. It was pretty hard."

But Mack watched him develop. As autumn neared, the legendary manager pulled him aside.

"You think it's about time?" Mack asked.

"I'm ready," Scheib told him.

"Go down and get a uniform."

On Labor Day, September 7, 1943, Scheib signed an American League contract at the age of 16 years, 9 months, and 7 days. Parents Oliver and Pauline had to come in from Gratz to co-sign, since Scheib was not yet of legal age.

Carl Scheib (courtesy of Carl Scheib).

Scheib made his debut against the Yankees, two innings of flawless mop-up work. He worked six games the rest of the way, going 0-1 with a 4.34 ERA.

In 1944, Scheib worked in 15 games in relief without a decision. In May 1945, Scheib entered the army, where he would serve until November 1946. While playing for various base and battalion teams, Scheib racked up a military record of 26-1, including a win in the "GI World Series" in Germany, where he won the title game to finish a season in which he averaged 16 strikeouts a game.

Scheib returned for the 1947 season, posting a 4-6 record. In 1948 the perennially pathetic A's were actually in the thick of the pennant race before fading at the end and finishing fourth. Scheib posted the best numbers of his career that year, going 14-8 with a 3.94 ERA. He was now a grizzled veteran at the age of 21.

Scheib went on to a respectable 11-year career, almost all with the Athletics; he finished his career with three games for the Cardinals at the tail end of 1954. His career stats: 45-65, 4.88 ERA. In 1955 he played with Portland, Oregon, but the rainy climate was not suitable for a pitcher suffering arm trouble. He headed south for San Antonio, where he played for two more years before retiring in 1957 at the age of 30. He settled in the area, operating service station and car wash businesses before retiring in 1988.

It could be assumed that Scheib could have benefited from some experience in the minors at the onset of his career. Even Mack acknowledged he had seen "too many young pitchers spoiled by working them in the majors too quickly." Scheib himself said he wonders, too, but adds he may have never gotten back.

"I don't know: Sometimes I think it might have been better," he said. "Then again, I might have fizzled in the minors."

Scheib said he has only one regret in the game. You see, he was a hitter. All right, almost all pitchers love to hit; Scheib actually could. He played two games in the outfield in 1948 and was regularly used as a right-handed pinch-hitter. He finished his career with a .250 batting average, including hitting marks of .298 in 1948 and an amazing .396 in his 53 at-bats in 1951. Could Scheib have become another Babe Ruth or Smokey Joe Wood: a pitcher turned outfielder?

"He could play there, or he could play any position," Mack said in 1948. "He's just naturally a ballplayer, potentially great, and with a little more confidence and experience he'd be a tremendous hitter."

Scheib agrees, if he only had had the chance.

"I wish I could have played the outfield," he said. "I felt like I could hit better than I could pitch. They talked about it, but they never had enough pitchers."

They even needed 16 year olds.

LOUIS SOCKALEXIS

First, the known facts on Louis Sockalexis:

One, he was an enormously talented baseball player, a potential all-timer arriving on the scene just prior to the turn of the century.

Two, he drank. A lot.

Three, he is the Cleveland Indian. Not a Cleveland Indian. *The* Cleveland Indian.

After that, the story of Louis Sockalexis gets a little trickier, but a lot more interesting. A mixture of fact, hyperbole, and pure fallacy, the tales of his athletic exploits are something out of a teen novel. In fact, it is widely believed that Gilbert Patten, who managed against Sockalexis in a Maine summer league, used Sockalexis as a model for his popular "Frank Merriwell" serial stories (written under the name Burt L. Standish). Consider that Sockalexis reportedly:

...could throw a baseball 400 feet.

...could hit one the length of two football fields, even during the "dead ball" era.

...once hit two home runs and two doubles in one college game and stole six bases in another.

...ran the 100-yard dash in 10 seconds flat.

...was a player that Hall-of-Famer Hughie Jennings said "should have been the greatest player of all times"—and Jennings managed Ty Cobb.

There is no doubt Sockalexis was a great athlete. It's just that much of his life has become fictionalized (there was even a fictional biography written on him), myths that expand on his very real on-field talents and very wild off-field inclinations.

"There is a grain of truth in all of it," Jay Feldman, a Californian writer who researched Sockalexis, said recently. "What I finally decided about it [was] this is mostly cock-and-bull."

But what stories. Some of the tales are contradictory, thanks in part to the fast-and-loose attitude some nineteenth and early twentieth century sportswriters had toward facts. But the stories—with a flourish here, an improbability there—were always colorful.

43

As Feldman wrote in the *Baseball Research Journal*:

> Stories with little or no factual basis get repeated and embellished in a sort of historical folk-process version of the old party game of "Telephone" until Sockalexis takes on a Paul Bunyanesque aspect. In the legend of Louis Sockalexis, the threads of fact and fiction are intricately woven together into a tapestry of heroic dimensions, and while separating those threads is often difficult and sometimes impossible, one thing remains absolutely clear: Without question, Louis Francis Sockalexis ranks among the truly tragic figures in baseball history, a man of immense talent and unlimited potential whose "tragic flaw" led inevitably and inexorably to his downfall.

Sockalexis' career was explosive but brief, snuffed out by alcohol and repeated problems in what were politely known as bordellos. But his popularity in his short stint in the bigs is evident today every time Cleveland takes the field. Sockalexis is there, if not in spirit then in name, not only for what he did, but what he was: an Indian.

Sockalexis was born October 24, 1871, on the Indian Island Reservation outside of Old Town, Maine. He was a three-sport star in high school in baseball, football, and track at Old Town High School, where his legend was born.

"He batted left and threw right with such prodigious strength that later, in semipro baseball, he gave throwing exhibitions before the games," wrote *Down East* magazine in 1963. "At Poland Spring on a dollar bet, he once threw a ball over the tower of Hiram Ricker's Hotel, thought to be an impossible heave. He used to give exhibitions at fair time in Bangor, throwing a baseball over the length of the grandstand to someone at the other end. His speed of foot enabled him to run the hundred, in full baseball regalia, in ten [seconds] flat."

Sockalexis was also a sensation in Maine summer leagues and was recruited to Holy Cross by team captain Mike "Doc" Powers, later a catcher with four major league teams over his 11-year career. Sockalexis decided to attend the Worcester, Massachusetts, college instead of signing with the professional New England League. In 1894 he was admitted as a "special student."

In one of his most famous collegiate games, against Brown, Sockalexis stole six bases (two for himself and four as a "designated runner" for injured players). In another game at Brown, he hit a home run that broke a chapel window on the fourth floor. He hit .444 at the school.

Sockalexis' throwing ability became as legendary as his hitting. In a game against Harvard, Sockalexis supposedly uncorked a 414-foot throw— as measured by a couple of Crimson professors—to hold a batter to a triple on a ball that rolled beyond the fenceless field, through some trees and onto a tennis court. From an 1886 game against Georgetown came this account in the *Worcester Telegram*: "The crowd went into ecstasies over many plays, but there was one which raised their hair. It was a throw by Sockalexis from center field which cut off a run at the plate. It was [a] magnificent liner from the shoulder passing through the air like a cannon ball and reaching home plate in plenty of time."

In 1897, Sockalexis transferred with Powers to Notre Dame. He was soon snatched up by the Cleveland Spiders for $1,500 a year. Before suiting up for his first game, Sockalexis was bigger than Lake Erie.

"SOCKALEXIS, THE INDIAN came to town Friday. ... He is a massive man, with gigantic bones and bulging muscles, and looks a ball player from the ground up on [*sic*] top of his five feet, 11 inches of solid frame work," wrote *Sporting Life*.

At first the chiseled 185-pound Sockalexis lived up to his billing, as he raced to a .338 average at the onset of his rookie year behind his lightning speed on the basepaths. Quickly becoming the biggest gate attraction in the league, also impressed onlookers with his throwing prowess from the outfield. New York Giants skipper John McGraw called him the best natural talent he had ever seen.

An unknown poet penned this tribute that year:

> *This is the bounding Sockalexis*
> *Fielder of the mighty Clevelands*
> *Like the catapult in action,*
> *For the plate he throws the baseball,*
> *Till the rooter, blithely rooting,*
> *Shouts until he shakes the bleachers.*
> *"Sockalexis, Sockalexis,*
> *Sock it to them Sockalexis."*

On his first visit to New York Sockalexis faced the Giants and Hall-of-Fame pitcher Amos Rusie. As fans were screaming for a strikeout, a small group of Penobscots, in full war outfits, let go a battle cry. Rusie, possibly the best curveball pitcher of his era, broke one over the plate. Sockalexis crushed it to center field for a home run.

There is the event. The Penobscot fans in the crowd may or may not have originated from the imagination of some sportswriter. As the story has been retold over the years, Sockalexis hit the homer in his first at-bat ever, on his first pitch. A grain of truth, but not the whole truth.

One Sockalexis story appears to be an incredible fabrication, but again one founded on a germ of fact. Sockalexis was supposedly the son of a tribal chief (some accounts had his grandfather as the chief) who was upset Louis

was playing baseball, "the white man's game." The elder Sockalexis supposedly hopped in his canoe in Maine, paddled 596 miles to Washington, D.C.,
met with his "good friend," President Grover Cleveland, had Cleveland sign
a proclamation naming Louis chief so he would have to return the reservation, then paddled the 596 miles back to Maine—only to find Louis gone.

Sockalexis' father very well could have disdained baseball (Sockalexis
also played football at Holy Cross), but did this 1,192-mile round-trip really
happen?

While the canoe trek seems implausible, there is absolutely no possibility
that all the stories surrounding Sockalexis' first step into alcoholism could be
true because they don't add up.

Story 1: While at Notre Dame, he was expelled in 1897 after he and
another schoolmate ransacked a nearby whorehouse. It was none other than
Cleveland Spiders manager Patsy Tabeau who bailed them out. Tabeau had
been in town trying to get Sockalexis to leave school, reportedly trying to
soften the prospect's reluctance with drink. After the drunken debacle in the
bordello, Tabeau then spirited Sockalexis out of Indiana into Ohio and put
him into the Cleveland lineup.

Story 2 (The "instant drunk" theory): After hitting a grand-slam and
making a game-saving catch, Sockalexis was taken out by a group of jubi-
lant fans (a variation has it being players) for a celebration. Sockalexis, "whose
lips never touched anything stronger than milk," became immediately hooked
on whiskey.

Story 3: Sockalexis, dazzled by the bright lights of the big city of Cleveland, became a drunk on his first payday.

Story 4: Sockalexis was a drinker before he met the Cleveland manager
or joined the majors but was able to keep it in check as long as he was playing regularly.

The instant-drunk theory was promoted by Jennings in a series he penned
in 1926 called "Rounding Third." The story was accepted as fact for decades:

> The turning point of his career happened in Chicago. It hap-
> pened as a result of a play in the opening game of the series.
> When Cleveland came to bat in the ninth, the score was 3–0 in
> favor of Chicago. Cleveland filled the bases with two outs, and
> Sockalexis came to bat. He hit a home run. Then, in the home
> half of the inning, Chicago got two men on bases with as many
> out.
>
> The batter smashed a long drive to the outfield. It almost
> looked like a home run, but Sockalexis made an almost impos-
> sible one-handed catch of the ball. His home run and his catch
> enabled Cleveland to win, 4–3.
>
> After the game the Spiders celebrated their unusual victory.

Sockalexis, the hero of the occasion, was finally induced to take a drink by the jibes of his more or less intoxicated teammates. It was the first taste he ever had of liquor, and he liked it. He liked the effects even better, and from that time on Sockalexis was a slave to whiskey.

The Jennings story became an oft-quoted account of Sockalexis' downfall. Too bad it's not true.

Feldman notes that not one of the three home runs Sockalexis hit in 1897 came against Chicago. None of the dingers were a grand slam. In a series against St. Louis, Sockalexis did make a great bases-loaded catch in one game and hit a home run in another and a bases-loaded triple in a third. The Jennings story could be an amalgamation of all three.

Also, as noted by Feldman, Sockalexis had been reprimanded at Holy Cross for drinking and tossed out of Notre Dame for public intoxication. A team official also told the *Sporting News* the team had reports of Sockalexis being drunk early in the season but received promises from the player to abstain.

Sockalexis' drinking problems became the grist of public ridicule, as evidenced by a July 13, 1897, *Cleveland Plain Dealer* story headlined "The Wooden Indian" that said Sockalexis "acted as if [he] had disposed of too many mint juleps previous to the game. A lame foot is the Indians' excuse, but a Turkish bath and a good rest might be an excellent remedy."

Added *Sporting Life*: "Much of the stuff written about his dalliance with grape juice and his trysts with paleface maidens is purely speculation. It is no longer a secret that the Cleveland management can no longer control Sockalexis."

As Feldman summarized: "He was a great athlete, no question about it. He was also a great drunkard. When he was playing he seemed to be doing fine."

But in July of 1897, Sockalexis hurt his ankle jumping from the second-story window of yet another bordello, and the injury knocked him out of the lineup. On July 3, Sockalexis was hitting .328 (81-for-247) with 40 runs scored, 39 RBIs, and 16 steals. Then he was out of the lineup until July 8; he played again July 11 and 12 and July 24 and 25, but only three times after that.

Sockalexis' injury was keeping him out of the game, but apparently not the bars. The next season he hit only .224 in 21 games and was cut 7 games into the 1899 season.

Sockalexis played several more years in the minors at Hartford and Lowell in the Eastern League before leaving the game and returning to the reservation, where he taught others baseball and worked as a woodcutter.

The Cleveland Indians franchise has played under the nicknames the Forest Citys (1889), the Spiders (1889), the Blues (1900), the Bronchos (1902), and the Naps (1903). Nicknames of many clubs of the time were fluid, the subject of the sportswriters' fancy and fan fashion that could change on a whimsy. Two years after Sockalexis' death in 1913, a Cleveland newspaper held a contest to come up with a new team nickname. In honor of Sockalexis, fans chose to rename the team, by then known as the Naps (after manager Napoleon Lajoie), to the Indians. Jim Thorpe and Al "Chief" Bender may have been the greatest Native Americans to play the game, but neither have a team named after them.

After Sockalexis' death, while the *Old Town Enterprise* was conducting a fund-raising drive to erect a monument at his gravesite, the Holy Cross *Alumnus* ran yet another poem from John A. Fitzgerald, Class of 1897:

> *Louis, we've gathered here today*
> *Tribesman and sportsmen, we all attend*
> *To mark the spot where your mortal clay*
> *Came to our universal end.*
> *More than one epitaph's been penned*
> *Of a player that has never had a peer*
> *But here's your meed, from an old-time friend:*
> *"He was loyal and brave, and his heart sincere."*
>
> *We could write: "At the start of the season's play,*
> *When the Bruins brown were all set to rend,*
> *You "stole" six times on that Patriot's Day,*
> *—A record that none can tie or mend—*
> *And crashed a homer its way to went*
> *Thro their chapel window, from out the clear,*
> *But no! Tis a finer tribute to send:*
> *"He was loyal and brave, and his heart sincere."*
>
> *As a batter, no pitcher could say you nay,*
> *You straightened whatever they could bend;*
> *And on Giant-Indian opening day,*
> *And the Gotham fans came in crowds to tend—*
> *"Rusie will fan him!" So they intend,*
> *But— "the first ball a homer into the clear!"*
>
> *What a line! But a greater one, old friend,*
>
> *Is: "Loyal and brave, and his heart sincere."*
> *Louis, with saddened hearts we send*
> *This tribute to one who had no peer,*
> *To one of the few who met his end*
> *Loyal and brave, and his heart sincere.*

In 1934, Maine honored Sockalexis in a ceremony unveiling his monument. In 1956 he was the inaugural inductee into the Holy Cross Athletic Hall of Fame.

Why was Sockalexis so remembered, so revered, for so long, when he had a career that was so short?

"There was something about him that captured people's imagination," Feldman said. "Maybe it was his exotic qualities. Every society loves its nonconformists and dead troublemakers."

All those years later fans in Cleveland and Maine remembered what Louis Sockalexis was and what he could have been. And so did he.

When he died, Sockalexis was 42, working as a woodcutter in Burlington, Maine, making $30 a month in a lumber camp. It was Christmas Eve, and when the shift returned to the camp Sockalexis was missing. A crewman found him dead in the woods. His body was taken back to the bunkhouse and his shirt was taken off. Inside was found a wad of paper: yellowed press clippings from his playing days.

There was the life of Louis Sockalexis, clear as black and white.

MARK FIDRYCH

There was a man once, not long ago, for whom loyalty to a team and its city was as much a part of him as the blood in his veins. This was a man who negotiated contracts not through agents, lawyers, or arbitrators, but through his dad; who was celebrated not just at home, but in the cold stadiums of his foes. This man walked among kings in a sphere he revered, and openly, honestly, reveled in it.

Oh, yeah, he also talked to baseballs.

The man is Mark Fidrych. The year is 1976. And no one is hotter on talk shows, on news and celebrity magazine covers, or on a pitcher's mound than the gawky 21-year-old who looked like a goofy Muppet. He was the Bird.

Yet by the time that year elapsed, the spell would be broken.

But what a spell it was.

The rural Massachusetts right-hander would go from not even getting his name on the Detroit Tigers' Opening Day roster to starting his first game a month later to starting the All-Star Game halfway through the season.

Along the way he admonished horsehides to break just so, pawed at mounds on his hands and knees to get the right feel, shook hands with infielders after each inning, and rejected baseballs for having too many hits in their souls. But Mark Fidrych was so much more.

Men on second and third, Hank Aaron steps up to the plate. The 21-year-old Fidrych rears back and fires. Three strikes later one of the greatest hitters who ever swung a bat is out.

Many pitchers would coolly wipe a brow, maybe dig absent-mindedly at the mound. But this was not, in any way, any pitcher.

"That was just weird," Fidrych said. "At the point where—here he is, I mean, a superstar, right? And here I am, a little guy, pitchin' to him. And knowin' he's a superstar. All of a sudden you get him out that one time ... and in the back of your mind, you're saying, 'Wow, this is Hank Aaron.'"

Pure Fidrych. Madison Avenue types would get millions to fabricate the persona the Bird was born with.

For all the stars that shined twice as bright for half as long, Mark Fidrych is the patron saint.

Consider 1976, his rookie season. He won 19 games and lost just 9, led the American League in ERA at 2.34; and with 24 complete games in 29 starts, despite not pitching until May, struck out 9; and he had a flawless fielding record. He was named Rookie of the Year and was the biggest attraction in baseball—honored at Mark Fidrych Days at ballparks on the road—all while making less than an honest plumber.

But there was more. Simultaneously he was the kid next door who kept running after a ball that rolled into your yard and one of the biggest flakes the game had seen. He was just a kid with too much hair and too many teeth who dreamed the same dreams as any fan and got lucky enough to make them real. He was also a pitcher who got outs, tough outs, and won ball games for the Tigers when they weren't winning many.

Fidrych signed for $16,500, the major's minimum wage. He would be told over and over again that players with half his talent were making millions. He didn't care.

"Play out my option and get more money?" Fidrych parroted back to the *New York Times* in the spring of his second year. "What for? I want to play for the Tigers, and they want me. When I got out of high school, they were the only team that offered me a job. Besides, I have all the money I need."

That second year he signed for a base of $55,000.

Refreshing. Crazy. Dangerous, even. This was at a time of widening major league player-owner tensions. Players were seeing how much they could flex their muscles, and they were worried about keeping their union together without allowing owners to convince fans that players were millionaire crybabies.

Somehow through it all, the same Bird who captured the hearts of fans to the point that he collected a bonus for drawing more than 900,000 fans that year appeared on news magazine covers, nearly had his own TV sitcom, and also captured the affection of his heroes, the major league players, whose bats he still collected as souvenirs.

"Mark Fidrych took over all of baseball in 1976," said a man who was there, the Bird's personal catcher, Bruce E. Kimm. "It was a playoff atmosphere whenever Mark pitched.... There were more fans in the stadiums, more writers in the press box and he just captivated all of baseball."

Kimm came up from Evansville with Fidrych in 1976 and caught the Bird's first major league game. Fidrych had a no-hitter through seven and a third innings. "They said we were like ham and eggs. I was just lucky to be part of it," said Kimm, who was named manager of the year in the Class AA Southern League and coached the world champion Florida Marlins.

Kimm, a lifetime .237 hitter who spent four years as a player in the majors and whose fortunes rose and fell with the Bird's, saw the electricity of that year up close. He saw time and again how Fidrych's car was stalled by fans who draped themselves over the hood for a look, and he watched city after city fall in love with the pitcher who talked to baseballs, sculpted mounds, and left batters talking to themselves.

"There was no fake to it," Kimm said. "He did the same thing back in the minors."

The Bird's secret? Simple. Great control, great speed, great fielding, great command of runners that glued them on base.

"He had a 93-mph sinker he could put anywhere and it was as strong in the ninth as in the first," Kimm said. "He put it where I wanted it and I just kept moving it around. He never feared any batter. Mark Fidrych was not just the best pitcher in baseball that year, but one of the best people ever in baseball."

Rarely has such a talent and personality been so quickly embraced by the media. Neal Bandlow, associate professor of journalism at the State University of New York at Morrisville College, who also is a Detroit-area native and Bird watcher, remembers:

> At the time it was kind of a lull in showmanship in baseball because the Mantles were gone, but The Bird was a breath of fresh air. Especially in Detroit. We had unemployment and all kinds of other problems. We needed someone to look to…. He gave a shot in the arm and a shot in the arm to baseball when baseball needed it.
>
> The media had a lot of fun with him. They had a difficult time writing anything bad about him because they liked him so much. Can you imagine that today?
>
> No one had that kind of impact in one year and continued to have an impact for years after when there was talk of a comeback.

That popularity, that devotion, was still waxing after that first magical season. By February and March of 1977, the rigors of spring training hadn't diminished Fidrych's popularity among players or fans, or his optimism.

"Sophomore jinx?" he confidently told the *New York Times* in the warm March sunshine of Florida. "There ain't no pressure on me. What's going to happen is going to happen."

It did.

In spring training in Lakeland, chasing a fly ball that many players of his fresh but solid stature would let drop, Fidrych hurt his arm. Weeks earlier he had torn cartilage in his left knee and had joked he always thought his arm would go before his legs.

Fidrych would be on the disabled list for most of the next three years. He never again pitched like he could. The Tigers, in a decision Detroit general manager Jim Campbell would call one of the most heart-wrenching he ever made, reluctantly released the Bird in 1981. He tried and tried to come back over three minor league seasons in the Boston farm system. His magnetism lingers in Detroit, long after comebacks in the Red Sox farm system failed, and he returned to his home state a thousand miles away.

"He can walk down the streets of Detroit today, and anyone 25 or 30 years old or older are going to recognize Mark Fidrych," Bandlow said. "You'd expect that kind of recognition for Al Kaline, but for a guy that had one good year and in four years was gone from Detroit? There is a magnetism about Mark Fidrych that still affects me."

In his last two years with the Class AAA Pawtucket (R.I.) Red Sox, Fidrych went 8-13 in 32 games, with an ERA of 6.30, including a one-inning relief appearance in May 1983 in which he gave up nine hits and nine earned runs. On June 30, 1983, at age 28, he retired to his 123-acre pig farm in Northboro, Massachussets.

"I got no regrets," quotes a one-page bio of Fidrych at the National Baseball Hall of Fame and Museum. "I got memories. I'll always keep them alive. Grab it while you can, 'cause you never know when it's gonna disappear."

PETE GRAY

Pete Gray knew he had talent to be a big leaguer. Yeah, yeah, World War II drained the pool of available ballplayers. But he was a minor league Most Valuable Player, a .333 hitter, and a record base-stealer. All he wanted was to be recognized as one of the guys, a player who belonged. A St. Louis Brown.

"He was always a little touchy," said Browns pitcher Nelson Potter. "He wanted to be accepted and judged just like everyone else on the team."

Owner Don Barnes even inserted a clause into Gray's contract stating the player was not to be exploited as a freak. Barnes then laid down the rules for manager Luke Sewell. This was fine by Sewell: he was going to judge him as solely as a ballplayer, and he made that clear to Gray when he showed up for spring training in 1945 in Cape Girardeau, Missouri.

"Don't expect any favors," Sewell told him.

"I don't want any," Gray responded.

But Gray saw slights real and imagined throughout the clubhouse. If there was one thing Gray despised, it was pity. Still, he saw it everywhere. He met it head-on with a snarl.

"Pete was the most ornery guy I ever met," said Ellis Clary, a Browns infielder. "You'd feel sorry for him and want to help him the first day you met him, but by the next day you'd hate his guts. He was no sideshow, but a darn good ballplayer. If he'd only had a better attitude, he might have stayed up."

Gray's worst enemy was not the fastball or the curve or fielding or throwing: it was suspicion. It made him sullen and withdrawn, alienating him from teammates. After achieving a childhood dream most believed he had no reason to hold onto, Gray was haunted by the conundrum: did the St. Louis Browns want him for the talent he had or the arm he didn't?

All Gray ever knew about the accident was what was told to him; he never remembered a thing about the day in 1923. The story of him losing his right arm as a six-year-old varied over the years from a train accident to a car accident. The final version had it that he and some playmates hooked a ride on the running boards of a truck that stopped short. Gray was thrown from the vehicle and bounced off an embankment and back toward the vehicle. His right arm became lodged between the spokes of the old-style wheels and was badly mangled. Supposedly, the driver left Gray on his family's porch and fled.

Gray was born on March 6, 1917, in Nanticoke, Pennsylvania, where he still lives today. Born right-handed, he had to relearn the basic necessities of life after his accident, from brushing his teeth to combing his hair. Yet Gray asked for no quarter and would give none: in an oft-told story from his youth, he barreled into a catcher at a play at home during a sandlot game, dislodging the ball.

"Why, if you had two arms I'd smash your nose," the catcher said.

Gray pounced and made the boy take back the barb.

The outfielder had to prove himself on every new diamond, for every new team. In 1939, while visiting the World's Fair, he talked his way into a tryout with the semipro Brooklyn Bushwicks. When Gray approached Bushwicks promoter/manager Max Rosner with the idea, Rosner laughed in his face.

"I've heard of a lot of ways of crashing the gate," Rosner said, "but this is a new one."

Gray, who obviously had heard of the cliche of putting your money where your mouth is, produced a crisp $10 bill. "Take this and keep it if I don't make good," he said.

Gray made good, hitting .449 with the Bushwicks and the Bay Parkways of Queens. News of the semipro hitting star spread. In 1942, Gray, who was born Pete Wyshner but changed his last name to the one his boxing brother, Whitey Gray, used in the ring, was signed by Three Rivers of the Canadian League.

One problem: the scouting reports sent north neglected to mention the 24-year-old player had only one arm.

But soon after, even before his first game, word of the unique newcomer spread quickly. An abnormally large crowd turned out, often breaking into chants of "We want Gray." Gray remained on the bench.

Into the bottom of the ninth the game went, with the home team trailing 1–0. Three Rivers loaded the bases, but there were two outs. Gray finally got the call, driving the crowd into a frenzy. A hit to win the game would have been so mawkish it would have seemed right out of a movie of the week. He hit one anyway, a line drive down the right-field line, driving in the tying and winning runs. Fans threw coins and cash on the field, about $700 in all. (The Pete Gray story did make the movies, as a so-so television drama called A *Winner Never Quits*, starring Keith Carradine.)

That season Gray broke his collarbone and tore ligaments, but he established himself as a blossoming star in just 42 games by hitting .381. The next season he had a tryout with Toronto, but did not hit it off with manager Burleigh Grimes, whom Gray apparently bad-mouthed. Gray was subsequently shipped south from Canada all the way to Memphis, where he hit a respectable .289 in 126 games for the Chicks.

But in 1944, Gray was to become a national sensation. He hit .343 with

5 home runs, struck out just 12 times (which still was a career high for him), led all Southern Association outfielders in fielding and stole 68 bases, tying KiKi Cuyler for the league record. In addition to winning the league MVP, Philadelphia sportswriters named him the Most Courageous Athlete of 1944. "With less, he achieved more" a citation read. After the season the Browns, coming off their one and only pennant, bought his contract for $20,000. The money was welcome.

"I've been turned down by more big-league managers than any other man in history," Gray said in 1945. "I spent more money trying to get into baseball than I've earned on the game."

But was he in "the Show" for just the show? Everyone, teammates included, had doubts over whether the one-armed player was being brought in solely as a gate-attraction.

"Gray is just like another ball player to me," Sewell said. "He has to stand on what he has. I know a lot of fans are pulling for him, and many will be curious to see him play. And he does put on a real good show. But Gray will be a gate attraction for us only if he can help our club. If we weakened the team by playing Pete, the Browns would cease to be an attraction."

At first, Gray proved he was a major leaguer. His first game was against the Detroit Tigers and Hal Newhouser in St. Louis, where he got his first hit on a single up the middle. On May 20, at home against the Yankees, Gray had an amazing doubleheader: 4-for-8, with 10 putouts in left field, 4 of them great catches. The Browns swept. The superlatives kept coming.

"What Gray might have accomplished in the big league if blessed with two arms is something for the imagination to play with," *Washington Post* columnist Shirley Povich wrote in midseason 1945. "Surely he would have be one of the greatest big leaguers of all time."

Years later Gray declined to be so presumptive. "Who's to say I'd have worked as hard at it, or had anywhere near the determination?"

Gray, who mostly batted second in the lineup, started to fade after one circuit through the league. He finished at .217 for 77 games. It was an off year for hitters: George Stirnweiss led the league with only a .309 average, while shortstop Vern Stephens led the Browns by hitting .289.

"He was OK the first time around the league," Sewell remembered years later. "Yeah, people wanted to see him. The New York writers drove me crazy to play him. But I kept telling them, 'I'm worrying about winning a pennant, not packing your ballpark.'"

Going into the season, it was assumed Gray would have the most trouble with fireballers who could bring it to the plate. But all major leaguers, including Gray, are essentially fastball hitters. It's what they do with the breaking stuff that determines their fate.

"He used a 35-ounce bat, but his wrist was real strong, and he would jump on a fastball and make good contact even against [Bob] Feller," Sewell said. "But then the pitchers got smart. They started throwing him junk, and he was way out in front of the ball. And the infielders started to crowd him to take away the bunt."

Gray was hitting .188 at the end of April, .189 after May, .224 after June and a high of .235 after July. But then his swoon began, and Sewell would be reluctant to bring him off the bench: Gray was only 1-for-12 as a pinch-hitter.

While people were at least at first impressed with his hitting, it was the ability of a one-armed man to field that had people shaking their heads. His catching style was somewhat reminiscent of that used by Jim Abbott, the one-armed pitcher, as he explained to the *Sun* of Baltimore years later:

"You know I had a shoemaker make that glove for me special. He'd take out most of the padding, and I'd use it like a first baseman's glove, keeping my pinkie outside. It helped me get rid of the glove quicker. I'd catch the ball, stick the glove under my stump, roll the ball across my chest, and throw it back in. No big deal. It was just grounders that gave me some trouble."

American League president Will Harridge issued a directive to umpires that if Gray dropped a ball on the transfer to his throwing position, the play should be ruled a catch and an out, similar to the ruling utilized by the Southern Association.

"I could field the ball in the air with any of them," Gray said.

Despite the remarkable feats, harsh feelings on both sides of the Gray divide remained. "Some of the guys thought Pete was being used to draw fans late in the season when the club was still in the pennant race and he wasn't hitting that well," second baseman Don Gutteridge.

In the book *Even the Browns*, player Mark Christman went as far as to say Gray cost the team the pennant:

"We finished third, only six games out. There were an awful lot of ground balls hit to him in center, and the hitters kept running right into second. That cost us eight games."

The argument doesn't hold up under scrutiny: the Browns played .600 ball with Gray in the lineup, and at a .425 clip with him on the bench. The Browns finished third, six games behind the Tigers, with a record of 81-70. The following season, without Gray, the Browns finished seventh with a 66-88 record. In fact, 1945 would be the franchise's last winning year before it moved to Baltimore for the 1954 season.

There have been several one-armed players in professional baseball, most notably Abbott, the University of Michigan pitcher who has thrown for several major league clubs. Another, Harry Connama, played in the 1910s in the Northern California League, once hitting .406 for a season with a no-hitter to his credit.

Hugh I. Daily—One Arm Daily—had his left hand blown off by a musket at a Baltimore theater, where he was a stagehand. But the right-handed pitcher was able to pitch six years in the majors in the 1880s, throwing a no-hitter for Cleveland against Philadelphia in 1883. The next year, when overhand pitching was legalized, he led the Union Association with 483 strike-outs in 500.2 innings, while tossing back-to-back one-hitters on his way to a 28-28 record.

Gray would not have such a career. In 1946, with major leaguers return-ing from World War II, Gray returned to the minors, playing sporadically for Toledo (.250), Elmira (.290), and Dallas (.214) before retiring after the 1949 season.

Gray went home to Nanticoke, where he lived with his mother and cared for his brother waylaid by too many flurries of punches. In the sporadic inter-views he granted over the years, he bragged that baseball was the only job he ever had, yet he never went on public assistance. Too much pride. But pride, if not friends or wealth, was what Gray was able to take away from the game.

"Well, I did prove something, didn't I?" he said years later. "I did show them something, didn't I? I wasn't very strong. That was the big thing. I was too skinny. I weighed, what? Maybe 145 pounds [he was listed as 6-foot-1, 169 pounds]. It just wasn't enough. If I'd been, say, 180 or 185…"

In the Bushes

DAVE BRESNAHAN

Dave Bresnahan made his last game memorable. In fact, making it memorable made it Bresnahan's last game.

Bresnahan should have been a forgotten also-ran among the tens of thousands who toiled in the minors without a call to the big leagues. While the catcher never reached the majors, he achieved something else—something if not greater, then rarer.

For lovers of a harmless gag, for those with no patience for the insufferably pompous, we present your patron saint, the Brez. While baseball history is rife with practical jokes, from the dugout hot foot to the prank calls from the bullpen, Bresnahan dared to bring humor to the field. His was no mere pedestrian gag: It was elaborate, requiring guile, skill, and an equal sense of humor and history; in short, style.

It also cost him his career, but it earned him the highest honor a prankster can achieve: a chuckle at the mere mention of his name, not to mention inclusion in baseball folklore, a story that should be passed from generation to generation.

Ian Shearn, a New Jersey newspaper editor, considered Bresnahan's sacrifice for the good humor of the game so great that he christened his Rotisserie team after the minor leaguer.

"I put him up there with Gandhi, Martin Luther and all the other great martyrs of Western and Eastern civilization," Shearn said.

Scary, but he was serious.

What gag did Bresnahan pull to cost him his job and secure his place in history? Set fire to the outfield? Give a hitter a wedgy? Put itching powder in an umpire's cup? No, no, and no.

Dave Bresnahan threw a potato. A Boise potato.

Baseball had the Tater, but it never had the Potato. For his contribution, a man who would have been remembered, if at all, as a weak-hitting catcher became a national hero, his number retired just like those of immortals such as Lou Gehrig.

"He said he felt like the luckiest man on the face of the earth," Bresnahan said soon after his claim to fame. "I feel even luckier, because Gehrig had to hit .340 and play in more than 2,000 consecutive games to get his number retired. All I had to do is hit less than .150 and throw a potato."

61

There was a Hall of Fame catcher named Roger Bresnahan. "The Duke of Tralee" hit .280 over 17 seasons from 1897 to 1915, which included leading the New York Giants to the 1905 world championship. Roger Bresnahan is remembered most as the first catcher to wear shin guards.

Then there was a catcher named David Bresnahan. A distant nephew. Not a great catcher. Still, a good one, good enough to rise to within two rungs of the majors.

After playing collegiately at Phoenix College and Grand Canyon University, Dave Bresnahan was an 18th-round selection in the 1984 amateur draft by the Seattle Mariners. Bresnahan takes pride in the fact that in 1986, while playing for Class A Waterloo of the Midwest League, he made the all-star team in a league that included Mark Grace, Dante Bichette, Larry Walker, and Walt Weiss. That year he also had a four RBI game in the playoffs, which Waterloo won.

Bresnahan hit .290 for the first half of that all-star season—and .230 for the season.

"I was a switch hitter—which means I couldn't hit from either side," Bresnahan says today. "I was a good defensive catcher; called a good game, could throw runners out at a little above-average rate. Hitting? I guess I couldn't adjust to Double-A pitching. All they had to do was throw it."

It didn't matter: Bresnahan, like any minor leaguer, held onto the hope that the big leagues would eventually come calling. Even in 1987, after being released by the Mariners and picked up by the Cleveland Indians, the 25-year-old backup catcher hitting .149 for Class AA Williamsport clung relentlessly to his shot at the bigs, as he notes:

"We all believe there is a glimmer of hope. As long as you got the uniform on ... if the whole big league team goes down, you could slide up to Triple A. We all wanted to get to the big leagues. There are guys that I played with and against who were far better than those who made it.

"I didn't play that much in '87. I had got injured that year. I was the backup. The glimmer of playing in the big leagues was slim. There were also talks late in that season that the organization, the Indians, was discussing coaching opportunities for me. I had no interest."

Bresnahan had his calling. The majors. But there was another calling in his head, over and over and over: the potato ... the potato ... the potato ...

The idea first hit him riding a bus in junior college. It lay dormant for years but had resurfaced in whatever portion of the brain houses benign mischief: What if a player threw a potato instead of the ball during a game? Bresnahan, one of the painfully few players who was also a student of the game, had heard a similar story from baseball's past but couldn't pin it down. He didn't know who threw a potato, or when, or from what position. It still sounded like fun.

Fun was just one of the few things missing from the 1987 Williamsport

Bills. The Eastern League team, despite having many players from the Class A champion at Waterloo the year before, was a bad baseball team. In a rare move the team's manager, Steve Swisher, was promoted early in the season to Triple A Buffalo, while the Bisons' skipper, Orlando Gomez, was sent down to Williamsport. The Bills then began their tailspin.

Gomez had been coaching and managing in the minors for about 10 years, but at Williamsport, he did not have the affection from players that Swisher had enjoyed. The low point in the season may have come when Bresnahan was shipped down to Class A for a stretch. Bresnahan was the type of player every team has, the guy whose banter and jokes can keep a team loose and winning (or at least loose). He was the player who would lead sing-a-longs on the bus, primarily so the coaching staff would not hear tabs being pulled from contraband beers in the back.

A month after his demotion Bresnahan was back after a Bills catcher got injured. But by then it was early August; the season was long lost.

"There was a lot of dissension on the ball club with him," Bresnahan said of Gomez. "Everyone was looking for getting the season over with."

The 1987 season was finally winding to a close. The Bills were more than 20 games out and fading. As August wore on, thoughts turned to the off-season. There was not much to get pumped up about.

Except the potato.

Bresnahan was in a bar with his roommate, third baseman Bob Swain, when the potato possibility came up again. The idea sped through the clubhouse like a wildfire: Brez was thinking of faking a guy into trying to score a run from third by throwing a spud. This was a team heading toward the end of a horrific season (final record: 60-79, seventh in an eight-team league, and 27 games out), with players worrying about whether they would have a job next spring. It's times like these that a team needs, well, a potato.

"It's a long freakin' year, and when you're losing, it's worse," Bresnahan said. "It got everyone so excited, it became fun. I was kind of puzzled to how it would work out."

One problem: Bresnahan said he didn't want to do the play if it cost his team. A joke is a joke, but no player wants to be responsible for losing a game, even when all pennant hopes were gone. In fact, one pitcher, former number one draft pick Mike Poehl, said the idea was fine so long as it wasn't in his game. The man had an ERA to worry about—and a point. This potato thing would take some research.

Bob Gergan, the team's first baseman and Bresnahan's roommate on the road, had a friend who was a major league umpire. Bresnahan broached the potato issue with the umpire, Tim Tshida. The ump said he would probably run the catcher from the game but send the runner back to third. "I checked with him; it really isn't in the books," Bresnahan said. "Based on Timmy Tshida, I could live with being thrown out as long as the run didn't score."

The potato proposition first came up again that season in a bar but took root in the bullpen. With time to kill during games, the backup tossed the concept back and forth with the pitchers. What kind of situation? What kind of potato? How can you make a potato pass, at least for a moment, for a baseball?

"The ideal situation in my mind was if there was a runner on third with two outs. I would tag him out and roll the ball back up the mound and all the players would go off the field."

That was the plan. Damned if it almost didn't work.

There was one doubleheader left in the season: Monday, August 31, against the Reading Phillies. A backup catcher is usually assured a start in the second game of a twin bill. Bresnahan figured if he was going to play, that was the day.

Williamsport played Reading in a series prior to the one that included the fateful doubleheader. Bresnahan got into a game and made sure to try to pick a runner off third. He was planting a seed ...

Bresnahan later made a trip to the local Weiss Market. He scanned the produce aisle looking for, well, a potato that looked like a baseball. But potatoes don't look like baseballs, at least naturally. Some experimentation was needed. He bought four large ones and went home.

First, the color was wrong, so he peeled one. Not bad, but a little too oval. Off went the top and bottom. Better. Stitches were a problem: Bresnahan couldn't draw them on the spud. Bresnahan now had doubts: *What if it didn't look like a baseball to the runner on third?* he asked Swain. The two tested one out back. In flight, for a moment, it could pass. Not bad at all.

Now Bresnahan only needed to be penciled into the lineup for that second game. Bresnahan's heart sank after he entered the clubhouse that day: he was scheduled to start the first game. Poehl's game. Rod Nichols, a future major leaguer, was angry: he was slated to start in game two and wanted to be on the mound for Bresnahan's feat.

Poehl was not as enthusiastic. He didn't want that earned run: "No way. I don't want the runner counting against me."

Bresnahan was going to let it go, but not his teammates, who began razzing the pitcher. But Poehl had a career to think about.

Finally, Gergan told him about the conversation with the umpire: Don't sweat it, Mike, it will be a do-over. Poehl gave in, reluctantly.

But, like crying, there are no do-overs in baseball.

A crowd of 3,258, swelled by the presence of the Philly Phanatic mascot in town, turned out for the doubleheader. Why else would anyone show up? It was the 138th game of a scheduled 140-game season, and Williamsport was 27 games out of first.

The Phillies were leading 1–0 going into the top of the fifth. Rick Lundblade, Reading's catcher, singled to start the inning. Phillies pitcher Mike Shelton then moved him to second on a sacrifice bunt. The moment was drawing close.

Dave Bresnahan (courtesy of Dave Bresnahan).

With a left-hander up, Bresnahan signaled Poehl he wanted a breaking ball, low and inside, the kind that results in grounders to the right side of the infield. Unbelievably, it worked perfectly: a ground ball out to second, moving the runner to third. Bresnahan was in the crosshairs of greatness: runner on third, two outs.

"There. There is the point of no return." Bresnahan said. "Everyone is saying, 'Oh, is he is going to do it?'"

Yes, yes he was. He turned to homeplate umpire Scott Potter. "Netting's busted," the catcher told him, waving his glove. Bresnahan trotted back to the dugout.

At third, Swain turned away to keep from laughing. Brez received the same reception down in the dugout. "Everyone was looking down," Bresnahan said. "I didn't look at anybody because I didn't want to start laughing."

With Gomez and coaches oblivious and players turning away, no one saw Bresnahan stash the spud in his mitt and run back to his position. "I squatted to give the sign. As the pitcher went into his windup I switched it from my glove hand to my bare hand."

After the pitch came in, Bresnahan fired to third, the idea being to sail the spud over the third baseman's head.

"I didn't want to make a real wild throw," Bresnahan said. "But if you throw a peeled Boise potato … well, instead of being inaccurate, I became too accurate."

It was a perfect strike. Bresnahan never considered the possibility of actually picking off the runner. Luckily, Swain called up all theatrical reserves he had not to catch the spud. He missed, and it bounded into the outfield.

"Go! Go! Go!" screamed third base coach Joe Lefebvre. Bresnahan threw down his mask and swore, kicking dirt. The man could have been an actor.

Lundblade was off for the plate.

Left-fielder Miguel Roman then gave chase. He went to scoop up the ball, or at least what was left of it. He stared at Swain; Roman wasn't in on the gag. "He was one of the Latin guys; maybe he didn't hear it," Bresnahan explained.

Meanwhile, Lundblade was trotting home with what he thought was a gift run. There was Bresnahan, standing at the plate. Suddenly, the catcher slapped the tag on the stunned runner.

"Hey, Rick, you're out," Bresnahan said.

Time seem to halt for a moment. Potter the umpire was struggling to figure out what had just happened.

"Brez," Potter screamed. "What the hell did you do?"

Lefebvre, having gone out to left to investigate, saw what was left of the projectile.

"It's a f———potato," he shouted.

"You can't bring another ball on the field," Potter said.

Bresnahan corrected him: "That was a potato—but I tagged him with the ball."

Confusion continued both on the field and in the stands, where fans were still clueless to what was going on. As Bresnahan noted: "Nobody said, 'Ladies and gentlemen, that was a potato.'"

Potter thought Brez was trying to "show him up." "The home plate umpire is all paranoid because he knows he has to make a ruling on what they don't teach in umpiring school," Bresnahan said years later. "Meanwhile, the Phillies are busting up."

Potter then made his call: "This is professional baseball; you guys can't be out here showing me up like that.

"That run counts."

Gergan tried to appeal to Potter's sense of humor. No way. "The run counts," he repeated. Next batter.

Gomez stifled a chuckle when he came out to the plate. "Why does the run count?"

The umpire came up with the best, and only, answer: "Because I'm ruling the run counts."

Mike Fitzpatrick has no trouble with Potter's logic. Fitzpatrick is the director of field supervision for the Major League Baseball Office for Umpire Development; in short, he scouts the minors for up-and-coming umps.

Fitzpatrick said Potter, who worked as a National League fill-in umpire as well as an International League regular in 1996, made the right call. He called Bresnahan's act "unsportsmanlike, and meant to deceive" and said that the field umpire was empowered to order the run scored under Rule 9.01(c), a wonderful catchall, if you are an umpire: "Each umpire has authority to rule on any point not specifically covered in these rules."

"I think there was good judgment involved there," Fitzpatrick said. "You can go through all the rules and you won't find anything about potatoes."

Bresnahan wasn't part of a Bill's winning rally capped by a triple by Turner Gill, the Nebraska quarterback who went back to be an assistant coach for the national champion Cornhuskers (Williamsport lost the second game). There is a misconception that Bresnahan, who was given an error on the potato play, was also booted by the umpire for the stunt. He wasn't. "Orlando Gomez pinch hit for me," Bresnahan said.

In fact, Gomez was on the phone with Jeff Scott, the Indians minor league director of operations who held the same position with the Mariners when Bresnahan was signed, while the Indians were retiring the last batter in the fifth. Then the manager benched Bresnahan.

"In the clubhouse he pulled me into his office," Bresnahan recalled, "and said, 'I'm going to have to fine you.'" As soon as the news hit the clubhouse, Players immediately took up a collection to cover the $50. "I thought that was the end of it," Brez said.

After the game Poehl was slightly ticked, while Gomez had grown indignant: "Bresnahan did an unthinkable thing for a professional."

The next morning Bresnahan went home and was with several other players when he received a call to report to the clubhouse at 10 A.M. Gomez handed the catcher the phone: it was Jeff Scott. To Bresnahan, Scott was a good guy who was now in a tough position.

Scott was laughing at the stunt but also knew he had to take action. He then told Bresnahan he was cut.

"I was perfectly fine with that," the now ex-catcher said. "It wasn't the end of my life. I said, 'See ya.'"

Bresnahan was now out of baseball. The local paper was bashing the catcher for "a foolish stunt." Maybe this potato thing was a dumb idea.

He then did what any kid in trouble would do, he called home. His dad back in Phoenix almost hurt himself laughing so hard. "He about fell off his chair," the son said. Maybe he wasn't so warped after all.

The next day he dumped 50 potatoes on Gomez' desk with a note: "Orlando, this spud's for you!"

Bresnahan came back for the last game of the year and found fans clamoring for his autograph. Soon newspapers all across the country were calling about the story. Letterman even talked about it.

"All the stuff that followed was a snowball effect," Bresnahan said. "It was embarrassing."

The *Chicago Tribune* named him its "Sports Person of the Year" for attempting to "have a little fun with life, to inject some lost levity into sports." Meanwhile, Gomez, who was demoted to Class A ball the following year, still didn't get the humor: "I love this game. What he did was to make a joke out of it."

For throwing a vegetable where no man had thrown one before, Bresnahan earned an honor reserved for greatness. On May 30, 1988, Williamsport retired his No. 59. (In 1996, when baseball returned to Williamsport in the form of the New York–Penn League, Bresnahan again had his jersey retired.) About 3,500 fans paid $1 and a potato to turn out for the ceremony at Bowman Field. The incident from the season before was reenacted, with Rick Lundblade on hand to recreate his fateful trot home.

"Baseball purists ask, 'Why? He made a travesty of the game,'" said Bills general manager Rick Mundean the night of the ceremony. "But we think Dave did something that is the essence of baseball; he had fun with it. At a time when the business of baseball dominates the headlines, he brought baseball back to the field."

Bresnahan is now a stockbroker living in Tempe, Arizona. He is the only player in history to throw away a career not with drugs, or alcohol, or sloth, but with a potato.

"It was my last play," Bresnahan said, still laughing years later. "It's a fun story to tell. At least I'm remembered by something. At least I'm known for something."

JOE BAUMAN

They used to call it fence money down in ballparks across the Southwest. Joe Bauman discovered the tradition in his second game for Amarillo in 1946, when he hit his first home run for his new team.

Bauman had just parked one into the right-field stands. Head down, he trotted the bases, tapped home plate, and returned to the dugout.

"Go get your money," a teammate said.

"What do you mean?" Bauman replied. "What money?"

"Look at the fence."

People were coming down from the stands behind home plate, sticking dollar bills into the fence. They did this for every home-team dinger. Once in a while you would catch a fiver; if some guy had a side bet in the stands, he might even slip a player a ten as part of the payoff. It was tradition down there. Besides, what's a buck?

Big money. "If you won a ball game, you could get one hundred, one fifty, two hundred dollars," the 6-foot-5, 235-pound first baseman said years later. "If it was just another run, it was thirty-five, forty, fifty dollars."

Bauman said he was embarrassed at first to emerge from the dugout and take the cash. He got over it before his first collection was over. "It didn't take me long to learn about going around the fence," he said. "You could make more money at that than in your salary."

Bauman was a career minor leaguer back in the days when the salary difference between the bigs and the bushes—or the rest of society, for that matter—wasn't as pronounced as today. But with fence money, well, you can say Joe Bauman did all right for himself.

Joe Willis Bauman played 9 minor league seasons over 16 years, never rising higher than the one game he played in 1948 for the Boston Braves' top farm team in Milwaukee (where the parent team would move in 1953). After his first season, 1941, he was out of organized baseball for four years, three taken up in the navy, where he played on a base team that could rival almost any minor league squad. After the 1948 campaign, he opted to play semipro ball and run a gas station. In 1952 he came back to organized ball with Artesia of the Longhorn League.

That year he hit 50 home runs, drove in 157 runs, and hit .375. He followed up in 1953 with equally impressive stats: 53 homers, 141 RBIs, and a

.371 average. By then Bauman was 32. But he was just warming up. In 1954, playing for the Class C Roswell Rockets of the Longhorn League, Bauman put up numbers that, as a group, may never be equaled.

He batted an even .400.

He scored 188 runs, or 1.36 runs for each of his team's 138 games (eight shy of Billy Hamilton's major league record).

He had 199 hits.

He racked up 224 RBIs (34 better than Hack Wilson's major league mark).

He walked 150 times.

He tallied 456 total bases (one less than Babe Ruth's major league record).

He banged out a .916 slugging percentage (69 points higher than Ruth's record).

He again eclipsed 50 home runs.

And 60.

And 70.

He finished the year with 72 homers, more than one every other game and better than anyone before or since in professional baseball.

"I kind of started out hot and stayed that way," he said with the understatement of a native Oklahoman.

The binge eclipsed pro baseball's single-season home run record of 69, set in 1933 by Joe Hauser of Minneapolis and tied in 1948 by Bob Crues of Amarillo. Hauser set his record four years after his last game in the majors; Crues never made it to the bigs.

Bauman almost never had a chance to reach the record. After the 1948 season, where he was a rung away from the majors, Bauman thought he was through with pro baseball after he had trouble reaching a deal with the Boston Braves.

"I had some money problems with that Boston organization," he said years later. "They offered a cut of $200 a month. I said go to hell. I said as far as I was concerned, I was done.

"Hindsight is 20/20; I should not have held out at all at that age, 24 or so," he continued. "I should have just gone back and played and given it a good shot. But I got stubborn. I made a mistake."

Bauman spent two years playing semipro ball and building up his Texaco business in Elk City, Oklahoma. He got lured back to the minors in Artesia, New Mexico, held onto his cash, and bought a gas station there. In two years he moved on to Roswell.

Bauman liked Roswell, best known for a purported UFO crash there in 1947. He liked the open spaces of the West. He liked the town's size and people. He liked the fact that Roswell had a Texaco station he could buy. And he really liked Park Field's whitewashed wooden right-field fence 329 feet from home plate.

Joe Bauman (courtesy of Joe Bauman).

Bauman had set a Longhorn League record for home runs in 1953, but in 1954 everything came together like it never has for any player before or since. He spent the year collecting cash—gas money from motorists at his Texaco station by day, fence money from fans behind home plate by night.

"I had never failed to have a slump, but that particular year I never had a slump," he said. "Oh, I had nights I had the collar, but not that many."

It took a while into the year before Bauman was able to realize his unbelievable season was inching into the historic.

"When we got to 60, that was a big number," he said. "We always knew that for 30 years Hauser had the record of 69. That always seemed way the hell on the horizon. That's just astronomical."

By September 1, Bauman had 64 home runs in 131 games. But with only seven games to go, the record appeared out of reach. Only 524 turned out at Park Field to see Roswell beat Sweetwater that night—and see Bauman hit four homers and a double while driving in 10 runs. All of the sudden the invincible record was within striking distance.

"When I got four in one ballgame, then it became a reality," Bauman said. "Then you start thinking about it. I did."

Bauman, moved to leadoff by his manager Pat Stasey to get more at-bats per game, was homerless the next night (Stasey moved into Bauman's cleanup spot and hit three homers). In his final home game, with national magazine writers in attendance, Bauman tied the record with an eighth-inning blast to right. Four games, all on the road, remained for him to go after the record.

The next two games were in Big Spring, Texas. The pitchers there were determined not to go into the record books with Bauman and never gave him a pitch to hit. "I even swung at some 3–0 pitches that were balls," he said. Heresy for a man who walked 150 times.

The last day of the season, Sunday, September 5, and a doubleheader in Artesia. Bauman was friendly with Artesia manager Jim Adair, who coincidentally had played in the same league as Hauser the year he hit 69. Adair and Bauman had a pregame chat.

"I heard about what happened in Big Spring," the opposing manager said. "We're going to pitch to you. If one of these guys walks you, I'll pull 'em."

True to his word, his pitchers threw strikes. Bauman set the record of 70 with a home run off Jose Galardo in his first at-bat and added two more in the night cap.

Bauman's record of 72 has stood longer than Babe Ruth's 60 or Roger Maris' 61. In 1956, Dick "Dr. Strangeglove" Stuart hit 66, but that is the only time Bauman's mark has been seriously threatened. Outside of Maris, no one has hit more than 60 home runs in a season until Mark McGuire (70) and Sammy Sosa (66) in 1998.

But by now Bauman was too old for the majors. The year after his record campaign Bauman didn't even get a raise, and his numbers at Roswell slipped to a mere mortal total of 46 home runs and 132 RBIs. Plagued by injuries in 1956, he called it quits halfway through the season with 17 homers. He finished his nine-year minor league career with 337 home runs, 1,116 hits, 1,057 RBIs, and a .337 average.

After leaving the game, Bauman worked at his service stations and for a beer distributorship before retiring in 1984. All these years later the question begs itself:

Would Bauman trade his one season of fame for one year in the bigs? No way, he answers.

"I never would have achieved anything like that in the majors." he said. Then he paused. Make that maybe.

"I might have exchanged it for a 10-year career," he adds.

Then he comes back around again. Nah, he'll take his career as it was.

"When it's all said and done it's not such a big deal," he said. "You get as much a kick out of hitting a home run in Roswell or Elk City as you do in Yankee Stadium. Because you love the game."

ODELL "RED" BARBARY

A world war raged. A dictator ravaged Europe. America suffered from the lingering depression and wartime rationing. Mothers with tear-streaked cheeks hung Gold Stars from windows to mourn dead sons.

The year was 1942. The world seemed to be coming apart.

America looked to baseball to forget, if only for a couple of hours at a time. But also to remember. Americans needed to remember the crack of a bat to muffle the crack of a rifle, to convince each other life could be fun. Life could be good. And that life's possibilities one day would, again, be limitless.

"I honestly feel that it would be best for the country to keep baseball going," President Franklin D. Roosevelt wrote to major league Commissioner Kenesaw Mountain Landis after the latter asked him if the game, like so much else, should be suspended for the duration. "There will be fewer people unemployed and everybody will work longer hours and harder than ever before. And that means that they ought to have a chance for recreation and for taking their minds off their work even more than before."

One who embodied that spirit of kindled hope was a small-town, red-haired Georgian who loved the game. His seven-year minor league career would yield a fame that was as brief; and a legacy as murky, as his pitching debut and finale was remarkable.

The legend was born on the long night of September 7, 1942, in Charlotte, North Carolina, in the Piedmont League. Second-string catcher Odell "Red" Barbaby finally had to put his arm where his mouth was. He had no choice because after a season bragging about his high school pitching prowess—often at the expense of his pitching teammates with growing ERAs and declining promise—he was sent to the hill.

Twenty-two innings later he would have a 4–3 win and a complete game. Both were his first. And his last.

The gushing of sports copy that followed helped him get a trip to the big leagues. It would be a one-game affair, but that's OK. Affairs are brief. His love was baseball.

The playoffs were a sure thing that year for the Charlotte Hornets (the NBA team recycled the name more than four decades later) that summer of '42. Not much was at stake when the Hornets took on the Asheville Tourists at Griffith Park the last night of the season. Charlotte was more concerned with saving its mound staff for the playoffs than notching one more meaningless win. The Hornets just wanted to get through the game, quick and easy.

Players were told they could pick any position they wanted to play that night. All spots were open—except pitcher.

Attention turned to the big red-headed catcher with a gun for an arm and a solid .300 average who sometimes pitched batting practice. As a pitcher he proved he was a good catcher: outside of missing a slider, changeup, or curveball he had all the tools. But he said he was a hot-shot pitcher back in high school in Simpsonville, Georgia, so Barbary got the nod, as much as a lark as anything else.

"All right, gentlemen, you're going to see the great Barbary pitch tonight," he told his teammates, who cheered and snickered.

Yet by the time that single game was over Barbary would add numbers to the record book that are nothing to laugh at: 21 scoreless innings, only 11 hits, 6 walks, and 13 Asheville runners stranded. At the plate he also slapped 2 hits, 2 sacrifices, and scored a run. He didn't commit an error or throw a wild pitch.

What made it all the more extraordinary was that in three and a half hours of baseball, after facing 72 batters, Barbary logged just 2 strikeouts. Moreover, the night also provided baseball with one of its greatest heartbreak kids: Asheville pitcher Larry Kempe went 22 innings, faced 79 batters, walked 3 and stranded 17, and went 3-for-8 at the plate with a double and 2 RBIs.

And lost. It had to be a long bus ride to Asheville.

But few gave it much thought. The night and the town's collective heart were with the catcher who wouldn't stop pitching. Herman Helms, executive sports editor of *The State*, a newspaper in Columbia, South Carolina, retold the tale 45 years later of "the catcher who pitched all night."

"Barbary, a noted clubhouse kidder, had boasted throughout the season about his talents as a pitcher," Helms wrote. "Any time a pitcher worked a good game, Barbary would say, 'Man, you pitched tonight the way I used to pitch in high school. It's a shame a talent like mine has to go to waste catching.'"

On the night that manager Harry Smythe took him up on the offer, the crowd was sparse, at least at the beginning. "But curious people got out of bed and rushed to the park to observe the miracle," Helms wrote. "The stands were pretty well filled as the thin man and Asheville carried their struggle into extra innings."

The *Charlotte Observer* captured the night with the prose of Jake Wade:

> The Hornets and Asheville Tourists kissed the Piedmont
> League season goodbye at Griffith Park last night by splitting
> a double header, one game of which was an amazing 22-inning
> struggle.

That's right, 22 long innings, count 'em. The marathon was the first game and Odell "Red" Barbary, of all persons, pitched it for the Hornets. And won it, 4 to 3.

Barbary, second string Hornet catcher, went to the hill more as a lark than anything else, the two wind-up games here meaning little to either ball club. But the lanky red-head, sold to Washington recently as a receiver, stayed in there to gain glory and become a hero. He'll have something to tell his grandchildren.

Barbary, who pitched a little in high school and once or twice before, has pitched in professional contests on such occasions as last night, did not show any dipsy-doodles on his pitches, but he had control and a strong arm to deliver it. He looked about as stout at the end as he did at the beginning. [The opposing pitcher Larry Kempe] also showed staying qualities but seemed to have little on the agate as the Hornets pounded a total of 22 hits, failing to convert them into runs. Kempe did not fan a hitter and Barbary whiffed only two.

Now Barbary talks of his years of living the dream of playing professional baseball with all modesty. With a laugh through a rich Southern drawl, he responds to requests to talk about his career with, "Sure, it won't take a long time." He doesn't mention he hit .370 in his first season in the minors in Greenville, Alabama, in 1939 or his strong arm ("that's from throwing to second base so many times") or that a knee injury cut short his rise through the ranks. He doesn't mention his permanent line in *The Baseball Encyclopedia* (Red Barbary, 1943, Washington, one game, one at-bat, no hits). He doesn't mention, or even know, that his minor league travels and misidentified ("Ronald Odell Barbary" and "Donald Barbary") major league tally along with a copy of the 1943 West Union telegram that called him up to "the Show" are on file at the Hall of Fame.

That's just not Red Barbary. At age 75, he referred to his remarkable, unparalleled night in baseball as simply "a fluke thing." Doesn't even remember much about it, he said years later, although the claim sounds more like a way to avoid talking about himself than an admission of old memories long faded.

"It was just one of those days.... It was just supposed to be a seven-inning game. It ended up a little longer," he said.

Barbary never pitched again. "No," he said with a laugh, "I had enough."

Years later Barbary still refused to take himself too seriously as a ballplayer. Maybe the Depression and a war or two will do that to you. Back in his playing days, while he savored every ball and strike, he knew it was a game and paled to what was going on beyond the foul lines. He knew he and

Odell "Red" Barbary (courtesy of Odell Barbary).

his teammates played for something more than the Piedmont League pennant. The country needed baseball and the stability it brought in an unstable time. One thing was still right in the world.

Barbary's bad knee, ripped up in a high school infield, kept him from serving: "A lot of boys went into the service ... that knee is what kept me out." Then he paused: "I had a lot of friends who didn't come back."

Years later he would rather talk about his son Eddie, who played on scholarship for Clemson and in the Pittsburgh farm system before getting his master's degree, or his grandson Travis, who played in the minors in Montana.

But make no mistake; he loved the game. "I just enjoyed every minute of it," he said. "I had legs broke, knees hurt, but I wouldn't trade it for anything."

The common perception of Barbary was that the 22-inning marathon ruined his arm and a chance at a prolonged major league career. Good excuse. Great bar story. But Red balks.

The day after he scrawled a bit of history into the record books he was ready to pitch batting practice.

There was also another fallacy, about that phenomenal high school pitching, that Red corrected for his teammates right after the game.

"To tell you the truth," the self-professed high school phenom said, "I never pitched a game before today in my life."

RON NECCIAI

In boxing, it's the knockout. In wrestling, the pin. In baseball, the ultimate moment of intimidation for a pitcher is the strikeout.

It's a moment of perfection, of absolute achievement over an opponent left flailing at the air, tilting at your windmill. Or, better yet, the batter is turned not only into defeated foe but into dumbfounded spectator as the third strike is called without so much as a check swing.

The strikeout. It can be just as sweet against Ted Williams or the loudmouth in the Kelly's Bar and Grill softball shirt strained against a beer belly.

Ron Necciai (pronounced NETCH-eye) is one who knows the strikeout's thrill well but also knows the chasm left when it's gone too soon, suddenly and forever.

In 1952 he did to an Appalachian League team what few even dream of. He struck out the side.

Eight times, and then some.

It was a cool night that May 15. Necciai had been a pitcher less than a year, after spending most of his American Legion and high school career at first base. After turning pro the year before, his first steps on the rubber were for the Salisbury, North Carolina, Pirates farm team, where he went 4-9. Not pack-it-in awful, but not good, either.

Then he was shipped to the Bristol, Virginia, Twins, which already had some serious pitching. There he soon faced the Class D team from Welch, West Virginia. They never faced anything like Necciai.

Even hustle, the great leveler, wouldn't work this night. After Necciai's catcher dropped a third strike and the runner sat at first base, thinking just maybe his team's nightmare was over, Necciai struck out another. The scorecard was a mess, and hard to believe: 4 Ks in an inning.

Imagine the frustration of the Welch Miners: Thirty batters up, twenty-seven batters fanned. It was the first time a no-hitter was almost an afterthought, secondary to an even greater feat. It was not a perfect game: it was better.

Yet it almost didn't happen. Halfway through the game Necciai approached his manager, George Datore. Necciai suffered from ulcers as the result of extreme nervousness that drove him to "smoking more cigarettes than Philip Morris could make in those days" in the clubhouse before a game. To make it through a game, he wolfed down milk, cottage cheese, and Melba toast between innings to keep his belly full and buffer the acid.

"I don't think I can make it," Necciai told the manager.

"Try another hitter," Datore responded.

The next inning, the same complaint, the same response: "Try another hitter." Then again the following inning: "Try another hitter."

Listening to his manager and not his stomach that night got him a mention in the National Baseball Hall of Fame, as the first to do the unthinkable.

"I knew during the game no one had a hit, but I didn't realize I had 'em all on strikes." He walked just one batter, hit another, and another hitter reached base on an error.

"When it was all over, none of us even realized what happened. They said, 'Hey! You struck out 27 guys!' I said, 'So what? The game's been around a hundred years, someone else must have done it.' It wasn't until the next morning that we realized no one ever had."

Welch hitters managed one groundout to second. Another hitter reached on a walk, another on a hit-by-pitch, and a third on an error. The fourth and final Miner to reach base was the wild-pitch strikeout in the ninth. Necciai went on to fan his 27th and final batter—and his fourth of the inning.

Necciai even went 1-for-4 at the plate. That performance was to be a jewel in a fantastic second professional year and his first full season as a pitcher. In 42⅔ innings at Bristol, he struck out 109, or better than 2 strikeouts an inning. He gave up just 10 hits, walked 20, and had an ERA that looks like a typo: 0.42.

He started four games for Bristol and appeared twice in relief roles, including one game that could have ended up a rattling tragedy for most pitchers, but instead put his name in the Hall of Fame: he struck out five batters in one inning.

It happened May 18, 1952, against Johnson City. That game he struck out eight in 2⅔ innings, including the eighth inning when his catcher couldn't handle two pitches that were good for third strikes. Both batters reached base. It was an unsettling yet surprisingly common sight for the fireballing right-hander, so Necciai just bore down and kept striking out overmatched hitters, as he did nearly every time he faced a man that summer at Bristol.

He was 19.

By the time that summer ended, he would shoot through the minors and pitch for the Pittsburgh Pirates, where Branch Rickey, the towering figure in Major League Baseball, offered praise usually voiced only by weekend Little League coaches.

"I've see a lot of baseball in my time," Rickey was quoted in *Branch Rickey* by Murray Polner. "There have only been two young pitchers I was certain were destined for greatness, simply because they had the meanest fastball a batter can face. One of those was Dizzy Dean. The other is Ron Necciai. And Necciai is harder to hit."

Necciai underscored that praise as he rocketed through the minors on the way to "the Show," developing his mean fastball and good curve. In Burlington of the Class B Carolina League, he led all pitchers with 172 Ks (in 126 innings) and a 1.57 ERA. His career stats show that in the minors he had 427 strikeouts in 338 innings. In one stretch of 69 minor league innings, he averaged 15 strikeouts every nine innings, according to Dennis Snelling's account in the book, *A Glimpse of Fame.*

Later that summer Necciai headed to Pittsburgh's Forbes Field, this time not as a fan, but as a phenom. The 6-foot, 5-inch rookie was the favorite son of a small steel-mill town called Monongahela outside Pittsburgh, and he compiled a respectable 1-6 major league debut on one of the most god-awful teams in major league history, one that bumbled to a 42-112 finish that year. But along they way, Necciai flashed portents of brilliance. In 54.2 innings he whiffed 31 at a time when talent made this one of baseball's most golden eras.

"I was either real good or real bad," Necciai recalls more than four decades later. "I either walked everybody or got everybody out."

The losses included a 2–0 heartbreaker to Cincinnati on Necciai's second night in the bigs and another "L" by a 3–2 margin. But that was OK. He was in the majors, striking out the best in the business, and he had just turned 20. The numbers were even a bit deceiving because the youngster was still working on his control against hitters who pounced on any mistake.

Some nights, like one relief appearance against Cincinnati, he struck out five of ten batters and had the stuff like back in the Appalachian League. On August 24, he beat the Boston Braves, 4–3. A major league win. But on other nights the pitches would inch up a little high or batters would pick up on his speed and motion, and he very much knew he was a kid in the majors.

"Those nights the same old thing would happen," he said. "I would throw balls, then half-assed fastballs. And those are line drives in the majors."

"When I left, I left early—when I got wracked, I got bombed. And when you're knocked out in the first inning, four runs gives you a 36.00 ERA for the day." His major league ERA in that rookie season would end up at 7.08.

"He's got a lot of stuff," said catcher Joe Garagiola in a 1952 *Sporting News* interview. "He's big and lean, 6 feet 5 and 180 pounds, the whippy Ewell Blackwell type, and he can throw as hard as anybody in this league. He stopped the Giants and Indians cold in training games and loosened up Sal Yvars, of the Giants, in a way Sal never will forget. He had a little trouble with the Browns and White Sox in New Orleans, but he showed me he has the makings of a great pitcher. ... He can throw as hard as [Bob] Feller or anybody else."

That winter the army called, but three months later the stomach ulcers that plagued Necciai throughout his baseball career tossed him out of military service on a medical discharge. So baseball was back and Necciai was ready to work into shape. That's what he was doing on a day in April 1953 outside the foul lines at Forbes Field when it happened.

Something tore. Something in his arm. His throwing arm.

Branch Rickey spared no expense, refusing to write off a sure thing, a can't-miss kid. Necciai was sent to hospitals at Duke University, at the University at California, at Johns Hopkins. All said surgery couldn't fix what throwing a wicked fastball had ripped apart.

"One of the doctors said he couldn't do it, and he recommended I go home and work in a gas station," Necciai remembers, bitterness at the harsh bedside manner still palpable today. "I was 20 years old. That's pretty hard to take. You grow up thinking old people don't heal, young people do."

Refusing to accept science over what his heart told him, Necciai just worked harder. For four or five months he trained and eventually went back to Burlington for a couple games, but the pain of the torn rotator cuff drove him out of the rotation.

He knew he had to face the unthinkable, that baseball might be over for him, that his white-hot potential might forever be just that.

Acceptance did not come easy, not for Necciai, not for Rickey. In 1954, Rickey wanted the righty back. Necciai did well for two innings against minor leaguers, but the pain shot back—a debilitating pain.

"You can't pitch two innings and then not be able to comb your hair for two weeks," he lamented.

But Rickey, who could have occupied himself with some of the best established stars in the game, wouldn't give up on Necciai. In 1955 he sent Necciai to Hollywood in the Pacific Coast League, along with a case of Cortisone pain-killer. The shots needled directly into the bad arm before game time gave Necciai an hour and 45 minutes of relief, and nothing but grief for opposing batters. Then it wore off. Two more weeks without use of the arm.

So Rickey paid Necciai to go to Waco, Texas, to lay in the sun. "Bake it out and rest," said Rickey, short on medical knowledge but long on optimism.

It didn't work. The injury that is commonly rectified by surgery today ended the career of Ronald Andrew Necciai. And by all accounts, the loss was suffered not only by the pitcher, not only by the Pirates and Branch Rickey, who placed Necciai on his all-time team with Christy Mathewson, but by the game's fans.

He had overcome so much—the nervousness, the ulcers, the hard times in the bushes, the army that could have taken a chunk of his prime, the attention, the mammoth expectation. He got through it all and flourished. What is left, it would seem to most, is a single stat line in *The Baseball Encyclopedia,* of his three months in the majors—not a flattering line at that—and some occasional pain, despair, bitterness, regret.

But not for Necciai.

"I got a lot more out of it than I gave," says Necciai, 64 years old by the 1996 All-Star Game, free from smoking and the ulcers.

Ron Necciai (courtesy of Ron Necciai).

Principal among the gifts are the memories, like the day he almost chucked baseball back in 1951 while nearly starving in Salisbury, North Carolina, in the Class D North State League.

"I threatened to quit because I was starving, even when hamburgers were a dime. So they let me drive the bus." Taking the wheel of that 17-passenger GMC dinosaur paid another $150 a month. It doubled his income. Necciai enjoys his minor league memories instead of thinking about what might have been.

"'Could I have?' or 'Would I have?' Those questions come to mind, but after a while you just accept it. ... You never miss what you never had, so you get over it."

"But I sure enjoyed it though, it was awful sweet," he said from his office in his Hays, Necciai & Associates sporting goods business in Charleroi, Pennsylvania, where his 1952 National League contract, with a $5,000 minimum wage, hangs framed on the wall.

Necciai looks upon it with pride, with satisfaction. There's nothing bitter in his vibrant voice. He figures that ultimately he got more than he paid. And if he has any doubt that he left a mark in the baseball world, he need only jump in his car and drive northwest five hours, as he did in 1995. To Cooperstown.

"I wanted to go up to the third floor, to the minor league section, and see my name," he said. "And there it is."

GENE RYE

The only thing oversized about Eugene Mercantelli was his name. Only 5-foot-6 but a stocky 165 pounds, Mercantelli went by the nickname "Half-Pint" while playing under the name Gene Rye, chosen at the suggestion of a friend to fit in a box score.

In 1930 the 23-year-old Chicagoan played left field for the Waco Cubs of the Texas League, a circuit he would tear up with a .367 average for the season. Batting left and throwing right, Rye was a dangerous player. Especially one hot Texas night.

In 1927, Waco had a player named Stump Edington who hit two home runs in an inning. The following year, while managing in the Class B Virginia League, he called his old team, telling the club to buy Rye. The man, he said, was made for Waco's home park. "He will hit more home runs in Katy Park than I ever could," Edington said. Doubt about Edington's prediction was understandable: Rye looked more like a bowling pin than a ballplayer.

Some sportswriters of the day fancied themselves to be poets. Jinx Tucker of the *Waco Times-Herald* was no exception.

> *So if a body meets a body.*
> *And it happens to be Rye.*
> *Just doff your hat and smile a smile*
> *As he waddles merrily by.*

"Yeah, he's the little bow-legged chap the big league scouts give the 'go by' because he is not much larger than a minute—doesn't have enough power or something at the bat," Tucker wrote. "All he can do is hit three home runs in one inning."

Night baseball had come to the Texas League in 1930, five years before the majors. A good crowd turned out for the midweek August 6 game against Beaumont, which was also the first night game broadcast on radio in league history. The Wednesday game appeared pedestrian, as Beaumont pitcher Jerry Mallett was cruising through the Waco Cubs lineup as he took a 6–2 lead into the bottom of the eighth.

Thus began one of the most wild and absurd half-innings in baseball history.

Gene Rye (courtesy of Baseball Hall of Fame Library, Cooperstown, New York).

The first batter up in the inning for Waco was Rye. He waddled to the plate "walking more like a duck than a human," one writer described him—his bow legs supplying him his unusual balance and power. Rye smashed a towering fly to right, going ... going ... foul, only by a foot or so. The groans barely ebbed when Rye leaned into an outside pitch and took it the other way to left and out of the park for a homer.

The listless crowd of about 2,000 briefly came to life, but Beaumont held a still-comfortable three-run cushion, 6–3. But Rye's homer rattled Mallet. He gave up a walk, a single, and another walk to load the bases and was relieved by Ed Green.

What Rye had started Green could not stop. All three runners left on by Mallet came around to score, as did three more. Suddenly, Waco had a 9–6 lead, and still nobody out. Exit Ed Green, enter Walter Newman.

Enter Gene Rye, this time with two men on. Newman came in with a fastball. Big mistake. "It's another homer," yelled a fan as Rye made contact. He was right: the ball disappeared over the right-field fence for a three-run shot.

Rye was 2-for-2 in home runs that inning. And still nobody out. The runs continued to pour in, and Walter Newman was hung out to dry. He was able to scrape a pair of outs. It looked like Rye, hitting fifth in the order that night, wouldn't get another chance.

But a walk and a pair of singles loaded the bases. There was that little guy again.

Rye was in the hole 0–2 when he took a ball. Then he fouled off a pitch. Newman, knowing what Rye did with his fastball, came back with a curve. Mistake again: Rye waited on the pitch and hit a rocket of a line drive to right. He then broke into his third home-run waddle of the game, and the inning.

Waco finished the inning with 18 runs, 8 driven in by Rye. And with 3 home runs in one inning, the shortest guy on the team accomplished a slugging feat never equaled before or since.

Wrote Tucker the sportswriter/poet:

> *If a body meet a body,*
> *And it happens to be Rye.*
> *If a body would walk a body,*
> *It would save a body a cry.*

As of this writing, 30 major leaguers have hit two home runs in an inning (Willie McCovey, Andre Dawson, and Jeff King each did it twice). But no one ever went deep three times in one frame. Tom Burns of Chicago hit two doubles and a home run in one inning in an 1883 National League game for the previous single-inning hitting standard.

Rye's contract was purchased for the next season by the Boston Red Sox. He was a man certain of his worth, and let Boston president Robert Quinn know it in turning down his first contract offer.

"I'm the best hitter you've got, Mr. Quinn, he said. "I found that out by looking at your club roster. I'm good. I know I'm good. And I'll show you that I'm good. But meantime I'd like to have you revise the stipend as the boys say, and revise it upward."

Rye would need money. A knee injury in 1931 limited him to 17 games and only 10 starts, in which he hit an anemic .179. It amounted to his career.

Rye would bounce around the minors until 1936. He hit .306 at Green Haven in 1932, .315 at Elmira in 1933, and a Western League–leading .378 in 1934. But he never got another shot at the bigs or recovered his long-ball stroke.

In 39 major league at-bats, Gene Rye didn't hit one home run. In the end he is remembered not for a shortened career, but an extended inning.

Moments
in
the Sun

Ron Blomberg

The future was ordained for the 17-year-old, No. 1 draft pick out of Georgia. He was going to be the new Pride of the Yankees, the Jewish Babe Ruth, the hero to the city's 2.5 million Jews and all of New York, just like Hank Greenberg of the Bronx would have been three decades before if the Yankees hadn't already had the power of Lou Gehrig.

"In time, The House That Ruth Built may be remembered as The House That Blomberg Remodeled," *New York Times* columnist Dave Anderson wrote in 1973.

Sportswriters even brought up the fabled M words. Ron Blomberg. The next Mickey Mantle.

"I hope you break some of my records," Mantle told the up-and-comer.

"I'll only be half of what you were," Blomberg replied.

Blomberg didn't shoot as high as Mickdom, but he set himself three goals. To play in a World Series. To make the All-Star team. And one more — a little memento at Yankee Stadium:

"You know, you always read about the place, and those monuments out there…. When I'm finished playing, I'd like them to have a monument of mine out there, too."

Fame was as reachable for Blomberg as the stadium's short porch in right. He should have been a star. For part of one season, 1973, he was. The 6-foot-1½, 195-pounder did Johnny Carson and Dick Cavett and Tom Snyder. He was on the covers of *Sports Illustrated* and the; *Sporting News*. "Not many guys get on the covers of those things," Blomberg said almost 23 years later. "I had it all. I had everything. I was out there, and it was great. I had it.

"Then I got injured."

Blomberg should have owned the Big Apple longer than he did, where for a time he was, in his own words, "the biggest thing to hit New York since Joe Namath." He should have been more than a trivia answer.

For all his potential, Blomberg's niche in baseball history was reached by merely walking up to the plate one Opening Day at Fenway Park. At 1:53 P.M. Friday, April 6, 1973, Blomberg, New York's fifth hitter in the top of the first, dug in against Boston's Luis Tiant and eventually worked out a bases-loaded walk. Blomberg thus became baseball's first designated hitter.

The distinction could have gone to Orlando Cepeda, Boston's DH, had the Yankees gone down in order. If it had rained that day in Boston, maybe Terry Crowley of the Orioles (called, in one Associated Press account the next day, a "designated pinch-hitter") or Ollie Brown of the Brewers, who played against each other later in the day, would have been remembered today.

Ron Blomberg shouldn't have been baseball's first designated hitter. He was slated to start the 1973 season opener in the outfield. But at the time Blomberg was injured. Appropriate.

"What do I do?" he asked before the game.

"Just hit the ball and knock people in," manager Ralph Houk replied.

Blomberg later joked he had been "a DH all my life—a designated Hebrew."

He was young then. He thought the first DH thing wouldn't really matter compared to the great career that was ahead of him. He knows better now.

"They took the ball and jersey [after the game] for the Hall of Fame, but I never thought it was a big deal," he said almost a quarter-century later. "Then the anniversaries go by: 10, 15, 20 [years]. All of the sudden you're on 'Jeopardy.' "

"Who was Ron Blomberg?" should have been the correct response to so much more.

"He had good tools, and he was ideal for Yankee Stadium because he really pulled the ball, line drives to right field," Yankee general manager Lee MacPhail would say 22 years after he drafted Blomberg. "He should have been a great major league player."

In the end, Ron Blomberg did turn out to be half of what Mickey Mantle was. The half that got hurt.

Blomberg told reporters early on that he was not a natural athlete growing up in Atlanta. "I taught myself to hit by pulling berries off a bush in our front yard and hitting them with a stick," he said. "I got to be a pretty good hitter, but no one ever hit the berries to me so I could learn to field."

The story goes like this: Ron tries out for his Little League team, but gets cut right away. "I couldn't catch," he explained. "I couldn't hit. I didn't know what to do with a baseball. I got blown away."

But he goes through the tryout line again, gets another number, and makes the team as a third baseman. His batting average for the season: .989.

"I think I got out one time," Blomberg says. Then he laughs at a confession: "My father was the scorekeeper."

Blomberg said that from that time on, making the majors was his goal.

"It seems like all my cousins and relatives became doctors or lawyers," said Blomberg, who often said his parents wanted him to be a doctor and a lawyer. "I wanted to do something different. While the other kids were studying, I was always outside, swinging a bat or throwing a ball."

At Druid Hills High School in Atlanta, Blomberg was an All-American in basketball as well as a star split end on the football team. "I turned down 150 basketball scholarships and 100 football scholarships," said Blomberg, who also ran track. He said many of these college recruiters were scared away by the baseball scouts showing up at his baseball games, crowing he would be the No. 1 draft pick. Blomberg, who hit left and threw right (he throws everything but a baseball lefty, but golfs righty, except when he putts), hit over .400 for his scholastic career. In his senior year he hit .472 with five home runs and 45 RBIs, despite the intense scrutiny.

"I had the ability. I didn't worry about pressure," he said. "I produced more when I had more people out in the stands. When you're an athlete, you're a showman."

The first round of the 1967 baseball amateur draft was impressive, producing Jon Matlack (4th pick), John Mayberry (6th), Ted Simmons (10th), Dave Radar (18th), and Bobby Grich (19th), among other future major leaguers. But it was Blomberg, blessed with the rare gifts of power, speed, and average, who was going to be the star.

"I can't imagine any high school boy being a better hitter than Ronnie," said MacPhail, who signed Blomberg to his first contract for $60,000.

Blomberg was up briefly in 1969 and was called up for good in June 1971, after a torrid stretch at Syracuse where he raised his average 40 points, to .326, over the span of several weeks. He would have been called up sooner, but he was hurt. This time it was his back.

"There's no doubt Blomberg has great potential," Houk said after the 1972 season. "He has so many plusses going for him that it has to be only a matter of time and experience before he realizes all his potential. With speed, power, the ability to make contact and all the other things he has going for him, Blomberg could wake up one morning and find himself a star."

That one morning was in 1973.

Like most lefties, "Boomer" was a deadly low-ball hitter. While he studied pitchers, he didn't try to outguess them. "I just operate on one idea about hitting—see, swing, hit," he said in 1973. While he obviously had home-run power, it was the searing line drives he sprayed across the outfield that made him the most feared hitter in the league against right-handers.

Starting in May of that year, Blomberg went on a tear, and by mid–June he was over .400 and had hit in 23 straight games as a starter. The consecutive-game streak was stopped at 17 by a failed pinch-hitting appearance.

"I was getting more of an opportunity to play," he said. "I was starting to fulfill my potential. I never felt like I was in a zone. I knew I was a hitter."

Blomberg made the All-Star team that year—as a write-in—but could not play. Injury. He finished the season hitting .329 in 100 games.

But even though *Sports Illustrated* made him a cover boy—"The New Pride of the Yankees"—Blomberg was still displaying an alarming ineptness in the field.

That season he muffed a sure triple play against the Texas Rangers. All he had to do was catch a throw from shortstop Gene Michael, who had caught a line drive from Rico Carty and stepped on second. The throw hit his glove, then his chest, then the ground.

"I wanted to watch the triple play, " he explained afterward. "I've never seen one before."

"The man can hit," said Bobby Bonds, a teammate with the Yanks and Chicago White Sox, "but he cannot play a position."

Blomberg was still defensive about his defense long after his career. "I did not like first base. My position was the outfield. I never hurt the team in right field."

There was another irritation with some teammates. In the cold type of print, some of the quotes Blomberg made over the years, especially when he was still carrying the tag of phenom, may have seemed like bragging in an era before it was acceptable. But as Boomer notes his accomplishments and goals today, a listener doesn't get the impression he is trying to show off, even if the notes on the page say otherwise. "That's Ronnie!" was the tag line after one Boomer quote at the end of one newspaper story in the early 1970s. It fit.

Blomberg, now a career consultant outside of Atlanta, believes that because he was such a high pick and had a good relationship with the media, he got a lot of press, too much for some people. He said some players—Graig Nettles, Dick Tidrow, Sparky Lyle—resented him for it.

"If you ask 15 guys," said an unnamed ex–Yankee teammate in 1978 to the *Chicago Sun-Times*, "you won't get one to say a nice thing about him."

Thurman Munson did. "Ronnie was a good kid, I liked him," said the catcher, who roomed with Blomberg for three years. Others were harsher.

"Tell Bloomie you've interviewed all his friends, and you couldn't get anyone to talk," Nettles told the *Sun-Times*. "I'm not going to say anything about Bloomie except he's an [expletive]. If you want me to say he's an [expletive], you ain't got no story."

"When I was in New York I got all the publicity," Blomberg explained years later. "People were always jealous of the people who got the publicity. It doesn't bother me. Although it hurt me when I read it in the paper."

One teammate thought Blomberg tried too hard to get the publicity.

"If you're not doing it, you shouldn't be talking about it," Roy White said in 1978. "I think a few guys here probably felt he didn't work hard enough to improve on his defense or hitting left-handers."

Duke Snider and Jim Gentile couldn't hit lefties. Neither could Blomberg, his managers thought. Even at his hottest, Boomer usually got pine time

Ron Blomberg (courtesy of Baseball Hall of Fame Library, Cooperstown, New York).

against southpaws. It got to the point where other teams would throw up lefties just to keep Blomberg out of the lineup.

"It's all up here," Blomberg said, pointing to his long blond locks. "I've never gotten a chance to hit that many left-handed pitchers, and now it's been all blown up and it's gotten psychological. I feel I have the ability to do it."

Soon Blomberg's historic first would be twisted by newspeople from New York to California as he continued to ride the bench against lefties. Invariably the headline would read: "Designated Sitter."

Years later the tag of platoon player still irked Boomer.

"If you can hit, you can hit anybody," he said. "Why didn't I play against left-handers? I cannot tell you. In the year I was hitting .400, they kept me out of the lineup against left-handers."

But it was injuries that doomed the muscular Southerner. They were of the nickel-and-dime variety: a sore back here, a hamstring pull there, a sore shoulder now and then. The injuries were nagging, frustrating. "I never get hurt," Blomberg said early in his career after pulling a right hamstring in Boston. "But every time I do, it's on a cold day like this."

Blomberg fought through the injuries in 1974, when he hit .311 in 90 games. Then the injuries became catastrophic. In 1975 he hit a home run and heard a pop in his shoulder. He took a week off. Boomer came back, hit another homer, and heard another pop. The tendon leading to his bicep had popped out of place. He was out for the season, and almost all of 1976.

In 1977, Blomberg went into spring training, a long shot to make the team. But he started to hit and hit and hit. "I was crushing the ball," he said.

March 30, 1977. A spring training game at Chain O' Lakes Park in Winter Haven, Florida. The last thing Blomberg remembers was Roy White screaming "Stop!" Then came the wall, the collision.

"The next thing I know I'm walking around in circles on the bad leg, and there's blood on my nose," Blomberg told writer Mike Lupica from a New York hospital bed. "Then I just started babbling, I guess: 'I can play, I'm fine, don't put me on the disabled list.' Stuff like that. In the back of my mind, I remembered that the Red Sox were using all right-handed pitchers that day."

That was all for 1977, and Boomer's New York career (he did get a World Series ring). Blomberg needed a new start. He had two at-bats in two-plus years. On November 14, 1977, he signed with the White Sox during what was the advent of free agency.

"I know if anything happens to my shoulder again and I can't throw, I can still be a DH in the American League," he said, a partial explanation why he chose Chicago over Atlanta and the Mets. The main reason was a $600,000, four-year, no-cut contract. He became the highest-paid player on the team.

In his first game for Chicago, Blomberg hit an upper-deck shot against Dick Drago that beat Boston. But he knew the end was near: "From that time on my shoulder was getting worse and worse and worse." He retired after the 1978 season.

"Being the first designated hitter is all right, but I'd trade it in a minute for 20 good major league seasons," Blomberg once said. For his eight-year career spanning 461 games, Blomberg batted .293 with 52 home runs and 224 RBIs. He played 144 games at DH, 143 at first base, 79 in the outfield, and the rest as a pinch hitter.

Blomberg now embraces his lasting legacy in the game. "To this day, even though I didn't get into the Hall of Fame the way I had liked to, being the first designated hitter means I'm still in baseball history," he said. "They can never take that away from you."

Still, there is sadness hidden in a voice that remains perpetually upbeat. Looking back, Blomberg calls his career a good one, not a great one.

"It was a career in which I lived up to half my potential," Blomberg said in a recent interview. "It hurts not being able to reach your potential. I would have liked to [have] seen what I could have done."

ARCHIBALD
"MOONLIGHT" GRAHAM

Archibald Wright Graham never became a star, but fame did come to him—more than a quarter-century after he died and 77 years after he played the game.

Make that played a game. An outfielder for the New York Giants, Graham was sent out to right field as a late-inning defensive replacement at Brooklyn for lead-off hitter George Browne. The move was trivial, as the Giants coasted to an 11–1 win on the road before just 2,000 fans. That brief stint June 29, 1905, amounted to the man's major league career.

The Fayetteville, North Carolina, native never got to bat, didn't get a chance in the field, and probably would have been buried in the annals of baseball if not for two things.

One, he had a great nickname.

Two, Burt Lancaster played him in the movie.

Archibald Graham died in 1965 in Chisholm, Minnesota, and would have been forgotten, if he was ever known, by all outside the tiny mining town if not for a short-story writer who liked to read *The Baseball Encyclopedia*.

William P. Kinsella, an avid fan who has written extensively on the game, came across Graham by chance while perusing the nearly 3,000-page records book. There it was: Moonlight Graham.

"It was his name," Kinsella said recently. "It was just accidental. And if he had played 10 games I probably wouldn't have used him."

Kinsella had a short story in mind. But then he went to Chisholm to find out who this Archibald Graham was. Kinsella figured he would find some palooka at the American Legion bar, reliving for the thousandth time his one-game career. No matter: Kinsella was a fiction writer. He planned to make up Graham's life, weaving fiction around the player's one game in the record books.

Kinsella's plans soon changed. Truth isn't always stranger than fiction, but sometimes it's a lot better.

"I had no idea when we went up to Chisholm we would find anything so interesting," Kinsella said. "He just turned out to be more interesting than anything I could have invented."

Kinsella scrapped plans for just a short story. He was working on this other project, one on J. D. Salinger, that he decided to weave in. The result was the 1982 novel *Shoeless Joe*.

That book became the basis for a movie six years later. And *Field of Dreams* turned Archie "Moonlight" Graham's brief bio into a metaphor for dreams grazed but lost.

While the book was for the most part true to history, several key facts of Graham's life and career were changed in the movie. For example, he was born in Fayetteville, North Carolina, not Chisholm, Minnesota, where he lived for many years and died. His one at-bat came in a June 1905 game, not the last game of the year in 1925. And contrary to the movie, he was a left-handed hitter, not a righty, and did not quit baseball after that one major league at-bat: Graham played four more years in the minors.

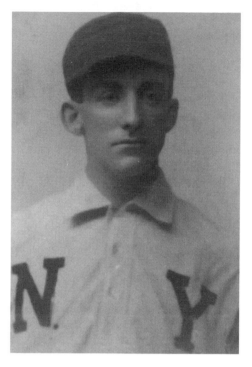

Moonlight Graham (courtesy of Veda Ponikvar).

One facet of the fictional accounts was very true: Dr. Graham was indeed a hero to a town that revered him both in life and long after his death.

Despite Graham's short stay in the majors, he was a player of some talent. In 1904, playing for Manchester of the New England League, he hit .272 with 15 stolen bases. In 1906 he played briefly for Memphis, then shifted to Scranton of the New York State League, where he led the league in hitting with a .335 average while swiping 38 bases. The 5-foot-10½, 170-pound outfielder had two more solid seasons for Scranton and ended his minor league career with a .291 average.

Graham, the older brother of Frank Porter Graham, a civil rights crusader who was briefly a U.S. senator and also a president of the University of North Carolina, did not have a baseball career much worth remembering. But his life's work, as a small-town doctor who made an everlasting impression in his community, is a noteworthy legacy.

"He was revered, that was true," said Bill Moose, a history instructor at

Mitchell Community College in Statesville, North Carolina, who is researching Moonlight's life. "He was the prototypical saintly, small-town doctor."

The town still remembers. It was 40 below zero in rural Minnesota the
day Veda Ponikvar was interviewed by one of the authors. If her name sounds
familiar to *Shoeless Joe* readers, it should: she was, in fact, the founder, editor, and publisher of the *Chisholm Free Press* and *Chisholm Tribune Press*,
the kindly older woman Ray Kinsella and J. D. Salinger—or, in the movie,
Kevin Costner (Kinsella) and James Earl Jones (Terrance Mann)—meet in
the newspaper office.

"Dr. Graham and I were real good friends and we worked on a lot of proj-
ects," said this former naval intelligence officer who founded the paper after
World War II. "He used to stop by every single day, in his big, black coat and
his hat."

Ponikvar sold the newspaper January 1, 1996. She stayed on as an adviser
and still writes the editorials for the paper that comes out Tuesdays and Thurs-
days. She handles all the questions about Dr. Graham.

She seems to relish the questions about a man she first met as a young
girl. She loved the movie, especially the scene where Moonlight Graham the
ballplayer steps off the Iowa ballfield and is transformed into Dr. Graham the
physician to save the life of Kinsella's daughter.

"It was beautiful, very beautiful," she said. "When he steps across the
line and saves that little girl, it couldn't have been done more beautifully or
more accurately. Because that was Dr. Graham."

Graham gave children inoculations and other forms of preventative med-
icine previously unknown in the mining town. Another of his revolutionary
procedures was criticized at the time but was later adopted as a model by the
Mayo Clinic and the University of Minnesota.

"He tested them for high blood pressure," she said. "There were a lot of
people who thought Dr. Graham was a quack. They didn't think kids could
get high blood pressure. They could."

Another program he implemented was making sure every child in kinder-
garten through sixth grade had a toothbrush and toothpaste at school. Dental hygiene was a rarity of the time, Ponikvar explained.

She said that's why she so loved that scene from the movie. "He saved
many a kid," she said.

Dr. Graham came to Chisholm, she said, after reading in a medical journal about the town looking for a doctor. It began a 40-year love affair. He
served as the school doctor, as well as working at nearby Root Hospital for
six years. His wife, Alecia, died in 1980.

Graham talked about his baseball career with the men who were his
peers, but he wouldn't tell the kids. They still knew he was athletic. He would
go out by the baseball park by Longyear Lake and play ball with the children.

"When he died, about two weeks later his wife Alecia brought to me his one and only miniature [photograph] of himself in his New York Giants uniform," Ponikvar said.

Sometimes Graham would travel with the Chisholm High School team, bringing along crates of apples and oranges, as well as a pocketful of dimes and quarters, for the team.

"Mining areas have ups and downs all the time," Ponikvar said. "During the Depression he was a hero."

Graham was popular enough to be elected to any local office of his choosing, but his only time in politics was serving several terms on the school board. "He got every vote," Ponikvar said.

Dr. Archibald Graham, aka "Moonlight" (courtesy of Veda Ponikvar).

Like Kinsella's search in the late 1970s, an effort today to find someone with an ill word for Graham is futile. "The only bad thing I can say about that fellow is he got old," said Chisholm basketball coach Bob McDonald, a former Chisholm player who is now the winningest scholastic hoops coach in Minnesota history.

Shoeless Joe and *Field of Dreams* are propelled by the power of the mystical, works where suspension of disbelief, necessary in most works of fiction, comes easily, welcomingly, for the reader and audience. In both we are expected to believe that a relative unknown is able to go to New England and get a writer famous for being a recluse—in the book, the real-life Salinger, in the movie, the fictitious Mann—to traipse around the country, all the way to Minnesota.

What requires an even greater effort to believe, yet according to Ponikvar is true, is that the book mirrored fact more than anyone ever thought.

It was known author William P. Kinsella did travel extensively researching for the book. What was not known, at least widely, was who went to Minnesota with him in 1978. Would you believe, as Ponikvar insists, Salinger himself?

"The two of them drove all the way from New York in an antique car," Ponikvar said. "They came into town and stopped right in front of the shop."

There, she said, she was met with one of the rarest of introductions: "This is J. D. Salinger," Kinsella said. They seemed surprised to hear Dr. Graham was in fact dead: he had died August 25, 1965, of pneumonia caused by lung cancer. He was buried in Rochester, Minnesota, home of the famous Mayo Clinic.

As in the book and movie, Ponikvar retrieved a clips file on Dr. Graham. Included was the editorial she had written upon his death (excerpted in the book), a piece of writing far more eloquent than you might expect from a small-town, north country newspaper.

"And as the community grew, Doc became an integral part of the population," she wrote in the August 31, 1965, edition of the *Chisholm Tribune Press*. "There were good years and lean ones. There were times when children could not afford eyeglasses or milk, or clothing because of economic upheavals, strikes and depressions. Yet no child was ever denied these essentials, because in the background, there was a benevolent, understanding Doctor Graham. Without a word, without any fanfare of publicity, the glasses or the milk, or the ticket to the ball game found their way into the child's pocket."

Did Ponikvar know, for sure, the man who sat at her desk by the window in her office was in fact Salinger? "Oh, yes I did," she said. "He didn't say much. It seems to me he was just making mental notes. It seems like he was fitting just everything into his mind."

Great story, Kinsella says. Too bad it isn't true, he adds.

"I was with my wife at the time," he said of his trip to Chisholm, adding the only contact he has ever had with the reclusive Salinger was through a lawyer who expressed concern about the litigiously minded author's name appearing in any other works. "I've been back and explained it to [Ponikvar]. You know the way the memory plays tricks."

You make the call.

In *Shoeless Joe*, Ray Kinsella tells Graham that it was a tragedy he never got to bat in the big leagues. Graham, for years known as Doc Graham, doesn't bite.

"If I'd only got to be a doctor for five minutes, now that would have been a tragedy," Graham said, in lines delivered in the movie by Lancaster. "You have to keep things in perspective. I mean, I love the game, but it's only that, a game."

The literary depiction was true to life. "I worked with the man about 20 years," said William Loushine, a member of Chisholm's state championship baseball team of 1948 (the team formed right before the regional tournament, then went 6-0 for the Minnesota title) and later a teacher in the district. "I don't remember ever hearing the name Moonlight."

But it was that one day on a major league diamond that made Graham into a legend, even if it took more than three-quarters of a century to do it.

That one game got him two lines in *The Baseball Encyclopedia*, lines that haunted William Kinsella enough that he traveled to Minnesota to find out more. Archie Graham was a hero not because of his baseball career but for what he did with his life after it. But if not for that one game, the world might never may have known.

EDDIE WAITKUS

He was hitting over .300 and was tops in the fans' balloting in the days of Musial, Robinson, Kiner, and Hodges. He was on his way to becoming the all-time Phillies first baseman.

Then in a Chicago hotel room in June 1949, the night, his career, and his life were shattered. A .22-caliber bullet shot by an obsessed teenage girl burst through Eddie Waitkus' chest.

Sound like a Hollywood movie? It was. *The Natural*, starring Robert Redford, was based on the story of Eddie Waitkus. But the real story of Eddie Waitkus was much more than Hollywood portrayed. His son, Edward "Ted" Waitkus, Jr., reported 43 years after the shooting:

> He was not the same after that. The Old Man told me that after that his stamina was down, his strength was down, he couldn't keep his weight up. He had to have three or four surgeries and was clinically dead three times on the operating table.
>
> He used to say he could handle the three-year break in his career for the war—everybody had to do their part—but he could never understand the shooting. His thought process was resentment, was anger. He could have had a good career—if he wasn't stopped by the war, or by the shooting, who knows what he could have done?

Waitkus' potential may best be comprehended by understanding that most fans fret over what Waitkus could have been, without realizing he battled back to have an enviable career.

It all began half a century ago, in the Pacific Coast League. Waitkus was the MVP and led the league in hitting. In late 1940 he chose the Chicago Cubs over the Yankees because the offers came just before Christmas 1940 and he needed the additional $100 signing bonus the Cubs offered for holiday presents. He went to the Cubs in 1941 but saw action in only 12 major league games. He hit only .179 in just 28 at-bats, but he was in the bigs, and the dream was becoming reality.

It would take five more years, not until 1946, before Waitkus would have his first full major league season. Three years of multiple beach landings in the Philippines and several Bronze and Silver stars from the army saw to that.

But when he arrived, he really arrived. He hit .304, rapped 24 doubles, scored 50 runs, and knocked 55 RBIs while hitting leadoff for Chicago. In the field, at first base, he had a .996 fielding average. In 1947 and 1948, he hit .292 and .295 while boosting his slugging average.

In the first half of the '49 season, after a trade to the briefly powerful Philadelphia Phillies, he was on a personal tear, hitting career highs in average (.306) and slugging percentage (.426) while on a pace to top his own highs in nearly every offensive category. He described himself as a "banjo-wrist hitter," for his quick hands that were, increasingly, putting the bat on the ball wherever it arrived. His fielding average was .994.

Dizzy Dean, a one-time roommate of Waitkus, figured he was the best first bagger he had ever seen.

Then the note arrived.

On the guest letterhead of the Edgewater Beach Hotel in Chicago, dated June 14, 1949, a simple, hand-scrawled message changed the 29-year-old Waitkus' life forever:

> Mr. Waitkus,
> It's extremely important that I see you as soon as possible.
> We're not acquainted but I have something of importance to speak to you about. I think it would be to your advantage to let me explain it to you.
> As I'm leaving the hotel the day after tomorrow, I'd appreciate it greatly if you could see me as soon as possible.
> My name is Ruth Ann Burns, and I'm in Room 1297A.
> I realize that this is a little out of the ordinary, but as I said, it's rather important.
> Please, come soon. I won't take up much of your time, I promise.

He found the note under the door of his room at the same hotel around 11 P.M., after a night out with some teammates celebrating that afternoon's win over his former employer, the Cubs.

Waitkus called her. She said something about him knowing her brother back in the Boston area. The woman, whose real name was Ruth Steinhagen, urged Waitkus to see her immediately at her room, again for a matter of great importance.

"There she tried to stab him," recounts Waitkus' son, Ted. "She tried to stab him and missed, so she pulled out a gun out of a closet and shot him."

Here's how the Chicago police and a local newspaper pieced it together.

"I intended to stab him and then shoot myself," said the 19-year-old stenographer, who had been obsessed with Waitkus since he had played for the Cubs. "But when he came in he sat down in a chair. I couldn't stab him that way." So she went to the closet and pulled out the old Remington .22 caliber, single-shot rifle she had bought at a pawn shop a month before.

"For heaven's sake, what's going on here?" Waitkus sputtered as he jumped from the chair.

"For two years you've bothered me," she said. "Now you're going to die."

Then the bullet ripped deep into Waitkus' chest.

Afterwards, she told the police she intended to kill Waitkus, reload, then kill herself. "But when I saw Eddie lying there moaning, I blacked out."

The day after the incident Steinhagen gave a contradictory account to reporters, including one from the *St. Louis Post-Dispatch*.

"I admire him now more than ever before," she said. "He showed so much courage as he lay there on the floor. The way he looked up at me and kept me smiling."

Steinhagen had dreamed of Waitkus the night before the shooting. After the incident, she said she was happy in jail and pleased that Waitkus had survived and was on the road to recovery. She told United Press she welcomed an assault charge because, "I deserve it."

"I'm happy in jail.... The people here seem to like me and I like them. They don't seem to understand me outside. If I did get out, I'd probably get into trouble again—maybe not in a shooting, but shoplifting or something."

A bewildered Waitkus spoke to reporters from his hospital bed. "I guess I zigged when I should have zagged.... When she shot me, she had the coldest face I ever saw on anyone.

"Before I could say anything—Whammy. Why should she want to pick on a nice guy like me, and with a rifle? Oh, brother."

Police later found in her room baseball charts, statistics, pennants, and emblems. On a bedside table was a gold-framed picture of Waitkus throwing, a cutout from the Sunday newspaper.

Looking back, the tragedy should have been picked up long before Waitkus walked into that Chicago hotel room. Her mother, Edith Steinhagen, told United Press that her daughter had talked a year before about killing Waitkus and then herself.

"She wrote Waitkus lots of letters," said a friend of the shooter, Joyce Stringly, "and phoned him whenever he was in town."

Edith Steinhagen said her daughter had even learned Lithuanian when she found out Waitkus was Lithuanian. And when Waitkus was traded to the Phillies, the daughter wanted to move to Philadelphia.

"She had been crazy about Eddie for about three years, and she had hundreds of pictures of him. Why, do you know she used to spread them out on the table and even on the floor to look at them for hours." Perhaps Ruth put it simplest, and the best: "I'm a good case for a psychiatrist," she told police.

Ted Waitkus picks up the story, from the heartfelt, father-to-son talks in which he learned it. "At 3 A.M. in the hospital, Chicago police brought her to my father's hospital bed for identification. He said, 'Why did you do it?' And his vitals went crazy."

The gash was deep from the surgeries made through Waitkus' back because the bullet lodged against his spine. Years later his son could put his finger into the gash up to the first joint. But the wound was far deeper.

"Prior to that point, my Old Man was a very verbal, very open and trustworthy man. After that event, he was afraid of people, withdrawn. He would question motives and he was a depressed soul when he got out of baseball," recalls Waitkus Jr., now a Colorado Springs attorney. "He didn't know if he could go on."

But he did.

As Steinhagen was tried, found mentally incompetent, and committed to an institution, Waitkus entered the painful road to recovery, first in operating rooms for repeated efforts to remove the bullet, then to correct subsequent problems like a collapsed lung. The table in his hospital room was capped by a tower of get-well wishes. Shortly after the incident, he received 376 letters and 12 telegrams in one morning, which followed 100 letters the day before. There were pain-wracked months in hospitals. When November arrived, Waitkus was off for four grueling months of conditioning in Clearwater, Florida.

"Looking back," Waitkus told the Associated Press in 1950, "they were the four most horrible months of my life. Worse than anything in the Army—worse than New Guinea or anything in the Philippines. The pain was so severe that more than once I found myself wishing that the girl had finished the job."

But he recovered with a vengeance. That spring Waitkus was starting and hitting leadoff for the powerhouse Whiz Kids, helping them grab their first National League flag in 35 years. In the World Series, Waitkus batted third and went 4-for-15 with a double off some awesome Yankees who won in a four-game sweep. Along the way that season, Waitkus played every game, hit .284, scored 102 runs with 44 RBIs, scooped at a .993 fielding rate, and won baseball's Comeback Player of the Year Award.

From 1951 to 1953, Waitkus continued to be a steady performer for the Phillies, hitting between .257 and .291, but he played fewer games and chalked up fewer runs. By 1953 he was out of the regular order but still had an enviable fielding average of .989. He was traded on March 16, 1954, to Baltimore for $40,000. That year he played in 95 games and hit .283, but the end was near. In 1955 he played 38 games for Baltimore before he returned to Philadelphia for his last 33 games, where he still managed to hit .280.

In 11 major league years, the line on Edward Stephen Waitkus is more than respectable: 1,140 games, 1,214 hits, a .285 lifetime average, and a fielding percentage matched by few in the game.

But the statement Eddie Waitkus made in baseball always will be

Eddie Waitkus and son "Ted" (courtesy of Ted Waitkus).

followed by a question: What would he have accomplished if not for a crazed fan's obsession?

He died September 15, 1972, in Boston at the age of 53.

Waitkus died supposedly of pneumonia a day after his children saw him healthy, tanned, and active, but an autopsy found cancer of the esophagus and lungs. Ted was 15. He had just spent August with his dad at Ted Williams' baseball camp in Cape Cod and had noticed some unusual hacking and an unexplained disdain for beer.

"My uncle, who's an orthopedic surgeon, strongly and firmly believes that the shock of the shooting and the stress of the surgeries really created a trauma he never healed from. There is a theory all those different surgeries contributed to his demise, even though there are questions of whether trauma can trigger cancer, it does take about 20 years to take hold and that's when he died."

Young Ted has heard stories about the fate of the woman who triggered his dad's fateful turn. He says he has heard reports that he never fully accepted that she again was free and living under another name, and building a new shrine to his dad. The son said she apparently was released after about 18 months in a psychiatric hospital, although he still bristles at the memory that his family was never informed of that at the time. Still, he harbors no animosity.

"In my mind, why foul her up? She was 19 then," Ted Jr. said. He has a degree in psychology and knows about obsessive behavior. He said the obsession probably ended as soon as the shot was fired. She was probably relieved, he said.

But Ted Waitkus is quick to note that the tragic twists in his father's life also brought him its highlight: meeting the woman he would marry.

Near his home outside of Albany, New York, Eddie Waitkus had a radio show, "The Sports Review." He would regularly relay mini-documentaries on great sports stories and stars of the day, closing with a sign-off of "Until then, keep hustling, and have a good day." On his wedding anniversary in 1953, however, Waitkus spoke of a sports star no fan had heard of.

He narrated a love story, his love story, about the most desperate moments of his life and career as well as the most hopeful, when he met 21-year-old Carol Webel of Albany on a Florida beach. Waitkus relayed the tale of his own life to the background music of their song, "My Foolish Heart":

> Our story for this morning is not only a sports story, but also a love story. It shows that sometimes truth is stranger than fiction.
>
> In 1949, the first baseman for the Philadelphia Phillies was shot by a deranged girl. For four weeks he hovered between life and death.

After his release he was called into the Phillies office and told he was being sent to Clearwater, Florida, with the club trainer to take the one in a thousand chance that he might recover enough to stand the competition of big league baseball. The grueling schedule laid out for him the first few weeks was a nightmare. And the ballplayer, already in a bad nervous condition from his accident, grew more depressed and reluctant to go on each day. He was tempted to give up the whole ordeal and the game of baseball that meant so much to him.

Then, he met a girl. A girl who knew nothing of baseball.... Their few "Hellos" on the beaches grew to infrequent dates. Slowly he started to withdraw from his shell and lose the fear he had developed of people. Slowly, through her influence, he started to take interest again in the world around him. And with her quiet confidence to help him, he went into his training with renewed interest. She had faith that he could come back, so he HAD to do it, for her sake.

When the going got rough, she was always there to cheer him up. When he felt like quitting she was there to prod him on. The months went on and spring training started with another battle to face, the battle to regain his job. He did, and with her comforting presence in the background he went on to a great season and a World Series.

That year the newspapers called his the Comeback of the Year, but he didn't do it alone. The season ended and the companionship grew into something deeper. As it happens in fiction, they were married, and went back into baseball together.

As you can see, it's not only a sports story, but a story behind an athletic figure; a story about how a woman's influence and a woman's inspiration helped a man fight the greatest battle of his life. It's the story of all the women behind all the men, a story as old as time.

Waitkus' son is left to contemplate what-ifs. What if the war didn't take away three years of his father's prime? What if the obsessed fan who built a shrine to Waitkus didn't act on her love of the handsome ball player she had never met? What if Waitkus had taken the Yankees' offer instead of the extra $100 the Cubs offered?

"It's the little things you miss when you lose your Dad at an early age," said Ted, who spent time with his father at big leaguers' baseball camps, at old-timers' games, and at countless ball games as fans. "It's like in that scene in the movie *Field of Dreams* when the guy asks his father, 'You wanna have a catch?' That's what I miss, because baseball was a big part of your lives. That's what I miss."

EMMETT ASHFORD

It was the most perfect of Opening Days. Emmett Ashford could smell the freshly cut grass of Griffith Stadium as he adjusted his short-billed blue cap and tugged at his blue suit.

Fifteen hard years in the minor leagues had passed, umpiring games in small towns for smaller wages on hot days, wondering if the patches and garter material sewn into the dark suit were going to hold the seams. But that was over. This is the major leagues, he figures. Emmett Littleton Ashford, you have arrived.

Then at the grandstand he was stopped by two stiff white men in dark suits, suspicious of a black man dressed as an umpire.

"Listen," one of them said to the stubby middle-aged man, "There are no Negro umpires in the major leagues."

"Well," Ashford replied to the Secret Service agent, "there will be a Negro umpire in the American League, if you let me into the park."

One of them then asked Ashford for his papers, according to the *Sporting News'* account of that day in 1966. It took only 10 minutes, but the incident summarized, as it foreshadowed, a lifetime.

By the time that game was over, the Secret Service men had done their duty, Vice President Hubert H. Humphrey, who threw out the first ball, was safe, and Emmett Ashford had become a trailblazer.

"Emmett, today you made history," American League president Joe Cronin said. "I'm proud of you."

At age 51, Ashford realized a dream that for most people would be a nightmare: Breaking the color barrier in a job where even the fairest of skin was hated. He hurdled a racial bar that some argue may have been even higher than the one cleared by Jackie Robinson. For Ashford's audacity was not to be a player under the direction of white men, but to direct on the field what was long the whitest of major professional sports. He dared to call white men out and toss white men out in a game that had for so long kept black men out.

"A pioneer of racial integration in sport, the courageous, determined Ashford used wit and charm to overcome the obstacles of racism on and off the field," wrote Larry R. Gerlach in the book *Biographical Dictionary of American Sports*. "Ashford may be of greater historical importance than Jackie Robinson because he represents the advancement of blacks in baseball to a role other than that of hired performer."

Ashford could have accepted quietly what many believed was too long denied him, but he didn't. He was a man who pushed, who would be his own man, who broke down fences with style—always with style. The stocky opera fan with more facial expressions than a Vegas comic did what he thought was best. He made baseball fun.

Writers of the day, and many pounded typewriters about Ashford, seemed to take great joy in describing the American Leaguer's style. One of the best descriptions was by the *Sporting News'* Bob Sudyk in 1966:

> Staying in a semi-squat, Emmett sweeps his right arm out to the side and up, and when it comes straight overhead, down it comes like a Karate chop. That's phase one. Then he teasingly reaches up as if pulling a train whistle and gives two short jerks for phase two. While in that squat, he reaches out to the side, grabs a handful of air and jerks it in as if yanking open a car door.
>
> When Emmett dusts the plate, he finishes by coming across sideways with the brush in a follow-through that leaves him on one foot. He runs on tip-toes like a guy trying to sneak into his house at 3 A.M., without waking the old lady, and sometimes executes a wobbly stiff-legged Charlie Chaplin exit down the first base line.

"Look, I just love umpiring," Ashford told that writer. "I think it's the greatest thing in the world. I can't do anything halfway. I guess I'm just so full of enthusiasm that it comes out of me that way."

Enthusiasm. It's as good a word as any to describe him. But the word, like many of the articles written about him during his brief major league career, fails to capture the adversity that Ashford's enthusiasm survived.

Like the letters Ashford recalled receiving: "One was scrawled on toilet tissue from a small town in Louisiana and it said, 'They should throw people like you and the NAACP in the river.'"

Ashford and the sportswriters downplayed the racial hatred, but those close to him apparently knew well what the man was going through off the diamond. At a gala birthday party for Ashford in 1971, at which white and black dignitaries and celebrities peppered the roster of well-wishers, Emmett's wife, Margaret, who had patched his worn minor league uniform with a black garter once because times were so tough, couldn't help but let it slip: "I wish all the bigots and militants could see this the way it really is."

Bigots and militants. For some, they finally had a common target for their anger in Ashford. For some militants, Ashford was a clown, a stooge of white business, a Steppin' Fetchit of baseball. For bigots, Ashford was a nightmare: an articulate man who overcame all the obstacles that could be thrown in his way and ended up wildly popular and powerful. They believed Ashford was given a chance to run the game because of pressure from politically correct league officials, civil rights groups, or the government.

It was an undercurrent felt by Ashford throughout his long umpiring career.

Ashford's story began back in Los Angeles. His father left the family when Emmett was young, and he grew up with an older brother and his mother, who was a secretary for a black newspaper, the *California Eagle*. When Ashford hit school, the firsts began, such as being the first black student body president and newspaper editor at Jefferson High School. From there he attended Los Angeles City College, earning a Bachelor of Science degree and playing baseball. He was also the sports editor at the school paper.

After spending 1944–47 in the navy, he played some semipro baseball and began umpiring. It was just sandlot and rec leagues at first. Then he started calling high school and college games while working for the post office.

In 1951 he became the first black umpire in pro baseball and began the first of 15 years in the minors, the last 11 of which were in Triple-A ball, tantalizingly close to the big leagues. From 1963 to 1965, he also was the Pacific Coast League umpire-in-chief. The rest of the year he spent as the first black to referee high school and college football and college basketball in California.

Ashford's five-year major league career, which ended when he faced the American League policy that mandated retirement at 55, included the 1967 All-Star Game and the 1970 World Series.

"This is the greatest thrill in my life," Ashford told columnist Jim Ogle of the *Star-Ledger* of Newark, New Jersey, in 1970 after his Fall Classic gig. "I never dreamed I would umpire in a World Series, but here I am. There's no way this could ever be topped, so I feel I have reached the top."

"No one ever loved baseball more," Ogle quoted legend Ralph Houk. "Emmett had his faults as an umpire, but he loved the work and tried his best. He was becoming a pretty good umpire."

Ogle concluded: "Ashford made friends among the writers, who must visit the umpires every once in a while following a controversial decision. Emmett always welcomed the writers and, what is more, answered their questions honestly and quickly. He never hedged. He never lied and he was always pleasant.

"Emmett Ashford wasn't around long, but he added something to the game."

His retirement was anything but. He went from the field to become West Coast public relations representative for Commissioner Bowie Kuhn and umpired major college baseball. He also was commissioner and umpire-in-chief of a league that mixed pros and amateurs.

Emmett Ashford (courtesy of Baseball Hall of Fame Library, Cooperstown, New York).

But more than lines on a résumé, Ashford's career was the stuff of oral history. Love him or hate him, you knew when he was working a game. Like the time:

...when Dick Williams, in 1969 as manager of the Red Sox, called Ashford a "little clown" after what Williams figured were blown calls. Players picked up on it with a chorus, "Are you Emmett Kelly, the clown, in the winter time?"

...or when Joe Pepitone, a Yankee in 1969, grabbed Ashford with both hands in a rage and was saved from a felony only by flying Yankee tackles. Pepitone, of course, got the afternoon off.

...or in 1964, when Dominican leaguer Julian Javier, later a St. Louis Cardinal, decked Ashford after a called third strike Javier suspected was a ball by a mile. When he got to his feet, eventually, Ashford nailed Javier with his umpire's mask on his way to ejecting the player from the game.

...when Ashford crossed paths with the granddaddy of all umpire bashers, Leo "the Lip" Durocher. It was the mid–1960s. An exhibition game in Arizona included a call the Cub manager thought might have been, let's say, in error.

"The hitter took a half-swing," Ashford told a newspaper reporter in 1971, "and Leo came out of the dugout like the lion he is, disputing my call vigorously. He yelled and he screamed that it was a strike. In accordance with our regulations, I took off my mask and walked down to first base and asked the umpire there if the batter had taken a full swing. He said the batter had not. That umpire was white, of course."

Leo kept yelling. "What have we got, what have we got?"

Ashford got right back in Leo's face.

"It was not a strike and you got it in black and white," Ashford said, pointing to the other umpire. "Him at first and me at the plate."

No small feat, talking back to Durocher. And winning.

But it was this type of high-profile questioning of Ashford's ability that, compounded by his role as a basher of barriers, plagued him throughout his career.

American League officials gave Ashford a reprieve on the mandatory retirement age for one season. Whether Ashford subsequently retired, as he said, of his own volition because he wanted to move on or was forced out, no one will know. What is known is that he loved umpiring and even after his retirement donned the chest protector for years at the college level and in exhibitions. He loved the game, and his contributions to it.

The *Sporting News* captured what would become a typical humble response from Ashford: "He bucked certain odds to give me the chance," he said of Cronin. "Somebody had to break in and I'm proud it's me."

New York Times sportswriter George Vecsey perhaps came closer to capturing all that Ashford had gone through, and accomplished, in this 1969 column:

The fans applaud Emmett Ashford the way they would applaud Jackie Gleason doing "a little traveling music, Ray," or Flip Wilson imitating some jivey Army sergeant.

But Ashford did not become the first Negro umpire in the Major Leagues merely because he was fast on his feet. He survived the near–race wars of the minor leagues because he could talk better and think faster than the lugs in uniform and the louts in the grandstand. He overwhelmed people with his endurance and his charm. You could call it "soul."

Ashford underscored that thought in his retirement message to baseball: "My five-year tenure in the majors has been one of extreme satisfaction and gratification at having conquered the biggest challenge of my life, and in some measure opening the door for black umpires now starting out in the minors."

Emmett Littleton Ashford died of a heart attack a month before Opening Day in 1980 at the age of 66.

In an interview with the Copley News Service upon his retirement nine years earlier, Ashford took a moment to make the call on his own life.

"Think of all the people who live an entire life and do not accomplish one thing they really wanted to do," he said. "I have done something I wanted to do. I have that satisfaction."

JIMMY O'CONNELL

From the annals of baseball comes this mystery story, full of liars, a bribe, a hanging judge, and a life sentence.

Worst of all, as more seasons go into the books, the more it seems possible that an innocent man who could have been one of baseball's great stars was unfairly banned for life before his prime—potentially the victim of a practical joke gone terribly wrong.

This baseball tragedy unfolded before a Saturday game on September 27, 1924. The three-time champion New York Giants, with a roster that resembled a wing in the Hall of Fame, faced the seventh-place Philadelphia Phillies. It was to be an easy home game for John McGraw's Giants, one that would clinch another pennant.

But it would almost cost baseball a World Series, and more.

It began when 23-year-old outfielder Jimmy O'Connell of the Giants was getting suited up in the locker room of the Polo Grounds. At the next locker was his coach, assistant manager Albert J. "Cozy" Dolan, 11 years O'Connell's senior and a former utility player who had bounced around six teams over seven years. The two chatted. O'Connell then dressed and immediately went out to the field to talk to Philadelphia shortstop Heinie Sand, who was warming up. Here's how Sand remembered it:

"Johnnie Couch, also a member of the Philadelphia ball club, and myself walked from the clubhouse to a position between short and home and started to warm up when Jimmy O'Connell came up to me. ... Couch walked about forty feet away from me toward the third-base line and started to warm up."

O'Connell then made his pitch to Sand.

"What does your club think of my club in winning the pennant?" O'Connell asked.

"Why I hope the best club wins, Jimmy," Sand replied.

"That is not it. How do you fellows feel toward us winning the pennant?"

"As far as I am concerned I would like to see you win, being a friend of mine."

Sand then explained his preference, although far-fetched, would be for his Philadelphia team to take two games from New York while Brooklyn would take two from Boston to force a long-odds, three-way tie.

"Would $500 change your opinion, Heinie?" O'Connell asked.

Sand looked at him in disgust: "Jimmy, I am not interested."

"All right, Heinie, this is just between you and I. It needn't go no further. You go out there and do your best."

Sand walked away to his bench, then on to batting practice.

Sand's story was the key testimony in the bribery investigation by the National League. Under questioning by the already legendary baseball commissioner, Judge Kenesaw Mountain Landis, several players provided witness accounts. The result was that O'Connell and Dolan were banned for life by a commissioner who believed harsh sentences were a way to save the game almost lost to the 1919 Black Sox bribery scandal.

This time, just five years later, Landis acted quickly and definitively before the World Series, eliminating the need to pursue dead-serious recommendations by some top baseball people to cancel the Series or to disqualify the Giants and send the Brooklyn Robins (as the Dodgers were also known, after manager Wilbert Robinson) instead to defend the National League flag.

For O'Connell, it was a crushing blow. Known as the "$75,000 Beauty from the Coast" because of his purchase price by the Giants, the Sacramento, California, native was one of baseball's rising stars. He batted lefty and threw right-handed, and he cut an imposing figure for the day at 5-foot-10½ and 175 pounds. He was purchased from San Francisco of the Pacific Coast League for the 1922 season, but the Giants let him mature another year at that minor league level. He hit .335 with 13 homers and stole 39 bases out West.

To put O'Connell's value and cost into perspective, $75,000 was more than major league teams had paid in total to then-independent minor league teams for the rights to 35 of the game's top players.

The fact wasn't lost on the skeptical New York sports press:

"Here is the ball player who cost the New York Giants $75,000 last week—the biggest price ever paid for a minor league player," the *New York World* reported in the winter of 1921. That past season in the minors O'Connell hit .387 with an arm measured by caliber and speed measured by superlatives.

The next year, at age 22 in his rookie major league season, most accounts show that O'Connell hit .262 for the Giants in 102 games at first base and in the outfield. His roommate and fellow Californian, Emil "Irish" Meusel (brother of the Yankees' Bob Meusel), said the relatively poor showing was the result of O'Connell's extreme homesickness. He played under unusual pressure, too, from fans, the press, and other players because of his price tag.

The following year the $75,000 Beauty came through. The first baseman hit .337, nailed 17 dingers, and stole 23 bases.

Then came 1924, and the bribe.

But was O'Connell guilty?

Decades later he would insist he was simply following the orders of his boss, Dolan, something a good small-town boy like himself was always told was the right thing to do. It was part of his simple code of honor, just like when he later refused to deny he offered Dolan's bribe to Sand, when the lie probably would have saved him as it did others.

Five months after Landis made his ruling, O'Connell broke his long silence to the press in a first-person article carried by the Allied News Feature Service. A contrite and frustrated O'Connell wrote that Dolan turned to him in the locker room that day before the Philadelphia game and started the whole terrible ordeal.

> "Do you know Heinie Sand?"
> O'Connell recalled Dolan asking him.
> "Yes," I said, "I played in the coast league with him when he was playing for Salt Lake."
> "Go out on the field," he said, "and tell Sand not to bear down too hard on us this afternoon. Tell him there'll be $500 in it for him."
> Dolan was the assistant manager of the team and we took orders from him. Now, I suppose, if I had stopped to think about it I might not have done it—although I don't know at that. Dolan was my boss and he told me to do something. I had no sense of responsibility in the matter. It was up to him.
> So as soon as I finished dressing I went out onto the field and found Sand there. I repeated Dolan's message to him, and he replied that he wouldn't do it—that he had always played the best he knew how, and he was always going to.
> I walked back to the dressing room and told Dolan what Sand had said. And then I forgot all about it. I never thought about it again until Tuesday [when he was interrogated by Landis].
> [Landis] asked me about my conversation with Sand. And I repeated it to him, word for word. I've often been asked if I felt at all nervous. Not in the least. I felt that I had nothing to be nervous about. I felt that I hadn't done anything wrong—I had simply carried out the instruction given me by the man for whom I was working.
> After Landis had talked to me, he called in Dolan, and a stenographer. You can imagine that I was considerably surprised when Dolan said he didn't remember any such conversation. I couldn't quite understand what he was trying to do. But Landis had always impressed me as a man who would get at the bottom of things if he could, and I assumed that he would sift it straight to the bottom.

I still wasn't disturbed when he dismissed me, and I went downstairs to join Mrs. O'Connell. I didn't even tell her about it, and never thought about it again.

The next morning, we went down to breakfast, and there was the story all over the front pages of the newspapers, with my picture, and the news that I had been disqualified. It was a pretty hard blow to me, I'll say.

I've been asked why I didn't lie about it when Judge Landis first asked me. It never occurred to me to lie. I never have been a liar, and it just never entered my mind to lie. I just told him what happened and let it go at that.

Now that's the story of the bribery scandal, exactly as it happened. I made a big mistake — naturally, I'm sorry. And if I had it to do over again, I suppose, knowing what I know now, I wouldn't do it, but if I were placed in similar circumstances, without the knowledge I now have, I suppose I'd do the same thing. I'd probably obey instructions from a superior officer.

I have no hard feelings for Judge Landis. I think he did what he thought was fair and right, and I believe that he honestly wants to find out all that he can about this affair.

Not everyone, though, has been so forgiving of Landis or believes he did get to the bottom of the scandal.

First, Landis found O'Connell honest enough to admit to taking the bribe offer from his boss to an opposing player. Landis also found O'Connell credible enough to convict Dolan, with some help by Dolan's hemming and hawing and I-don't-remembers under questioning. But Landis couldn't find O'Connell as simply the pawn in the affair, who didn't even know or ask where the $500 was supposed to have come from. Landis also refused to chalk up the whole incident to the running gags among players at the time, joking each other with talk of a bribe to throw a game.

Instead, O'Connell became the scapegoat.

Some fans, sportswriters, and baseball people sympathized with O'Connell. After all, he was hitting .317 and was a rising star on a team that — with or without a bribe — was a sure thing to collect another World Series check. His future was too bright, physically and financially, to risk it all on a poorly placed bribe in a game against the seventh-place team, his supporters reasoned.

One was Chicago Cubs owner William Wrigley, Jr. He said the Beauty was a victim of circumstances and innocent of any wrong doing.

"The whole thing, in my opinion, was a rather crude practical joke on the part of Dolan," Wrigley said. "He figured O'Connell for a kid and thought he was putting over a clever joke, never dreaming any investigation would come of it.

"For one thing, there was no need for the Giants to try to buy the game—they had it clinched. For another—why bribe a shortstop? He has but a few chances to affect winning or losing a game. It was a terrible, crude joke on Dolan's part. Basically there was nothing wrong."

Even Landis, upon reflection, may have had some reservations about O'Connell's sentence. A 1945 article in the *New York Daily Mirror* stated: "In later years Landis, without mentioning O'Connell, observed in a mellow mood: 'Perhaps sometimes the indirect offender suffers during the vigil for spotless baseball, but the importance is so profound it transcends the individual.'"

In Landis' defense, some historians said the O'Connell-Dolan banishment did more to discourage bribes than the Black Sox scandal.

As for O'Connell, he was devastated by his ejection from baseball.

As his team was about to take on its ill-fated attempt to knock off Washington in the World Series in 1924 without a star outfielder and veteran coach, and just days after Landis' banishment, O'Connell shocked everyone by showing up at the Polo Grounds for a scheduled practice. John McGraw called O'Connell to his office, according to the account by the *New York Times*.

"Well," McGraw said to O'Connell, "What have you to say, Jimmy?"

"I don't know what to say," O'Connell responded.

"How did you ever get yourself into a thing like this?" McGraw pressed.

"I don't know," O'Connell cried. Then, the man who had suffered such homesickness in his recent rookie year and who said he had simply tried to do what he was told by a boss, broke down and sobbed into his hands.

"I can't go home. I can't go home."

Half a year after he died in 1976, his hometown paper, the *Sacramento Bee*, carried an item on his passing:

"We have been belatedly informed that Jim O'Connell, who could be classed as Sacramento's greatest ball player, passed away in Bakersfield at the age of 75. Jimmo, before reporting to the San Francisco Seals in 1920, played for the Sacramento High School club in 1918 and with Santa Clara University in 1919.

"While with Sac High in 1918, he was a member of a club which almost went all the way to the State Title only to be beaten by San Diego by a 2–0 score."

The Beauty probably wouldn't have liked the play his item got in the paper—buried in the second leg of a column on minor league baseball on page 8. But he would have loved it just the same. Nowhere is there a mention of the bribe.

Art Shires

He was Deion before Deion, Bo before Bo, a two-sport star whose words were calculated to get him ink and an angle on another buck. Art Shires wanted to be called Art the Great, a man who fancied himself not only as the best baseball player in the game from the moment he hit the majors, but also a boxer who could lick anyone in the ring. Or the clubhouse.

Shires played only four years in the majors and was out of the game by the time he was 27. He hit .291 for his 290-game career over four years, besting .300 in three of those seasons. But he never played more than 100 games in any major league season, in part because of his habit for getting suspended. He was a supernova on the sports scene, burning brightly but quickly, a legend—at least in his own mind.

Art the Great chewed the biggest wad of tobacco, wore the snazziest clothes, walked with the cockiest swagger, broke the most rules, and punched out his manager the most times. The first baseman was the brashest and the wittiest, a quote machine off the field and the king of trash-talkers on it. The persona far outshadowed the performer, but his talents and potential were great enough to keep him in the game.

"There is a grave suspicion," *New York Times* John Kiernan wrote in Shires' rookie year, "that he may be a real ballplayer."

From as soon as he hit the majors in 1928 with the White Sox—when he tripled in his first plate appearance and went 4-for-5 in his first game—until he departed the bigs from the Boston Braves in 1932, Shires was news almost daily, whether for his mouth, his bat, or his fists.

Shires was a nickname cottage industry. "Art the Great." "The Great Shires." "Whataman." "Dude." "Big Shot." Sportswriters, giddy with the reams of clippings Shires was supplying, threw in a few more, such as "I, I," "the Texas Terror" and "the Texas Wind-bag."

Charles Arthur Shires also went by a handful of other names, especially while playing college football—for pay—at several schools over the course of several years.

The following comments, appearing in the June 22, 1929, *St. Louis Star*, clearly illustrate Art Shires the player and Art Shires the person:

"Baseball is getting too darned sissy when a guy can't go out and take a few drinks without getting suspended," he said. "There's too much of this 'Hello George' and 'Hello Bill' in the business, and when you slide into second spikes first and try to bump the second sacker to cut off a double play, the poor boob looks at you with the eyes of a wounded deer.

"It's too darned sissy."

Shires was a lot of things—a ballplayer, a buffoon, a boxer, a blowhard— but he was no darned sissy.

Shires was born on August 13, 1907, the son of Irish immigrants who settled in Texas. At the tender age of 11, he struck out on his own, working odd jobs and playing ball. In 1922, after playing for a semipro baseball team in Texas, Shires played football for Wesley College in Greeneville, Texas. The next year he played minor league baseball and then returned to Wesley to play football and basketball. His vagabond days were just beginning.

In 1924 he again played in the minors in Texas, then "was hired" by Marshall College in Huntington, West Virginia, where he played football under the name Dana Prince. Shires also played basketball and baseball for the school, despite already being a professional ballplayer. In 1925, Shires got called up to the Washington Senators but didn't play. He told sportswriters he reported under the name Robert Lowe. In the fall he returned to Marshall for more football.

The year 1926 was particularly busy for Shires. He agreed to play football for Canisius College in Buffalo, New York, under the name Bill French. (Some accounts had his alias as Edward French; he said once he played there under the name Adair.) But Shires thought he wasn't getting paid regularly enough, so he bolted to Geneva College in Beaver Falls, Pennsylvania. There he was told to stay so as to be eligible for football the following fall, but instead he bolted to Buffalo to play professional football. In the fall of 1927, he was off to Westminster College in Wilmington, Delaware.

Shires said he got paid $75 to $100 a month in the fall playing college football. Think how NCAA regulators of today would have reacted to his collegiate career, which seems to have broken every rule.

Five colleges in six years. That had to be a record—especially for a kid who never graduated from high school. At least he attended classes. "I certainly did," he said, "when there was nothing else to do."

Shires' boastful ways were well established by the time he joined the White Sox in August 1928. But Shires, who hit left and threw right, was able to back up the talk, hitting .341 in 33 games while playing a skillful first base. He also ousted Leo Durocher as the most ferocious bench jockey in the game and was labeled the best-dressed player in baseball. The only player in the league to carry two trunks on road trips, Shires was said to have in his closets 50 suits, 100 hats, 40 pairs of spats, 300 neckties, and 20 walking canes.

Manager Lena Blackburne saw beyond the glitz and the hype to Shire's potential as a player—and a leader. Shocking teammates and sportswriters,

Blackburne named the 21-year-old rookie the team's captain in spring training 1929, hoping the new responsibility would tone down the rambunctious great one.

Shires responded by breaking team training rules that March while the club practiced in Texas, a bonehead move that cost him his captaincy and a suspension. "Meeting too many home folks," Shires explained. "I wasn't exactly crocked when I returned to the hotel at 1:30 A.M., but I had broken training, stayed out too late and set a bad example, as captain, for the rest of the team."

Shires was sent home for a week. He returned and was benched. There was an argument, then another suspension. Shires, 6-foot-1 and a solid 190 pounds, responded as he normally did: with his fists. There was a fight, and Blackburne left the clubhouse with a black eye.

"Now the truth about it is that I got an awful clip on the jaw from Blackburne, but all the papers said about it was that I blackened his eye," Shires said after the season. "He gave me as good as he took."

So ended round one.

The bell for round two sounded less than two months later. On May 15, during batting practice, Shires stepped to the plate wearing a ridiculous red felt hat. Blackburne was not amused. Take off the hat, the manager said. Shires liked a lot of things; authority was not one of them.

Instead of complying, Shires grew furious. "I'll run you out of baseball," he yelled in a tirade. Blackburne stuck to his guns: "while you're taking off the hat, Shires, take off your uniform." Shires was fined $100 and suspended indefinitely. The player left the park.

Art the Great was not a man to let anyone get in the last word. He returned to the clubhouse after the game: "I can whip anyone," he brayed, including the manager in his glance. Blackburne took him up on it, and the fight was on. It was quickly broken up, but not before manager and player had each gotten in a shot to the face. Shires then cried, probably realizing he had screwed up for sure this time, and then left the park.

So ended round two. Round three came four months later, and it was the best of the Shires-Blackburne brawls. Art had bristled all season at the "spying" he thought the manager was doing on him. In a Philadelphia hotel room, the issue boiled over into a free-for-all.

Blackburne was notified by hotel management that there was an out-of-control ballplayer making after-hours "whoopee"—which in 1929 did not have the same Bob Eubanks/"Newlywed Game" sort of sexual connotation. Blackburne knew where to look.

A drunken Shires was in the process of tearing up his room. The manager looked in and got a closeup of Shire's fist. Traveling secretary Lou Barbour jumped in, but he soon was cornered, fending off haymakers from Shires, who now had Blackburne in a headlock. When a pair of house detectives arrived, Shires went after them with a bottle.

Blackburne again ended up with a black eye. Barbour had a bite wound on his thumb. It was self-inflicted; he thought he had Shires.

"I like Lena Blackburne," Shires said the following season. "He knows I like him. But I just had to sock somebody and he was the nearest. From now on, though, that rough stuff is strictly out."

But Blackburne had had enough of his petulant star. He had grown tired of being the player's personal punching bag and afterward fumed:

> The Great Shires is through forever, as far as I'm concerned. Never in my 22 years of baseball did I treat a fellow better or was treated more scurvily in return than I was by him. Art will practice his pugilistic art on somebody else in the future, not me.
>
> I didn't mind the first few times he gave me a black eye, but there's a limit to everything. When a fellow starts making a habit of it, you've just got to do something drastic about it. I couldn't keep telling people forever that I walked into a door in the dark; that's too old.

But Shires was still around the next spring training, and Blackburne was not. Shires had won the war, but he had lost more than $3,000 in fines and salary over the course of the year. He needed cash.

One October 1929 day (weeks before the stock market crash) Shires needed to borrow money from the cigar store of the Pershing Hotel, the White Sox home base. The store was operated by local fight promoter Nessie Blumenthal and his wife, May. During a conversation with May, Shires revealed his rent was overdue, bills were piling up, and there was no chance the Chi-Sox would advance him a portion of the next year's salary.

"I don't know what I'm going to do," Shires said. "Maybe Nessie can give me some advice." "Why don't you become a boxer?" May Blumenthal replied.

Shires smiled, and May made the call to her husband. Nessie Blumenthal, once confirming Art the Great was serious, signed him to a five-year contract to fight as a heavyweight.

Shires' first fight was December 9, 1929, in the White City Arena on Chicago's South Side. His opponent was "Mysterious" Dan Daly, mysterious because no one knew of him. The fight was over in 21 seconds, with Shires winning by a knockout.

The baseball player, who entered the ring in a robe emblazoned with "Art the Great" on the back, next chose a football player to fight. Only 17 days after his first bout, Shires took on Chicago Bears center George Trafton.

The fight resembled a street brawl, with both men flailing roundhouses rather than executing tactical plans—other than to beat the hell out of each other. Shires was saved by the bell in the first round after he was rocked by an overhand right.

Shires was sent reeling in the second but stayed on his feet. In the last three rounds, the already exhausted fighters mostly clutched and grabbed and punched at air. Trafton won a decision in the five-round fight.

"I did it for the good of Chicago," Trafton said afterward. "This Shires is just a big noise. That's all he is, and I proved it."

"I didn't want to fight that big bum anyhow," the Great One said in typical Shires fashion. "Get Wilson for me."

Wilson was Hack Wilson, the Chicago Cubs star. Shires wanted to fight him for the baseball boxing title in his next bout. Wilson was signed to do the fight, but Cubs owner William Wrigley, Jr. was overcome by sanity and refused to let his star get into the ring.

Shires then fought a palooka named Bad Bill Bailey, knocking him out in the first, then another baseball player, Cleveland Indian Neal Ball, whom he KO'd. in the third round of their January 1930 fight. Shires proceeded to knock out another baseball player/boxer, Boston Braves catcher Al Spohrer, for his next win.

But like his baseball career, Shires' boxing life was cut short. He soon was hauled into Commissioner Kenesaw Mountain Landis' office, where he was given an ultimatum.

"You can either play baseball or fight," Landis told him, "but you can't do both."

Shires chose baseball. He returned to the White Sox for the 1930 season. During spring training, Shires tried a new approach: concentrating on keeping his mouth shut, not getting into fights and playing baseball.

"I have discovered that publicity is the easiest thing to get and the hardest thing to cash," he said. "All you fellows knew I wasn't the chump I sounded like in print. I used to sit down cold-bloodedly with the Chicago writers, and frame some startling stunt to catch the front pages."

But after 37 games, the Great One was shipped to Washington. He got injured, wallowed in the minors in 1931, and resurfaced for 82 games with the Boston Braves in 1932. After that, his major league career was finished. Shires went on to operate a diner in Texas, dying in 1967 at the age of 60.

An incident in Shires' rookie season of 1928 best illustrates the man. During an off-day in New York, Art the Great decided to take in a Broadway show. As he walked down the aisle of the theater, the crowd burst into applause.

It was the type of moment the cocky kid lived for. He bowed dramatically and low to his left and to his right, soaking in the adulation. He then turned to acknowledge the cheers from the rear of the theater.

That's when he bumped into actor Douglas Fairbanks, Jr., and his wife, Joan Crawford, waving to their fans.

The Utility Man Who Turned on the Power

MIKE BENJAMIN

Mike Benjamin still doesn't know where it came from and probably never will. It overcame him swiftly, unexpectedly, historically. Before he realized it, the moment was over.

In all likelihood Benjamin never will have much of a career. He has yet to have much of a season. Or a half-season. Or a month. But for one week in June 1995, or at least three days of it, the utility infielder was the best ever.

In a strike-shortened season that included Albert Belle hitting 50 home runs in a 144-game schedule, Greg Maddux going 19-2 with an ERA under 2.00, and the Cleveland Indians rising from a four-decade slumber to run away with a divisional title and pennant, San Francisco Giant Mike Benjamin was the most unexpected story of 1995.

Mike Benjamin, a Euclid, Ohio, native who grew up in Southern California, was a third-round draft choice of the Giants in 1987, after an All-America season at Arizona State. He reached the bigs in 1989 but bounced back and forth to the minors over the next several years before sticking for good in 1991. A natural shortstop, Benjamin's strength is that he can play throughout the infield. But the cliché "Good field/No Hit" was written for him.

Going into the 1995 season, the 29-year-old San Francisco Giant was a career .186 hitter. When all-star third baseman Matt Williams went down with an injury in June, the Giants turned to Benjamin, hitting a measly .150 (3-for-20), to fill-in. He was actually manager Dusty Baker's second choice, but an abdominal strain to backup Steve Scarsone left the manager with no other option.

Filling in for Williams in a June home game, Benjamin hit a home run the opposite way to right field against the Montreal Expos. "I've never done that," Benjamin said. "That gave me confidence. That, in a sense, got me going."

Some hot hitters enter what's known as the Zone. Benjamin proceeded to enter the Twilight Zone.

"It was like flicking a switch," he tried to explain. "Something came over me. It was an instant feeling."

The next game, on June 11 at home again against the Expos, Benjamin slapped four singles while going 4-for-6. Impressive, especially for this 6-foot-3, 195-pound infielder.

A travel day and a trip to Chicago didn't cool him off. His torrid hitting continued on June 13 against the Cubs at Wrigley Field, as Benjamin went 4-for-5 with a home run and three singles. That's beyond impressive. That's unthinkable.

The next day, again against the Cubs, Benjamin exploded and went 6-for-7 with a double and five singles, including a game-winning hit in the 13th inning. The streak thus stretched beyond unlikely into the realm of unparalleled.

Fourteen hits in 18 at-bats, a torrid .778 average.

"It seems like every time I went up, I had a good idea what pitch was coming," Benjamin said weeks before the start of the 1996 spring training, after he had had most of the off-season to ponder his achievement. "I knew what was coming. I thought, 'I'm going to get a hit.' Wait a minute, let me say I knew I was going to hit the ball. After that was out of my control."

The 14 hits over such a span broke the major league record of 13; Benjamin's 10 hits in two games tied the National League mark. On June 15, against the Cubs, Benjamin went 1-for-4 (which still raised his career average), which made him the first player since Walt Dropo of the Detroit Tigers in 1952 to get 15 hits in four consecutive games.

How stunning was the outburst? The 14 hits bettered the 13 hits Benjamin had between June 10, 1994, and June 11, 1995. Previously, Benjamin never had a four-hit game, or consecutive multihit games.

"It happened so quick," he said. "I was swinging the same way I was before. The ball looked a little bigger—you seemed to know what pitch was coming."

Benjamin managed to keep his perspective during the streak. "Why don't you ever jump up and down, or yell?" his wife, Karen, had asked on several occasions. The answer, he believes, is baseball has too long a season to get worked up over one game or series.

"I'm more of a realist," he said after the season. "The next day you can absolutely suck. It's a humbling game."

How right he is.

The binge got the unheralded Benjamin notice for the first time. But as quickly as his hitting prowess came, it disappeared. After the three-game splurge, Benjamin hit .198 (24-148) over the rest of the season. Discounting the three-game streak, he hit .161 for 1995 with 51 strikeouts in 168 at-bats.

"In St. Louis [after the Cubs series] I got a day off. That's all it took," he said. "I went from the top of the world ... to under it."

Benjamin tried everything. Extra batting practice. Watching films. Changing his swing, his stance. Everything.

"I was trying to find that feeling, and I just couldn't," he said, the frustration and the bewilderment still in his voice months later. "You feel like your swing is messed up. One day [in mid–August] I said I had enough. I was beating my brains out in the batting cage. I decided to get back to basics."

Benjamin finished the season batting .229. After the season he was traded to the Philadelphia Phillies. Hardly anyone noticed.

THE MAY 18, 1912, TIGERS

Baseball's history is full of teams of numbing ineptitude. The 1962 Mets. The 1952 Pirates. The 1935 Boston Braves. The 1988 Baltimore Orioles.

Some of these teams had character, others merely characters. All were losers. But none — not the 43-109 Phillies of 1928, not the 36-117 Philadelphia Athletics of 1916, not even the 20-134 Cleveland Spiders of 1899, who finished 84 games out of first — could compare to the 1912 Detroit Tigers.

Make that the May 18, 1912, Detroit Tigers, the worst "major league" team ever to take a baseball diamond.

Note the quotation marks because this team wasn't even a team, and its players were in no way major leaguers. These were the original strikebreakers.

This group made the wanna-be replacement players of 1995 look like all-stars. While, thankfully, the strikebreakers of the most recent vintage never had to take the field for a regular season game, the 1912 Tiger replacements did. Mercifully, for only one game.

This story, like most involving the Tigers of this era, begins with Ty Cobb.

Hilltop Park was the uptown Manhattan home of the New York Highlanders, the forerunners of the Yankees. The 16,000-seat park on Broadway and 165th Street had almost no foul territory behind home plate, allowing fans to be in easy shouting — and throwing — distance of players. While George Steinbrenner is the most notorious owner in New York sports history, the Highlanders' owners may have been the most nefarious: Bill Devery was a former New York police chief and alleged bag man for Tammany Hall, while Frank Farrell was the boss of the regional bookie syndicate.

Cobb hated Hilltop Park, and the fans of Hilltop Park hated Cobb. With a man whose fuse was as short as Cobb's, it was inevitable there would be trouble. The inevitable arrived May 15, 1912, and it would lead to the first strike in major league history.

The Georgia Peach arrived at the park early for batting practice, and a fan behind Cobb's bench began razzing him right away. By the player's account the abuse went beyond anything that could be accepted, including statements about the sex habits of his mother and sister. Cobb went to see Highlander manager Harry Wolverton.

"There is going to be trouble if that fellow isn't stopped," Cobb said. He didn't stop. There was trouble.

Ty Cobb (courtesy of Baseball Hall of Fame Library, Cooperstown, New York).

Cobb said he did nothing more than yell back, "You rotten dog" at the fan during the four innings of abuse. After seeing Wolverton, Cobb went over to Farrell's box. Again, the fan stayed.

According to Al Stump's book *Cobb*, the fan, Claude Lueker, was handicapped: he had no fingers on one hand and two on the other, the result of an industrial accident. Apparently Cobb didn't know, or care.

Soon Cobb jumped the railing and went after Lueker, stepping over and on fans in his path. Once he reached the abuser about 12 rows up, he let loose with haymakers to the fan's head. After Lueker was knocked to the ground, Cobb did what was natural for him: he spiked him with repeated kicks.

"He has no hands," some fans shouted.

"I don't care if he has no legs," Cobb was said to have responded.

After the pummeling, Cobb fought his way back to the field, while his teammates waited at the railing in his defense, bats in hand. As he was throughout baseball, Cobb was disliked by his teammates—80 percent according to Stump's book—but they thought their leader was wronged.

That perceived injustice was no matter to League president Ban Johnson, one of the most impetuous executives in baseball history. He suspended Cobb indefinitely, leaving open the door to a permanent expulsion. All Cobb should have done, Johnson reasoned, was appeal to the umpire.

Cobb met with Johnson and testified he had repeatedly asked umpire Silk O'Loughlin to have the fan ejected. The other Tigers backed him. Johnson conceded Lueker started the verbal parrying, but the suspension would stand.

Sixteen Tigers sent Johnson a wire: lift the suspension or we strike. Individual players had gone on strike, sometimes as many as two or three in a group, but never an entire team. This was pre–1994, pre-union.

"Feeling that Mr. Cobb is being done a grave injustice, we, the undersigned, refuse to play another game until such action is adjusted to our satisfaction," read a statement sent to Johnson by the players. "He was fully justified in what he did, as no one could stand such personal abuse. We want him reinstated or there will be no game. If players cannot have protection, we must protect ourselves."

Meanwhile, the Tigers traveled on an off-day to Philadelphia, where they were scheduled to play the Athletics. The team hoped Johnson would back off, but instead he issued an ultimatum in person: any team that failed to play for reasons other than "train wreck, flood or other act of God" was subject to a $5,000 fine per game, and individuals were subject to suspension.

Connie Mack, the venerable A's manager, decried the striking Tigers as "quitters." He also approached Detroit manager Hughie Jennings with an idea: recruit Philadelphia-area players as a stand-by team. "That way Detroit won't be fined and we'll keep the schedule intact," Mack said. Word spread through Philly on May 17: You want to be a major leaguer? Show up at the Aldine Hotel tomorrow morning.

The next morning a lined formed outside the hotel, as semipros, college players, former minor leaguers, sandlot players, and others sought their one shot at glory. Jennings held his "tryout" by going down the line and tapping potential prospects on the shoulder. Interviews were conducted, and 18 players were selected.

That day the regulars showed up at the park, dressed, and went out for batting practice. Cobb was among them but was shooed off the field by umpires Bill Binneen and Bull Perrine. Jim Delahanty, a Tiger second baseman/outfielder and one of five Delahanty brothers to play in the majors (including Hall of Famer Big Ed), approached the umpires as team spokesman.

"Has Cobb's suspension been lifted?" he asked.

Delahanty was told no. The Tigers left the field, changed out of their uniforms, and returned to the hotel. Even though Cobb himself told the players to play, baseball's first strike was on.

The Aldine 18 were going to play. The "Tigers" that did take the field that day were an unusual assortment. Aloysius Travers, a St. Joseph's College theology student, was to start on the mound. His battery mate was Deacon Jim McGuire, a .278 lifetime hitter who was also 48 years old and a Detroit coach. At first base was another coach, 42-year-old Joe Sugden, a utility player who had last played in 1905 and had broken his leg in a game two decades earlier. At third base, Billy Maharg—his real last name Graham reversed. This local boxer actually would play in another game, in 1916 for the Phillies. He never got a hit in two career at-bats.

The rest of the team was filled out by students from St. Joseph's as well as Georgetown University, along with other players from throughout Philadelphia. Cobb's replacement in center was a puzzle: the box score listed him as "L'n'h's'r." Historians later pieced his name together: Bill Leinhauser, an 18-year-old Philadelphian.

For the right to be sacrificed against the mighty A's, the pseudo–Tigers were paid $10 to $20 per man. They may have never had a chance, but the game would count in the standings.

It didn't help that the Athletics had their ace, Jack Coombs, on the mound. Coombs worked only the early innings, giving way to Boardwalk Brown. Brown allowed a couple of runs, scored by McGuire and Sugden, while 30-year-old sandlot player Ed Irvin shockingly went 2-for-3 with a pair of triples. Hey, teams have won with two runs before.

But not when you are giving up at least two runs an inning, which the Tigers did every frame but the second and fourth. Eddie Collins rapped five hits and scored four runs, while Amos Strunk had four hits. While some of the 15,000 in attendance screamed for refunds and tore up seats in disgust, A's were practically running to the plate, bat in hand.

Final score: 24–2.

Pity Al Travers. He learned all he would need to know about suffering as he went the distance. The right-hander surrendered twenty-six hits, walked seven, and struck out one. His ERA was only 15.75 because ten of Philadelphia's runs were unearned, the result of nine errors.

Travers later entered the priesthood.

"These bums in disguise didn't try for a double play, they were lucky to make a putout now and then against the A's great Eddie Collins, Stuffy McInnis and Frank Baker," sportswriter Arthur "Bugs" Baer wrote. "The sandlotter who replaced Cobb in the outfield wouldn't give his right name. When he came home late and told his wife he'd been playing at Shibe in place of Ty Cobb, she hit him with a skillet."

Johnson was now furious, stating all the Tigers would join Cobb on indefinite suspension. Cobb again pleaded with his teammates to play, and they relented. Their $100 fines were covered by the Tigers' owner.

Johnson then reversed field, setting Cobb's suspension at 10 days and fining him $50. The Tiger Revolt of 1912 was officially over.

History shows the Tigers that year finished 69-84, in fourth place and 21 games out from the pennant-winning Athletics. Ty Cobb led the league in hitting with a .410 batting average, while shortstop Donie Bush and catcher Oscar Stanage led the league for their positions in assists. This was not a great team but clearly not a horrid one, featuring a pitching staff with a pair of 17-game winners, Jean Dubuc and Ed Willett.

But the Tigers of 1912 will not be remembered for their season, but for one game, a game they didn't play.

DANNY GARDELLA

Check today's sports section. We'll wait.

Note the references to multimillion dollar paychecks, salary arbitrations, and free agents that crowd out the box scores, write-ups on late games, and hot minor league prospects.

What started all this? And when?

The money-hungry '80s?

The anything-goes, me-first '70s?

The counter-culture '60s?

Try 1946.

That's right, post–World War II America. A nation that in Europe, the Pacific, and at home had just won a pitched battle for all that was American— not a small slice of which was baseball.

It was against this backdrop that a powerfully built little man named Danny Gardella took on major league baseball. And long before Curt Flood filed an anti-trust suit against baseball in 1970 to try to strike down the reserve clause, before Andy Messersmith and Dave McNally forced open the door to free agency in 1975, Danny Gardella won. It cost him his career, but he won.

Baseball players today as a group are notoriously suspect when it comes to the game's history, but the above are people to whom they should privately thank every time a paycheck rolls in. The first blow was struck by Gardella, the New York Giant outfielder no one remembers.

"I have no regrets about suing baseball," he said. "They needed it. And I think that I helped the marginal player make some more money, and I was happy to be instrumental in it."

Daniel Lewis Gardella was baseball's first free agent.

The year is 1945. America and Americans know the darkest hour of the war is over. Less than a year after D-Day, America reads and listens as Nazis surrender by the thousands in the field, and as their high command eventually surrenders unconditionally on May 7, days after Adolf Hitler takes his own life. In the Pacific, Japanese cities are bombed, and there's some loose talk about a U.S. super-secret weapon.

Fans knew that baseball, after limping through the war in the absence of stars, would soon return to normal. In the interim, some kids, over-the-hill veterans, marginal minor leaguers, and legit major leaguers kept the game alive.

Danny Gardella in the 1940s (courtesy of Danny Gardella).

One of them was Gardella. A military 4F because of a punctured eardrum, Gardella was in his second season in the majors in 1945, a season that would prove to be a career year. The 25-year-old hit .272 for the Giants with 18 homers and 71 RBIs. He roamed the outfield and played some first base. On top of that he was a bit of a clown, or at least a lovable mug. Either trait made him a hot commodity for major league owners hoping to fill seats.

The 160-pound, 5-foot-7 dynamo could mishandle a play on occasion that would be fodder around the assembly line for days. Or he could get the crowd roaring with laughter, as when he was adjusting his belt in the outfield when a fly ball flew his way. He gave chase and gathered in the ball, all the while using his lefty throwing arm to hold up his pants.

The Giants, managed by Mel Ott, went 78-74 that year, good for fifth place in the National League behind Chicago, St. Louis, Brooklyn, and Pittsburgh. It wasn't a great year, but it was one to build on. Gardella figured he was a solid block in that foundation and wanted the Giants to recognize it, especially on payday.

It's not that the Giants didn't agree he was a strong player, it was that the team wasn't quite as forthcoming with cash as Gardella figured they should be. The Giants offered him a $500 raise, a somewhat hefty 11 percent, to $5,000.

Gardella was more than a bit disappointed. But all ballplayers gripe. The difference was that, in a way unlike anyone else in past years, he did something about it.

He looked south. What he found there was an offer that would give him nine times the raise the Giants were willing to give. All he had to do was play in Mexico, in the growing league down there, and along the way throw organized American baseball a curve.

He did it.

"We doubled our salaries," Gardella said at the age of 78 in 1996 during a rare interview. He said he and a bunch of other major leaguers were courted by Mexican millionaires with lavish nights on the town and wads of thousands of dollars. Stars like Phil Rizzuto and others walked away from the money. Others knew they would probably never see piles of cash like that again, at least not from the owners north of the border who held all the cards in those days.

In an America that was still struggling out of a depression and preparing to get a postwar economy underway, cash was a formidable negotiating tool. So Gardella, Giants pitcher Sal Maglie, and 14 other major leaguers headed to Mexico.

Commissioner A. B. "Happy" Chandler was anything but. He nailed the bunch with a five-year ban. A year later Gardella did what was nearly unthinkable then, but which today has become as automatic a reaction as a catcher throwing his mask to chase a foul ball: He sued.

Gardella filed his $300,000 suit in October 1947, claiming among other things a conspiracy to keep him out of American baseball. The kid from the Bronx who just wanted to play baseball had been blackballed.

That's what hurt because after a couple years with the Vera Cruz Blues, the Mexican experience petered out. The millionaires who courted American players turned out to be trying to score votes for their presidential candidate, and when he lost, the league's interest in scoring American ballplayers waned.

So Gardella and the others played anywhere they could for a few pesos here, a few dollars there: Mexican semipro games, Cuban pro-ball, a new Canadian league, barnstorming through America as Max Lanier's All Stars.

But, as it turns out, the powerful arm of major league baseball extended much further than most thought.

"They went out of their way to keep us from making a living," Gardella said. A call from the commissioner to a ballpark, any ballpark, was all it took to send the All Stars packing.

It got personal. It got serious.

Gardella lost his lawsuit in federal court in Manhattan, but appeal brought an order for a new trial. Lawyers argued. Owners worried.

The judge, Learned Hand, said in 1949 that radio and television might have put major league baseball in the jurisdiction of federal trade and antitrust laws. For owners, that meant they might have to play by the rules of all employers and no longer as a small group of chess players pushing around pawns.

"The owners even sent [Dodger catcher] Mickey Owens to my house to beg me to call off the case," Gardella told the New York *Daily News* in 1994. "Owens said if I dropped the case, the ban would be lifted and we could all play again. The pressure was enormous."

Danny Gardella stretching to apply the tag on baserunner (courtesy of Danny Gardella).

By the All-Star break of 1949, the owners balked. They lifted the ban on all players who had skipped to Mexico. By the end of the World Series, Gardella settled out of court for $60,000. Gardella said that after paying his two lawyers, he kept $29,000. But more importantly, the air of owner infallibility when it came to their handling of players was gone.

In 1950, at age 30, Gardella was back in the National League, now with St. Louis. This was not the same league the boy from the Bronx had left four years before: the stars were back. He played in only one game, had only one at-bat.

He played a couple more years in Class D ball, was even invited to a spring training once, but he knew his major league career was finished. He busted the five-year ban, but it took four of his best years to do it. The layoff from major league curve balls and the pressure of legal wrangling and tight finances took their toll, and then some.

"That was one of the most important events in the post-war era to happen to baseball," said Stephen Rocco Acee, a Niagara Falls, New York, freelance baseball writer and expert on Maglie. "Overall, it was good for baseball as a whole because it made the pension fund come around."

Acee said that not only did the Mexican clash lead to development of the pension system, but salaries inched up and players began to band together.

Mexican millionaires who ran the league wanted to use the defection of U.S. baseball talent as a plank in a presidential election platform, Acee said, and throwing $10,000 around and offering salaries two and three times higher than those of the major leagues turned a lot of heads.

But those Mexican promises and paychecks eventually dried up, and many major leaguers left Mexico in the late 1940s, having spent a good part of their prime in a league that left no line in *The Baseball Encyclopedia*. Still, it showed that American baseball players who didn't think they got a fair shake from management had other places to go—Mexico, pre–Castro Cuba, even Canada.

Sal Maglie took a $15,000 signing bonus and an $18,000-a-year paycheck to play in Mexico, when the average major league salary was about $5,000. He stayed two years, learned to be a better pitcher, and was the only one of the American expatriates to return to a solid major league career.

"In some ways I considered the settlement a sellout, a moral defeat," Gardella told the *Daily News* in 1994. "I think they would have lost if the case went all the way to the Supreme Court. But my lawyer told me they could delay it for years, and still find a way to keep me out of the game. I loved playing for the Giants. They were my home team. I still feel as though I beat them."

That $29,000 he ended up with in the settlement was only slightly more than he would made if he had stayed in the majors at the salary he rebelled against. And for all the empowerment he may have sparked among players, he receives no baseball pension.

Gardella was no egomaniac who sought personal gain at whatever cost— the game of baseball be damned—he was a man who figured out his priorities early in life.

"Having just made it to the major leagues was enough for me," he said. "I enjoyed playing for the Giants and in the Polo Grounds. It was the realization of a boy's dream ... having just played a couple of years was good enough for me. I didn't have an inflated opinion of myself."

So the line on Danny Gardella reads that he played 169 major league games, hit 24 homers, and had a lifetime batting average of .267.

But he knows his baseball career left a greater mark than any he made in a scorebook.

"I think that I probably will be mentioned by serious writers as someone who exposed the reserve clause [which would tie a player to a team as long as the club wanted]. I think I helped players get more money—I think a little too much today. But the indiscretion of owners is not my fault."

"I have since worked in many places where they had unions," Gardella said of his days in several labor jobs and at the phone company. "And unions did very well by us. They've always served me well and I think the American worker is served well by unions, because human nature is human nature. It will always sink to the lowest level."

So who won? As a result of the Gardella conflict and the judges' rulings in the case, baseball owners were put on the road to facing a powerful players union. And owners now can no longer stave off free market pressures easily with a reserve clause.

Danny Gardella, on the other hand, bought a nice house in Yonkers with $13,000 of his out-of-court settlement. He has raised nine kids in that house, where he still lives comfortably in retirement. And he has one more thing: satisfaction. Lots of satisfaction.

AMANDA CLEMENT

BERNICE GERA

PAM POSTEMA

Many days, when Postema, Gera, and Clement took the field, they faced cat-calls, insults, physical threats, and even lawsuits designed to keep them off the diamond forever.

They were determined to take it. Although the abuse was as up-and-up as a spitball against a corked bat, they loved a game some thought women should love only from a distance—the bleachers, a family room, a kitchen. It mattered little that they knew the game well: Postema had hit for power and Clement could peg a ball 275 feet on the money.

None of that mattered, you see, because these names, legendary today only to their few successors, belong to women, and these woman had tried to do the unthinkable: run a game that for so long had been the exclusive domain of men. They were the pioneering women umpires.

Much of the everyday abuse heaped upon Pam Postema (1970s and 1980s), Bernice Gera (early 1970s), and Amanda Clement (early 1900s) was cruel, even for umpires. This was especially true if a woman tried to break beyond the ranks of the minor leagues, where novelty and oddball promotions are as common as ERAs over 5.00. That's OK in the bushes, some thought, but don't be takin' that to the Show.

The gender barrier these and a few women like Christine Wren (Class A, 1975–77) tried to overcome was formidable. Consider that Jackie Robinson, Hank Aaron, and other African Americans not only busted the color barrier in major league baseball, but through their ability and fortitude rewrote the history of the days of whites-only with a permanent and embarrassing blotch. Before them there were others who brought down other barriers, like the bans official and otherwise that ranged from prohibitions against wearing glasses to playing Latin American players.

Today major league baseball is still a boys club, integrated and sometimes bespectacled, but a boys club nonetheless.

Pamela A. Postema was one who dared to knock on their clubhouse door.

137

It should have come as little surprise to those around her. She was used to doing what people were unused to. As a girl in Willard, Ohio, she toured the boondocks as a power-hitting catcher with a fast-pitch softball team comprised mostly of girls two to three years her senior. Later she handled third base on a boys' softball team. Her father, Phil Postema, was a farmer who spent a life facing adversity with hard work and more hard work. His philosophy of resiliency against life's storms and droughts reflected that and stuck with his daughter.

"You can do anything you want," he told her, "as long as you do a good job at it." Then there was the advice he gave her before his 11-year-old catcher hit the road.

"Be good ... and I wasn't talking about morally," he recalled to *Newsday*. "I was talking about playing the game well." Be good. Play hard. Work hard. Oughta be enough. By God, in post-integration baseball at least, it oughta be enough.

It wasn't.

At 21, Postema forced a major break. She broke in with one of the top producers of major league umpires in the country, the Somers Umpire School in Daytona Beach, Florida. She did well, finishing 17th in a class of 130.

Ahead lay long days and nights in the bushes. Along the way she drew lots of attention, much of it condescending. Her umpiring attributes, the *Sporting News* said in 1977, included her "engaging smile and a direct gaze from hazel eyes." The article also described her as "an attractive farm lass." A couple of years later another publication reported her experience and regard were growing, while dutifully noting she spoke of it with "bright hazel eyes aglow."

The special attention focused on her was not reserved for the press. There was the time a frying pan was left on home plate, the game when a manager grabbed and kissed her, the mascot who waved a bra. And the talk. There were comments from fans about breasts and chest protectors and sexual orientation as subtle as a Nolan Ryan fastball.

Some of the most egregious assaults on Postema and other female umpires have lingered long after they hang up their spikes: the God-awful sexist puns and misplay on words in the press that still evoke a cringe:

GAL UMP WINS THE DECISION;
COURT PUTS HOUSEWIFE AT HOME PLATE

THE LADY IS AN UMP

WOMEN SHOULDN'T BE AT HOME (PLATE)

Bernice Gera of Jackson Heights in Queens, New York, found out how difficult it would be to enter the men-only domain of baseball when she began her quest to umpire in the New York–Penn League in 1969. Already an experienced umpire in semipro and other leagues, she secured a contract in 1969 to call games in the minors. But as the New York *Daily News* reported, a funny thing happened to her on her way to calling a game in Auburn, New York: her contract was rescinded.

Court action and sexual discrimination filings followed. And although the battle received some media attention in the depths of the sports pages, her serious effort was often met with less-than-serious attention. For example, her picture ran with a January 14, 1972, *Daily News* story about her victory on appeal in the state's highest court. It was a stately portrait of an older woman in pearls with conservatively styled hair. Beaver Cleaver's mom.

Next to it, ten times the size of the photo, was a cartoon of a wild-eyed, big-breasted woman with, inexplicably, five arms, wearing a short, tight skirt and baseball spikes. No explanation. No caption. Just funny, apparently.

Here's how the Associated Press reported the battle in November 1971:

"The baseball officials contend that the diamond is no place for a lady because of the physical strain, inadequate dressing rooms, and heated tempers and harsh language among ballplayers. They say that umpires must be big men because they have to control big men. And they suggest that by standing behind a brawny catcher Mrs. Gera would not be able to see and properly call a pitch."

Less than three months later, the battle was won: "I am overjoyed at the decision," Gera told AP. "I love baseball and I want to be part of the game."

As a result of the court decision, Gera finally was granted the right to umpire a New York–Penn League game that season. The pressure of the court battles, the fans, the baseball people, and in the game itself apparently proved too much.

She blew it.

Gera hastened her exit from baseball, not so much as a result of making a mistake, but by correcting one.

In the fourth inning of the first game of a doubleheader, in front of network television and 3,000 fans the Auburn Phillies were unaccustomed to hosting, Gera called a runner safe at second.

Wrong. And she knew it.

It was a force play, Gera realized a few long seconds later. Her fist shot up in the air, accurately but belatedly. Out!

Auburn manager Nolan Campbell charged out, screaming. Gera conceded her error. As columnist Dick Schaap correctly noted: "She committed the cardinal sin of baseball—she admitted she made a mistake."

Campbell kept on ranting, and Gera tossed him from the game.

"That's two mistakes," Campbell said to her. "The first was putting on the uniform."

"I made one bad call," Gera told *Referee* magazine in 1979. "And I have to admit, and I admitted it to the world, I made a bad call, and nowhere does

Bernice Gera (courtesy of Baseball Hall of Fame Library, Cooperstown, New York).

it say that you can't reverse it if you are wrong.... I openly admitted it to the manager and he came running out and had every right to be mad. I have to say this, because I wouldn't lie about it, he never cursed. The only thing I said to him was that I had made a mistake and he said, 'You made two mistakes— putting on a uniform and coming out here on the field,' or something like that. 'And your second mistake, you should never have left the kitchen, you should be home peeling potatoes' or something like that. That's when he left the game."

After that first game, Gera quit.

"People are saying I'm a quitter, but I'm not," Gera told *Esquire* magazine in 1973. "Not after what baseball put me through. Someone else might have quit earlier, but I stayed with it."

"I wasn't scared off," she told *Referee* magazine, "I was just disgusted. I was fed up with it.... I could win in the courts but how could I force them to make the umpires work with me?"

Gera stayed around baseball, in a front-office job with the New York Mets farm system and in promotions, but never again as an umpire. In a 1989 interview Gera said she was comfortable with her place in the game's history. Years after her quick entrance and exit from the field, she still signed baseballs: "Bernice Gera, First Lady Umpire."

"I quit baseball after the game because I was physically, mentally and financially drained," she said. "I knew what I was going into, but it is hard to get used to having people spit at you and threaten your life. But I was determined to do it.

"I know I had broken the barrier, and that is what I wanted to accomplish. If nothing else, I had opened the doors for others to follow."

But Gera was not really the first. Just after the turn of the century Amanda Clement umpired seasons of games and drew decent paychecks for the time, although she never took on the professional baseball establishment as Gera did. But to Clement's credit, she did her umping in the early 1900s, an era when women in many states not only had precious few opportunities in male-dominated fields but couldn't even vote or own property.

Amanda Clement of South Dakota umpired 300 games over six years in five states, during which she called balls and strikes and well as worked the bases in a one-ump era, according to a 1972 article in the *Connecticut Herald*. She turned to umpiring after she found her playing opportunities limited, despite breaking the women's record for a baseball toss.

Her big break was in 1906.

She learned to play baseball in the park she had lived next to in Hudson, South Dakota. That's where she broke the state girl's softball toss record. An old chronicle, the *Original Baseball Magazine*, picked up her story there in a 1952 article that was rewritten in the *Connecticut Herald* 20 years later. According to the *Herald*:

> She became an ardent student of the game's rules and recognition of her resultant knowledge led to her being drafted to work sandlot games. Folks like[d] the way she officiated and before long she was hired to handle a torrid annual series between Hudson and the team from nearby Canton.
>
> It was a home-and-home rivalry and she did so well in the opener that she was engaged for the return game, altogether acquitting herself so ably before partisan fans that she was on her way to bigger things as a semi-pro arbiter.
>
> She received as much as $25 a game, big money for those days. Over her career she averaged 50 games a year.

It was that reputation that began to be a major draw, sometimes the major draw, for games. She was in such good shape and so physically capable of the task that she once officiated a 17-inning marathon—running into positions to call balls and strikes and then plays at the bags—in 100-degree heat, despite her common attire of long skirt, white blouse, black tie, and hat.

She umpired amid much fanfare, and her widely accepted good reputation in the job gained congratulations from campaigning presidential candidate Teddy Roosevelt as well as—more impressively—a man who lost a $2,000 bet on a game she called. She went on to teach physical education in college and eventually became the city and county welfare manager in Sioux Falls, South Dakota. Umpiring in the majors was never an option.

Postema knew from history she shouldn't expect the road to the majors to be easy, but it's hard to imagine anyone anticipating the roadblocks she would encounter. Like Houston Astros pitcher Bob Knepper, who said she would have to answer to God for trying to do a job for which only men had been ordained.

"This is not an occupation a woman should be in," Knepper said. "In God's society, woman was created in a role of submission to the husband. It's not that woman is inferior, but I don't believe women should be in a leadership role."

Must have been Commandment 10a.

But there were supporters: even Knepper conceded Postema did a good job behind the plate. So did Pete Rose, as well as Mets pitcher Ron Darling, who offered an analysis to the New York *Daily News* in 1988:

"The point is, I'm not too impressed with the guys we have umpiring now. So what's wrong with a woman, especially if she's good? I've known Pam since I was in Double-A [1982], so she's definitely paid her dues. And she's not bad. This isn't any affirmative-action thing."

Yet Postema was still getting ripped from all angles. Not only did the more boorish fans and players heap abuse upon her during games (she got a reputation in the minors for having a quick thumb, and said she learned to spell every dirty word there is by writing up verbatim ejection reports to league offices), but she even caught some grief from feminists. In a 1988 column in *New York Woman* magazine titled "The Umpire Won't Strike Back," Postema was subtly taken to task for not lashing back more at the boys club that was and is baseball. But critics on that end of the spectrum were in the minority; most saw her as a hero, a pioneer.

"Last summer, from the quiet of their Park Avenue offices, some of the most powerful executives in baseball started a revolution as significant as the signing of Jackie Robinson," the *New York Woman* article read. "The National League was considering Pam Postema, a Class AAA umpire and the only woman ump in baseball, for a Major League contract. 'The Lady Is an Ump' trumpeted *Sports Illustrated*'s cover, and for several weeks Postema's was the most anomalous story in sports."

That attention flickered out quickly after she was dropped before the start of 1990 spring training after five years in Triple-A and, as she said, "13 long, lonely hellish seasons." Such weeding to allow newcomers coming up the ranks is a common fate for umpires who don't make the majors within that five-year window. But Postema filed a sexual discrimination lawsuit in federal court. (She settled for an undisclosed sum and the condition she wouldn't apply for any umpiring jobs affiliated with major league baseball.) Then she wrote a stinging book, *You've Got to Have B*lls to Make It in This League: My Life as an Umpire.*

"I tried to change the rules," Postema wrote in a May 1992 guest column in *The Sporting News.* "I made it further than any woman umpire ever had. But then I got too close, close enough that I started to make the baseball purists [translation: sexists] nervous." Postema listed just a few of the big-name players with whom she had worked, such as José Canseco and Carlton Fisk. And she closed her column with bitter words:

> I should be there. That's what I keep telling myself. I should be working a ballgame right now, not driving a Federal Express truck. But until baseball's good ol' sexists network begins treating women as equals—fat chance—rather than threats, no female umpire will ever know how it feels to call a major league game. I'm proof of that.

Postema just wanted to be part of baseball, this Ohio farm kid. When she outgrew the girls' fast-pitch softball team, when she outgrew the boys' softball team, she advanced. What she didn't know was baseball wouldn't.

RAY CHAPMAN

At what sounded like the crack of the bat, Yankee catcher Muddy Ruel bounded out from his crouch behind the plate.

"I saw the ball roll toward the pitcher's box," he said more than a quarter century after the 1920 game against the Cleveland Indians. "I was just a kid then, and pretty fast on my feet. I pounced across the plate, snatched up the ball and fired it toward first base. Only then did I see the look on Carl Mays' face. I turned around, Chappie was half-sitting, half-sprawling in the batter's box. I tried to rush to him, but Speaker and Steve O'Neill and Jack Graney got there ahead of me. I guess I was glued to the ground."

The hitter, Ray Chapman, had never gotten his bat on the ball. The squibber Ruel thought he was chasing had in fact ricocheted off Chapman's skull. Umpire Thomas Connolly went to the stands to request a doctor, and two came to the field. Chapman, with player/manager Tris Speaker by his side, rose to his feet, to the applause of the opposing crowd at the Polo Grounds. He started to make his way to the center-field clubhouse under his own power but collapsed into the arms of two teammates.

In the clubhouse, Chapman, married the previous October to socialite Kathleen Daly in Cleveland's "social event of the fall," asked for his wedding ring back from a trainer who was holding it for the game. He then spoke to a friend in town for the game, pleading with him not to tell his wife about the incident. If he had to tell her, Chapman added, say he was OK.

Raymond Johnson Chapman died in a New York hospital the following morning. He was survived by his wife, who gave birth to their child, a daughter, the following February.

What Ruel had seen when he turned back toward home plate stayed with him the rest of his life.

"I knew right then," he said, "that I had seen a man killed by a baseball."

Ray Chapman, a Cleveland Indians shortstop, and Carl Mays, a New York Yankees pitcher, could not have been more different. Chappie, as he was known, was wildly popular with fans and fellow players, a fine singer and admired storyteller.

Carl Mays may have been the most hated man in baseball, even on his own team. He could be surly. And whiny. And gruff. In short, he rubbed people the wrong way, hard.

"Any player who ever worked for me, if he was down in his luck, can come to me for help," said Yankee manager Miller Huggins. "I make only two exceptions, Carl Mays and Joe Bush. If they were in the gutter, I'd give them another kick."

F. C. Lane wrote in *Baseball Magazine* that Mays was virtually friendless and had "aroused more ill will, more positive resentment than any other ball player on record." Even Mays acknowledged as much, stating he was not popular with his peers dating to his minor league days.

"The unpopularity which had come to be as natural as my own shadow continued to follow me," Mays told the magazine, speaking of his minor league career. Later he added a postscript:

"It was long ago made very apparent to me that I was not one of those individuals who were fated to be popular."

What Chapman and Mays did have in common was that they were both stars. Chapman was born on a farm in Beaver Dam, Kentucky, and his baseball skills saved him from a life in the mines. After starring in the Three-I League, Chapman rose to the majors in 1912. His first few years were plagued by various injuries, but his potential was apparent.

Bill Wambsganss, the Tribe's second baseman who also would gain fame that 1920 season, came up as a shortstop in 1914 and was expected to wrest the job from Chapman. *Chicago Tribune* writer Ring Lardner knew better, as the literary legend penned this ditty:

> *The Naps bought a shortstop named Wambsganss*
> *Who is slated to fill Ray Chapman's pants.*
> *But when he saw Ray*
> *And the way he could play*
> *He muttered, "I haven't a clam's chance."*

In 1917, Chapman hit .302, stole 52 bases (during a charity competition that year he circled the bases in a then-record 14 seconds), scored 98, and led the league in assists and putouts at short. The following year he led the league in runs and walks. In 1919, despite a bout with lumbago, he again hit .300 and was regarded as one of the best shortstops in the game, comparable even to all-timer Honus Wagner.

"For sheer versatility for excellence of performance in every department of the game [Chapman] has proved for one season at least a not unworthy rival to the Dutchman at his best," *Baseball Magazine* wrote.

Chapman was having his best year in 1920; in July he was hitting .306 and riding a 16-game hitting streak. He wanted the year to be his finest moment, capped by an Indians' world title. If all went well, Chapman, only 29, planned to retire after the season.

Mays was foundering in the minors until he saw 42-year-old Iron Man Joe McGinnity pitch for an opposing team in 1913. McGinnity, already past his Hall-of-Fame career in the majors (he would pitch until 1923 in the minors), was still pitching in the minors using a "submarine" pitch—a below-sidearm delivery that was the fashion before overhand pitching was legalized in 1885. Mays adopted the style—a modern-day parallel would be former Kansas City Royals reliever Dan Quisenberry—and his career flourished. The 5-foot-11½, 195-pound right-hander was promoted to Providence and later the Red Sox, where he went 18-13 his second year in 1916. He blossomed into a star, winning more than 20 games the next two years for the BoSox and forming a dangerous rotation along with a left-hander named Babe Ruth.

In 1919, amid a dispute with team officials, Mays walked out on the club and demanded to be traded. He was 5-11 at the time. He was shipped to the Yankees, where he finished the season 9-3 for an overall record of 14-14.

Mays' pitching style, while not revolutionary, was virtually unique to the majors during this time. "He looks like a cross between an octopus and a bowler," *Baseball Magazine* wrote. On most days right-handers couldn't touch him; on good days no one could.

"His under-handed motion is not natural and at times some of the balls he throws take remarkable shoots, jumps, ducks and twists," Ruel said in 1920. "I have never been able to understand how any batter ever gets a hit off him."

While Mays had a reputation as a winner, he also was tagged as a moody whiner (although Mays and Ruth were teammates on three teams—Providence, Boston, and the Yankees—they were never friends). Of greater concern to opposing hitters, Mays also was known as a headhunter.

"[Mays] was known to be a duster, at least that was the general thought of the guys that didn't like him," Wambsganss said. "He came from that Boston club. They were told not to be afraid to knock 'em down. A lot of those fellows just got that in their head. Of course, they'd lose control once in a while."

Mays' reputation was widely accepted, but not by the pitcher.

"I merely wish to say I am not a murderer nor do I aim to take any unfair advantage of anyone," he said before the Chapman incident. "I depend largely on a peculiar delivery. ... And due either to the freak breaks of this delivery or my desire to take the corners of the plate to which I'm entitled, I have been unfortunate enough to hit a number of batters, though very seldom on the head."

But hitters knew otherwise, including the doomed Chapman.

"Carl Mays throws it so he'll dust you off the plate," he said the season before the fatal beanball. "But I'll stand right up there. He doesn't bother me. He's not going to intimidate me."

In 1920 the Indians had jumped out to the league lead with a 16-6 start

Ray Chapman (courtesy of Baseball Hall of Fame Library, Cooperstown, New York).

and had a 4½ game lead on the Yankees as of August 9. But after New York swept a four-game series at League Park in Cleveland, the two teams and the Chicago White Sox found themselves almost in a dead heat. A pivotal series loomed in New York the following weekend.

The August 16 game was big to Mays, not only because of the pennant race, but because he was shooting for his 100th major league win. He once owned the Tribe, going 12-2 over his first three years, but then had lost six of seven. The day in New York was hot and muggy, but rain fell over the first three innings.

Chapman had laid down a sacrifice bunt in the first inning and bunted out in the third. Cleveland held a 3–0 lead when Chappie came to the plate to lead off the fifth.

On his first pitch of the frame, Mays went into his windup, bringing back his right arm at a 50-degree angle, dropping his left shoulder low, and shielding his chin. Chapman slid back his right foot, a sign from a right-handed batter that a bunt was coming.

The pitch came at his head. Chapman froze. "I saw Ray standing there never moving so much as a muscle," Ruel said. "He must have been paralyzed, fascinated like the rabbit by the snake." Other players talk about instances where the hitter becomes mesmerized by the ball and doesn't get out of the way.

"You simply can't get out of the way of the bean ball, though you see it coming and you know it's going to crash into your skull," former Cleveland infielder Terry Turner told the *Cleveland Press* just after the Chapman incident.

While Mays was known for throwing tight on hitters, Chapman was also known for crowding the plate, cutting down on a pitcher's margin for error.

"I was closer to Chapman than anyone else on earth, and right now, almost 30 years later, I still believe it was an accident, pure and simple," Ruel said in a 1948 *Sporting News* article. "You know, Chapman had a peculiar stance. It is literally true that he could have been hit on the head by a perfect strike. He crowded the plate and hunched over it. His head was in the strike zone."

Noted *New York Telegram* sportswriter Fred Lieb, who was seated behind home plate at the game, exonerated Mays in a column more than 52 years later.

"Though Mays had the reputation of pitching bean balls, going back to his Red Sox days, I always felt that the submarine ball that exploded against Chapman's left temple in 1920 was wholly accidental," he wrote. "Chapman ... had a habit of leaning over the plate. As the Mays pitch approached, Ray acted as though he were mesmerized."

Mays believed Chapman actually moved somewhat into the pitch. "It was a straight fastball and not a curve," he said. "When Chapman came to bat I got the signal for a straight fastball, which I delivered. It was a little too close and I saw Chapman duck his head to get out of the path of the ball. He was too late, however, and a second later he fell to the ground. It was the most regrettable incident of my career and I would give anything to undo what happened."

Wambsganss said he could not necessarily disagree with Mays' contention that Chapman stepped into the pitch and the pitch didn't break. "I suppose it's possible, yes," he said. "It's possible that was the case."

In 1963 Mays, by then a scout with the Milwaukee Braves, wrote an astold-to column with the *Sporting News*. In the column, Mays put some of the onus on Chapman himself.

> The man I hit was a batter like that, crowding the plate with his hand and head over it.
>
> I didn't mean to hit him, of course. But I had to pitch in the strike zone.
>
> I don't like the idea of pitchers deliberately throwing at batters. I don't think many ever have.
>
> But I don't like the idea of batters taking a foothold, digging in, right on top of the plate and almost defying the pitcher to throw to the inside corner of the plate.
>
> Any batter who does that bears equal responsibility. He has to take his chances if he wants to gamble."

The Rev. Dr. William A. Scullen delivered the eulogy for Chapman before an overflow crowd of mourners at St. John's Roman Catholic Cathedral in Cleveland.

"May there be no hostility in any heart to the man who was the unfortunate occasion of this accident. He feels it more deeply than you, and no one regrets it as much as he. This great game we play, that is our national pastime, could not produce anybody who would willingly do a thing like that. Remember those would be the words of him who lies here. Do not hold any animosity."

But many did. The Indians, Red Sox, Tigers, and Browns were debating whether to boycott any game Mays appeared in. Ty Cobb later sent Mays a note through an intermediary:

"If it was within my power, I would have inscribed on Ray Chapman's tombstone these words: 'Here lies a victim of arrogance, viciousness and greed.'"

American League president Ban Johnson, who like many in baseball had a strong dislike for Mays, later exonerated him of guilt. But on the day of Chapman's funeral, Johnson sounded like he wanted to bury the pitcher's career as well: "I could not conscientiously attempt to make any trouble for

Mr. Mays, but it is my honest belief that Mr. Mays will never pitch again," he said. "From what I have learned he is greatly affected and may never be capable temperamentally of pitching again. Then I also know the feeling against him to be so bitter among the members of other teams that it would be inadvisable for him to attempt to pitch this year at any rate."

Ever defiant, Mays thought otherwise. "I intend to keep on and work as well as I can to provide a home and comfortable future for my family. This is what I shall try to do, for that is my lookout. What people may wish to think about me or say about me is their lookout."

Mays had his supporters.

"It is unfortunate for Mays that he has not been as popular as the dead player," the *New York Tribune* wrote, "but he must not be sacrificed because of his unpopularity." Even Speaker, whose disdain for Mays dated to their days as teammates at Boston, said, "I do not hold Carl responsible in any way." Mays met with reporters at his home after the incident. He promised to go on. "If I were not absolutely sure in my own heart that it was an accident pure and simple, I do not think that I could stand it," he said. "As to my pitching future, I do not think that this thing will unnerve me. My conscience is absolutely clear. It was an accident for which I am absolutely blameless." He then went on to blame Connolly for not throwing out a disfigured ball. "It was the umpire's fault."

Mays did go on, taking his next turn in the rotation against the White Sox. While Mays did yell "Look out!" on several of his breaking pitches, he eventually regained his composure and finished the season 26-11.

The Tribe went on as well: a week after Chapman's death, rookie Joe Sewell was called up as a replacement. He hit .329 for the season, and Cleveland won that first world title Chapman had so coveted.

In his insightful book, *The Pitch That Killed: Carl Mays, Ray Chapman and the Pennant Race of 1920*, author Mike Sowell noted that an average nine-inning game sees about 200 to 250 pitches. That means that since big-league ball began in 1871, there have been roughly 25 million pitches. "Only one of them has killed a man," Sowell wrote.

Other professional ballplayers had been killed on the diamond before and since, but never in the majors. The first is believed to have been James Creighton, a pitcher for the Brooklyn Excelsiors. October 15, 1862, he suffered an internal injury "occasioned by strain" against the Morrisania Unions. He died four days later of a ruptured bladder. There would be other deaths:

• On August 9, 1906, Tom Burke of Lynn, Massachusetts, was hit in the head in a New England League game and died two days later. A manslaughter charge was filed against pitcher Joseph Yeager but soon was dropped.

• On September 23, 1910, Charles Tenkuy was hit in the head by Kirk Hageman in a game at Grand Rapids, Michigan.

• Former major leaguer Johnny Dodge was killed in a Southern League game June 18, 1916. A third baseman for the Mobile Bears, Dodge was hit in the face by a pitch from Tom Rogers.

• The last known fatal beaning on the field occurred June 2, 1951, when Ottis Johnson of Dothan of the Class D Alabama-Florida League was hit by Jack Clifton of Headland. Johnson died eight days later.

• Two other players, Herb Gorman (1953) and Dixie Howell (1960), died of heart attacks suffered on the field. Both were former major leaguers.

• On Opening Day of 1996 in Cincinnati, veteran umpire John McSherry called time, walked away from home plate, collapsed, and died of a massive heart attack just moments into the game.

On the day Chapman died, many newspapers carried a small news item: Carl Jager of Plainwell, Michigan, was hit on the head in an amateur game in Kalamazoo the day before Chapman; he died the same day as the Indians shortstop.

After the beaning Mays went on to play nine more seasons. For his career he finished 208-126 over 15 seasons, a .623 winning percentage. During his career with the Red Sox, Yankees, Reds, and Giants, he led the league for a season in wins and winning percentage (27-9, .750, in 1921), complete games, shutouts, and saves (twice each), and games, innings pitched, and wins in relief. He had a better winning percentage than Bob Feller, Waite Hoyt, Bob Lemon, Herb Pennock, Cy Young, and several other Hall of Famers and more wins than the enshrined Dizzy Dean, Jack Chesbro, Sandy Koufax, or Rube Marquard, among others. Yet the Hall of Fame has eluded him.

"There was once some [support], but it was not great," said Shirley Povich, the famed *Washington Post* columnist and a member of the Hall's Veterans Committee from 1987–95. "On the numbers I think he was deserving. He was an unpopular person; that was a factor. I think there was some carry-over from the Chapman incident."

Even as years passed? Even now?

"Then," said the writer, "they forgot about him."

Gone and a tumultuous but successful career forgotten. Mays died April 4, 1971, in El Cajon, California. He was 79 and bitter, bitter over the Hall of Fame's snub, which he attributed to the Chapman incident.

"I won over 200 big league games, but no one today remembers that," he said. "When they think of me, I'm the guy who killed Chapman with a fastball."

ALEXANDER CARTWRIGHT

Author's Note: Coauthor Michael Gormley, who along with Abner Doubleday claims Ballston Spa, New York, as his hometown, disavows any involvement with the following chapter. Doesn't even want to read it. As far as he's concerned, Cooperstown is the birthplace of baseball, period. He even has a cheesy souvenir pen to prove it. It says: COOPERSTOWN HOME OF BASEBALL.

Tucked along the southern shore of Otsego Lake where it meets the Susquehanna River, Cooperstown is a village that screams "quaint," from its Victorian homes to its antique shops and rolling farms. Founded by the father of novelist James Fenimore Cooper, the village is the home to a fine opera, several museums (including ones dedicated to farming), a renowned regional hospital, and 2,300 residents or so.

It's also the home of baseball.

It's just not the game's hometown.

Many kids first learning about the history of the sport can tell you baseball was invented by Abner Doubleday. Coauthor Gormley excluded (the homer), most historians today acknowledge the tale is a myth concocted with the thinnest of evidence early in the century and promoted by a sporting goods magnate determined to prove the American game was a uniquely American invention.

And Doubleday was definitely a historic American. A West Point graduate, he served in the Mexican War in 1846–48. At Fort Sumter, South Carolina, he fired the first shot of the Civil War, and he was later a brigadier general commanding volunteers in charge of defending Washington, D.C. In 1862 he was promoted to major general, and he served in the army until his retirement in 1873. Thousands saw him lie in state after his death in 1893.

In the short vernacular, he did it all—except invent baseball.

"I don't think there's much likelihood that [Doubleday] was in Cooperstown or had anything to do with the birth of baseball," Bill Deane, then a senior research associate at the National Baseball Library in Cooperstown, said in 1990. "It seems, in retrospect, kind of silly."

Had history got it right, Hoboken, New Jersey—that Yuppie bastion on the shores of the Hudson River a PATH train away from the World Trade Center—would be called the birthplace of baseball and Alexander Cartwright its father. Then again, maybe Manhattan island should have the distinction, although it has enough already.

Then again still, maybe no one can take credit for the exact evolutionary moment where baseball arose from the dozens of bat-and-ball games being played at the time. The exercise may be akin to trying to identify the first man, even if baseball's birth was only 150 or so years ago.

From time to time, elected officials from New York and New Jersey have gotten into spats over which state could claim the game as its own. Senators from across the Hudson would fire off bills in Congress calling for their home state's designation as baseball's birthplace. Governors would hold news conferences, proclaiming baseball as a native son. The political rhetoric neither added to nor resolved the debate.

After more than one and a half centuries, only two things are sure:

Cartwright is enshrined in the National Baseball Hall of Fame in Cooperstown.

Doubleday isn't.

This comes from the Hall of Fame's own yearbook:

> ALEXANDER CARTWRIGHT Born April 17, 1820 at New York, N.Y. Died July 12, 1892 at Honolulu, HI. Elected to the Hall of Fame in 1938. Alexander Cartwright is called "The Father of Modern Baseball." Using his ability as an engineer and draftsman, he ingeniously located the bases 90 feet apart. His rules also established 9 innings as a game and 9 players as a team. He provided for three outs per side, set an unalterable batting order, and eliminated throwing the ball at a runner to retire him. Cartwright organized the first team—the New York Knickerbockers in 1845.

People have been hitting roundish things with sticks probably dating back to the Stone Age. The British had two games based on the concept: cricket, the sport of men, and roundball, a child's game. In America various derivations of the games arose under many different names: old cat, one old cat, two old cat, three old cat, goal ball, town ball, barn ball, sting ball, soak ball, stick ball, burn ball, and base ball (not the same game) were among them.

Town ball seems to have been the most uniform. The game was played with a square infield and no foul lines. Anywhere from 8 to 15 players could play on a side, although up to 50 could be accommodated. Teams got a single out to a side, with outs tallied by either catching a ball on a fly or "soaking" a runner—nailing him with a throw (soaking is still used in some versions of backyard Wiffle Ball).

The last rung of the game's evolutionary ladder was New York City, where in the first half of 1842, men gathered in Manhattan to play the game.

They first played at Madison Avenue and 27th Street and later at the foot of Murray Hill. Baseball began to resemble the game it is today.

On September 23, 1845, Cartwright, a tall, 25-year-old shipping clerk, corralled 28 of these men to establish the New York Knickerbocker Base Ball Club, named after a volunteer fire company to which Cartwright and several others belonged. Rules were drawn up, as well as a schedule of fines for ungentlemanly conduct: profanity, 6.25 cents; arguing with an umpire, 12.5 cents; expressing an opinion on a proper call before the umpire's decision, 12.5 cents, and disobeying your captain, 50 cents. All fines had to be paid to the umpire before leaving the field, under penalty of suspension. The game's codification began.

Cartwright and the Knickerbockers decreed the infield should be diamond rather than square. First and third bases were 42 paces apart. The balk was identified and outlawed. Foul lines were implemented. Pitchers threw underhand from 45 feet, elbow and wrist straight. Batters got three missed swings. Runners could either be tagged or thrown out. Soaking was banned.

As Manhattan grew denser and more urban, the men needed an open place to play; their spot was found a ferry ride away in Hoboken.

Elysian Fields was a grassy picnic clearing with a view of downtown. Doc Adams, president of the Knickerbockers and a New Hampshire physician, recalled the outings:

> Once there we were free from all restraint, and throwing off our coats we played until it was too dark to see any longer. I was a left-handed batter, and sometimes used to [hit] the ball into the river. People began to take an interest in the game presently, and sometimes we had as many as a hundred spectators watching.... The first professional English cricket team that came to this country ... used to come over and watch our game. They rather turned up their noses at it, and thought it was a tame sport, until we invited them to try it. Then they found it was not so easy as it looked.

On June 19, 1846, Elysian Fields was the site of the first prearranged game, pitting the Knickerbockers against the New York Baseball Club. The Nine, as the New York Baseball Club was also known, won 23–1. Historians, using the scorebook as a guide, believe the Knickerbockers did not play their first string: Cartwright umpired and in fact levied a six-cent fine against a Nine player for profanity. The Knickerbockers would play solely intrasquad games over the next four years.

Even these historically substantiated events leave doubts as to whether this was in fact the first game. In the preface to his book *Great Baseball Feats, Facts & Firsts*, novelist and baseball historian David Nemec raises some

Alexander Cartwright (courtesy of Baseball Hall of Fame Library, Cooperstown, New York).

interesting questions about whether the Elysian Fields contest was in fact the inaugural:

> If so, how did the Knickerbockers, purportedly the first club ever to organize mainly for the purpose of playing baseball, manage to lose so egregiously? Who were the New York Nine? When and where did they assemble and start mastering the intricacies of the new sport? How sure are we that they didn't secretly play a slew of games to prepare for Cartwright's bunch and that those games were the first ones? Well, the unhappy truth is that we're not at all sure; nor, probably will we ever be.

In 1849, Cartwright left Manhattan for California, taking with him a bat a ball and a Knickerbocker rule book in a quest for gold and riches.

"During the past week we have passed the time in fixing wagon-covers, stowing property, etc., varied by hunting and fishing and playing base ball," Cartwright wrote in a diary entry from April 23, 1849, in Independence, Missouri. "It is comical to see mountain men and Indians playing the new game. I have the ball with me that we used back home [New York]."

Cartwright would not find his riches in California; rather, he became a wealthy merchant in Hawaii. Along his trek he left behind seeds of a game that would mushroom into a national craze during the Civil War.

So where does Abner Doubleday come in?

The story goes that in 1839 kids from Otsego Academy were playing Green's Select School in a game of town ball. One Otsego player, Abner Doubleday, sat down and at that moment drew up the rules for a new game to be called baseball. First he and the others had to chase the cows out of Elihu Phinney's pasture so the new game could be played.

It is a wonderful story, Rockwellian to the core, one that has survived not because of fact but because it is such a powerful fable worthy of retelling. Even today, the Hall labels the story "folklore."

The origins debate raged before the game was 70 years old. It crested in a tête-à-tête between two future Hall of Famers.

Henry Chadwick, an English-born newspaperman, was converted from cricket to baseball and even played shortstop for the Knickerbockers. Possibly more than Cartwright himself he promoted the game out of its infancy, convincing the *New York Times* and other dailies to run scores of games. He later became the first newspaper baseball editor, for the *New York Clipper*, and worked for more than 40 years at the *Brooklyn Eagle*. In addition to writing baseball guides and yearbooks, Chadwick also devised baseball's shorthand, the box score.

In 1905, Albert Spalding was 55, a former pitcher, manager, club owner and executive. For years he and Chadwick were in the midst of a friendly argument over the origins of the game. When Chadwick wrote that baseball had evolved from the British games of crickets and rounders, Spalding had had enough.

Spalding was sure, or at least hoping, that the game flowed forth from the fountain "of some ingenious American lad." Spalding, of Spalding Sporting Goods fame, appointed a commission to find out.

The Mills Commission was named after Col. A. G. Mills, a New Yorker who had played the game before and during the Civil War and was past president of the National League (1882–84). The commission was rounded out by three former ballplayers, Albert J. Reach of Philadelphia, George Wright of Boston (both successful businessmen), and Nicholas E. Young (also a former National League president), a pair of U.S. senators, Arthur P. Gorman of Maryland, and Morgan G. Bulkely of Connecticut (who was also a former governor and the first National League president), and James E. Sullivan of New York, president of the Amateur Athletic Union (A.A.U.).

For the first two years, no conclusive evidence was unearthed. Then came a letter from Abner Graves, a mining engineer from Denver. The old man claimed that when he was a boy in 1839, his Cooperstown classmate Doubleday had designed and named baseball, abandoning the rules of town ball in favor of his own concoction. Doubleday had drawn it out on a piece of paper, Graves said, although the paper was now long gone.

Spalding pleaded with other commissioners that the letter be given serious consideration. "It certainly appeals to an American's pride to have the great national game of baseball created and named by a major-general in the United States Army," he said. On December 30, 1907, the commission complied, declaring:

"The first scheme for playing baseball, according to the best evidence obtainable to date, was devised by Abner Doubleday at Cooperstown, New York, in 1839."

Spalding was ecstatic, as well as alphabetic: "I claim that Base Ball owes its prestige as our National Game to the fact that as no other form of sport it is the exponent of American Courage, Confidence, Combativeness; American Dash, Discipline, Determination, American Energy, Eagerness and Enthusiasm; American Pluck, Persistency, Performance; American Spirit, Sagacity, Success; American Vim, Vigor, Virility."

In short, what's the word we're looking for ... American?

The fact is that of the four major sports in America, only basketball can claim pure American origins—and that game was invented by a Canadian, James Naismith, albeit in Massachusetts.

Some of the evidence available and or later unearthed would debunk the Doubleday declaration:

• Doubleday was at West Point the entire summer of 1839, at a time when cadets were not allowed off campus. There were plenty of Doubledays living in Cooperstown at the time, however, including another Abner Doubleday.
• Graves was 5 years old at the time he was supposed to have witnessed the historic birth of the game. He also said he was a classmate of Doubleday, but Doubleday was 15 years older.
• This "reputable gentleman" was later declared criminally insane, and he died in a sanitarium after shooting his wife to death.
• After his death in 1893, Doubleday left behind more than 20 journals. Not one mentioned baseball.

Twenty-seven years after the Mills Commission's findings, there was another find in an old trunk that once belonged to Graves in an attic in Fly's Creek, New York, just outside of Cooperstown. It was a baseball—misshapen, undersized, homemade, but a baseball nonetheless. Stuffed with cloth with a criss-cross stitched cover, it was dubbed the "Doubleday baseball." As far as Cooperstown theorists were concerned, it was a smoking gun.

A local philanthropist, Stephen C. Clark, purchased the ball with the idea of displaying it and other baseball memorabilia in the Village Club, now the Village Hall. The idea grew to establish a museum and enshrine the game's greats. In 1936 the first five inductees were selected by the Baseball Writers Association of America: Ty Cobb (the high vote-getter), Babe Ruth, Honus Wagner, Christy Mathewson and Walter Johnson. The National Baseball Hall of Fame and Museum was dedicated on June 12, 1939: Main Street Cooperstown, which now handles more than 400,000 pilgrims to the museum every year, was changed forever.

The Hall of Fame is a remarkable depository that transcends sport, offering an insightful perspective of a maturing nation. It is a graceful place, and its overseers handle the Doubleday dilemma in a graceful manner. Again, from the 1995 Hall of Fame yearbook:

> From time to time over the years, various critics have challenged the speculation on Doubleday, although most of the original documentation was lost in a fire in 1916. ... Whatever may or may not be proved in the future concerning Baseball's true origin is in many respects irrelevant at this time. If baseball was not actually first played here in Cooperstown by Doubleday in 1839, it undoubtedly originated about that time in a similar rural atmosphere. The Hall of Fame is in Cooperstown to stay; and at the very least, the village is certainly an acceptable symbolic site for the game's origin.

In the movie *Miracle on 34th Street*, a man is able to prove in court he is in fact the real Santa Claus because of all the mail he receives addressed to St. Nick. U.S. Rep. Sherwood Boehlert, whose New York congressional district includes Cooperstown, offers a similar argument:

"If Cooperstown was not the home of baseball, why would Stan Musial and Ted Williams and the commissioner of baseball and the president of the National League and the president of the American league and hundreds of thousands of fans make the annual trek here?"

The answer is, with apologies to Mount Everest explorer George Leigh Mallory—and Alexander Cartwright—because it's there.

COOKIE LAVAGETTO

AND BILL BEVENS

Dodgers manager Burt Shotton paced the dugout and turned to his bench. Bottom of the ninth, Brooklyn down one, two on and two out. Game Four of the 1947 World Series would come down to his next decision.

"Cookie!" the manager shouted.

Veteran Harry "Cookie" Lavagetto, 34 and on his last legs of a war-shortened career, was so attuned to the game and so unprepared for the call that he didn't hear the manager at first. Shotton called his name again: this time Lavagetto bounded up from the bench, prepared to trot out to first base to pinch-run for the injured Pete Reiser, who had just walked.

"No ... you hit for [Eddie] Stanky," Shotton said as Lavagetto headed toward first. "I want Miksis to run for Reiser."

Meanwhile, Stanky was trying to sneak up to the plate to get his cuts. "Stanky's a smart little bugger," Shotton said afterward. "He could hear me hollering but he wouldn't look around. He didn't want to come back."

On the mound, Floyd Bevens, a man known by the simple nickname of Bill, was waiting and sweating in the autumn air. The New York Yankee right-hander had struggled throughout the game, walking his ninth and tenth batter of the game in the final inning, but he clung to a 2–1 lead. The 30-year-old Oregonian needed just one more batter, just one, for the game, for history.

Bevens wiped his brow as Lavagetto finally ambled to the plate. It was now just him and Lavagetto, the man between Bevens and baseball's first World Series no-hitter.

Bevens had thrown no-hitters before, two of them, in fact. But they were in the minor league outpost of Wenatchee, and while one was in a playoff game, it was not in the heart of New York, in a World Series contest.

And Bevens was coming off a bleak season, 7-13, after two promising campaigns in which he went 13-9 in 1945 and 16-13 in 1946. But in 1947 he had looked good in only two of those games: a shutout against the Indians and Bob Feller (part of a Yankee 19-game winning streak) and a three-hit shutout toward the end of the season against the Athletics.

161

Bevens was a thrower more than a pitcher, with a heavy fastball and a good sinker. Even his manager acknowledged as much, telling him just to rear back and fire.

"You're big and strong, Bill, and you have a live fastball," then-manager Joe McCarthy told Bevens when he reached the majors in 1944. "Never mind trying to pitch to spots. Just rear back and fire away. If you are around the plate, they're going to be swinging. And they're not going to be able to do much with your stuff."

In 1947, however, they were smacking more than a hit an inning off Bevens. He had nothing left, except one more game.

Never before had a pitcher gone beyond 7⅔ innings of no-hit ball in a Series, which Yankee Red Ruffing did in beating the Cards 7–4 in the 1942 opener. Two Chicago Cubs, Ed Reulbach in 1906 and Claude Passeau in 1945, hurled one-hitters.

What made Bevens' pitching that October day more remarkable was that the Dodgers were coming off a 13-hit, 9–8 slugfest in Game Three. Now in Game Four, nothing. "We had been talking about the no-hitter from the sixth inning on," Lavagetto said. "He'd walked all those people, but Joe DiMaggio and Tommy Heinrich had been climbing all over the outfield fences catching fly balls. I don't know how many hits they took away from us."

The Dodgers' lone run had come in the fifth, on two walks, a sacrifice, and a groundout. It took a little while for Bevens to grasp his chance at the record books. "With all the walks and so many men on base and the Dodgers getting a run, I didn't know I had a no-hitter until about the eighth inning," he said. "Then I went after it."

Bevens retired Brooklyn catcher Bruce Edwards to start the ninth. After Carl Furillo walked, first baseman Johnny Jorgensen fouled out. Al Gionfriddo was sent in to pinch-run for Furillo and promptly stole second. Then came Reiser's walk and Eddie Miksis' substitution. The fact that Yankee manager Bucky Harris had decided to walk a sore-legged Reiser after ball three and put the winning run on base in contravention to conventional wisdom would be second-guessed for a generation. ("I have no regrets," Harris said afterward. "I would do it all over again if the same situation came up again.")

Lavagetto, who had skipped running his father's trash business to sign with hometown Oakland of the Pacific Coast League, came up with Pittsburgh in 1934 and was a fixture as the Dodgers No. 2 hitter and third baseman from 1937 to 1941. He hit .273 or better with at least 70 RBIs in four of those five years and hit .269 for his 10-year career. But Lavagetto lost four years to the navy starting with 1942, and he played in only 41 games in 1947. "I was washed up," he later said. He knew his time had passed: in fact, the Series was being broadcast for the first time on the East Coast via a medium that didn't exist in Lavagetto's prime—television.

As Lavagetto dug into the right side of the batter's box, Bevens knew

Harry "Cookie" Lavagetto (courtesy of Baseball Hall of Fame Library, Cooperstown, New York).

how to pitch him. He had the scouting report from Charlie Dressen and Red Corriden, Yankee coaches who had been with the Dodgers the year before. He remembered the line on Cookie given to him by Dressen—one of Lavagetto's closest friends.

"When they sent Lavagetto up I remembered he said Lavagetto couldn't handle hard stuff away," Bevens recalled years later. "That's what I gave him."

Bevens came with heat, and Lavagetto swung at the first pitch for strike one. Bevens came back again with the same stuff, hard and outside, just as he was told. Catcher Yogi Berra, another righty who would become known for hitting pitches well out of the strike zone, said the pitch was clearly a ball. It still looked good to Lavagetto.

"This is it," Lavagetto thought. "This is the one."

Bevens got the scouting report dead right ... except the scouting report was dead wrong.

"If they were pitching fast and outside me to me, they were almost exactly wrong," Lavagetto said. "Fast and tight was the way to handle me. I thought Bill tried to pitch inside to me and the ball got away from him."

In a year that would mark the debut of a televised World Series, as well as the postseason coming out of Jackie Robinson, Lavagetto took a swing that defined the Series.

Lavagetto lunged, hitting a rocket the opposite way to right. Right-fielder Heinrich went back on the ball quickly, debating whether to try for a leaping catch or play the ball off the wall. "All I could think of was, 'That ball wasn't more than a few inches over Heinrich's head,'" Lavagetto recalled. "If it had been a half a foot lower, nobody would have remembered me."

Heinrich, who took away a hit at the wall with two outs in the eighth, remembered it differently right after the game. "I could not have come within eight feet of it had I been playing right on the wall. It struck the upper half of the wall."

Heinrich gave up the chase on Lavagetto's smash and stopped short to play the ricochet. "I thought the ball was a routine fly to right," Bevens said. "I saw Tommy Heinrich going back as far as he could and when the ball hit the wall, I ran home to back up the plate."

Gionfriddo, who would gain his own slice of lore with a miraculous catch on Joe DiMaggio in Game Six of the Series, was around third and easing home. Miksis was waved around, too: with this being the Dodgers' first hit, they weren't taking any chances that another would come. Miksis soon followed Gionfriddo around third as Heinrich hurried the ball in, still with a chance for a play at the plate. But first baseman George McQuinn inexplicably cut the ball off as Miksis raced home. The game, and baseball history, was turned upside down on a single pitch.

Pandemonium erupted at Ebbets Field and throughout Brooklyn. The astonishing and abrupt ending to the game even left home plate umpire Larry Goetz somewhat stunned: after the winning run scored, Goetz brushed off home, as if the game were to go on.

From his "catbird seat" atop Ebbets Field, Dodgers announcer Red Barber called the ensuing melee for his radio audience:

"Friends, they're killing Lavagetto, his own teammates. They are beating him to pieces. And it's taken a police escort to get Lavagetto away from the Dodgers."

Cops, at least the ones who were not hugging ushers and players in joy, gently but firmly cleared a path through the fans, players, press, and others so Cookie could get to the clubhouse.

"I never saw anything so nutty as afterward," Lavagetto recalled. "On the way to the bench, three or four cops were patting my back. Here came these fans. One of them stole my cap. I had to run for it before they stripped me."

The hit came at 3:50 P.M. October 3, 1947. A half-hour after the game was over about 100 fans swarmed out in right field. They just stared at the wall, the grass, a baseball Medjugorje, a home of a miracle where Cookie Lavagetto had broken up Bill Bevens' no-hitter.

Barber closed his radio broadcast with a statement of astonishment shared by all of Brooklyn and of baseball: "I'll be a suck-egg mule ..."

We're not sure what it means, either, but you can guess the sentiment.

The only place in and around Ebbets that was not in chaos after the game was the Yankee locker room. Harris had ordered the doors closed to the media for 10 minutes. When the press was finally allowed in, they found that gloom still hung heavy.

Berra, a rookie who was demonized that Series by a press which did not foresee his Hall of Fame potential, was still amazed Lavagetto had clubbed a ball out of the strike zone like that. "You can't ask for more than that," he said. "It was still good pitching even though that guy got a hold of it."

DiMaggio didn't realize a no-hitter was within reach until he was told in a hushed Yankee locker room after the game: "Are you kidding me? This is the first time I knew about it." Instead of a no-hitter, Bevens dejectedly left the mound that day with only one World Series record: most walks in a game, 10.

In the very next game of the Series, Lavagetto again came to bat in the ninth with the Dodgers losing 2–1. This time he ran the count to 3–2 against Frank "Spec" Shea, before striking out on a changeup. The Yankees went on to win the Series in seven games, but the title would be lost among the Bombers' string of world crowns. What history marks is Lavagetto's at-bat.

The historic double would be Lavagetto's last major league hit. Starting in 1948, he went back to the Pacific Coast League for three seasons before taking a coaching job—at Dressen's request—with the Dodgers. He went on to manage the Washington Senators/Minnesota Twins and coached for the Mets, Cardinals, and Giants before retiring in 1967 on the day marking the 20th anniversary of his double. He died on August 10, 1990, in Orinda, California, at the age of 77.

As for Bevens, a man who was expected to anchor the Yankees pitching staff for years to come, the near no-no marked his last start in the majors, although he did relieve in Game Seven of the 1947 World Series. Bevens had stumbled in 1947 in part because of a sore arm that got worse. He tried to come back in 1948 with no luck and sat out 1949. He returned to the low minors in 1950, never to return to the majors. His career mark in the bigs was 40-36 over four years.

One anecdote shows how quickly Bevens fell. After his World Series near-miss, he returned to Salem, Oregon, welcomed as a hero. He took a $600-a-month off-season job for a local beer company, with his duties comprised mainly of glad-handing potential customers. The next year, his pitching arm shot, Bevens returned to the beer company. This time they put him to work at half the previous year's salary, loading cases onto trucks.

Bevens died on October 26, 1991, in his native Salem. But before he went, he was able to get some satisfaction.

In August 1966 his 17-year-old son, Bob Bevens, pitched a 5–0 no-hitter for Salem's Capital Post 9 American Legion team. Newspapers across the country ran a photograph of the beaming father and son.

American Legion games last only seven innings.

FRED SNODGRASS

Fred Carlisle Snodgrass had a career batting average of .275, stole 51 bases one season, played in three World Series, and racked up a fielding percentage of .965, primarily in center field.

Yet to the day he died in 1974 at 86, he knew *the* Question before it could be finished:

"Weren't you the guy who dropped the fly ball and lost the 1912 World Series?"

The answer was yes ... and no.

After a while, he didn't even get sore. Yes, he dropped a fly ball. But no, he did not lose the Series. In fact, most would agree that the New York Giants could not have even been in the World Series had it not been for Snodgrass. In fact, few could ask for a player to have done more, or performed better, during that Series against the Boston Red Sox.

But, in fact, baseball lore often has little to do with fact. Snodgrass, an aggressive converted catcher, lived that hard lesson.

The right-hander broke into the majors in 1908 with New York and played eight years in the bigs, mostly with John McGraw's Giants, one of the best teams ever. In his career, Snodgrass played in more than 900 games, hit .300 or better two years in a row, collected 211 stolen bases, and registered 1,752 putouts against just 68 errors. At just over 5-foot-11 and 175 pounds, "Snow" was a steady regular outfielder who also saw action at first base and a game at second.

In three consecutive World Series from 1911 to 1913, he managed 10 hits and 3 runs in 16 games, fielded perfectly the first two Series, and made but one error in the third.

It was that one error that loomed so large it has its own nickname: "The $30,000 Muff." That's how much a World Series winning share was worth to a team, a paycheck that many to this day maintain was canceled for the Giants by Snodgrass.

The disappointment of the Series was compounded by dashed anticipation because this was a stellar year for the Gothams. They won 103 games against 48 losses, thanks in no small measure to one of history's best pitchers, Christy Mathewson. "Big Six" went 23-12, the tenth of twelve straight years he would win 20. Still, Mathewson's stats weren't even the best on the team that year: fellow Hall of Famer Rube Marquard went 26-11, while spit-baller Jeff Tesreau had a league-leading 1.96 ERA.

This was one mighty team, but this was an era when legends roamed the majors. The Red Sox, playing in a new park called Fenway, were led by Smokey Joe Wood's 34 wins on their way to a 105-win season and first place in the American League. They finished 14 games ahead of the Washington Senators, despite Walter "Big Train" Johnson's 33 wins for the Nats.

It was a year that deserved a memorable and momentous World Series. The Giants, the Red Sox, and Fred Snodgrass obliged.

Snodgrass' haunting fly ball came in a game that never would have been played today: Game Eight. Game Four was called a draw after 11 innings because of darkness, deadlocked at six.

That final game would go into the 10th, an inning *Oldtyme Baseball News* would call a half-century later "probably the wildest single inning of base-ball ever played in a World Series."

The Giants had gone ahead 2–1, an edge that looked like enough for the title in a game of legendary pitchers: Mathewson vs. Wood. Wood was pitch-ing like the Hall of Famer he would become, even knocking down a line drive with his throwing hand and making the putout. But the extraordinary play came at a price: the hand swelled and Wood had to exit, a break for New York not only because he was pitching well, but also because Wood was a .290 hit-ter slated to lead off in the bottom of the 10th. (Wood was such a good hitter he finished his career as an outfielder after blowing out his arm and compiled a career .283 average.)

Enter Clyde Engle. Engle played in less than half of the Sox' games that year, posting a meager .234 average. He promptly popped up. To center. To Snodgrass. To history.

"He hit a great, big, lazy high fly ball halfway between Red Murray in left field and me," Snodgrass recalled years later in Lawrence S. Ritter's *The Glory of Their Times* (Quill Books, 1992).

"Murray called for it first, but as center fielder I had preference over left and right, so there'd never be a collision. I yelled that I'd take it and waved Murray off, and—well—I dropped the darn thing."

Engle watched his towering fly drop through Snodgrass' glove on his way to second base.

But this was a game that wouldn't, couldn't, end the way any old game usually did. In most games, the next batter would bunt Engle to third, setting up a sacrifice or hit to get him in. That didn't happen. What did happen was the kind of moment that turns baseball games into legend.

Outfielder Harry Hooper, yet another Hall of Famer in this series, saw it from the batter's box, as everyone—including Snodgrass—played in tight in hopes of thwarting the sac bunt or fly:

"I was up next and I tried to bunt, but I fouled it off. On the next pitch

I hit a line drive into left center and looked like a sure triple. Ninety-nine times out of a hundred no outfielder could possibly have come close to that ball. But in some way, I don't know how, Snodgrass ran like the wind, and dang if he didn't catch it. I think he outran the ball. Robbed me of a sure triple."

Snodgrass would call it his best catch ever. No one disagreed.

But Snow didn't stop there. After making the catch, he fired a ball back to second to nearly nab Engle, who had rounded third on what looked like an uncatchable shot.

The inning got weirder. Mathewson, the model of control who the next season would average a mere .62 walks per nine innings, walked .252 hitter Steve Yerkes. The winning run was on.

Enter still another all-time great, Tris Speaker. Mathewson got the "Grey Eagle" to pop up just foul of first base. Mathewson, first baseman Fred Merkle, and catcher Chief Myers took off in pursuit. Mathewson called for the slow-footed Myers to make the catch, even though Merkle may have had a better shot. The backstop never got there, and the ball fell harmlessly inches from his mitt.

Speaker, talking trash to Mathewson for his bad directions, lined the next pitch to right field. Engle came home.

The score was tied, and Yerkes, the go-ahead run, stood on third.

Larry Garner's deep sacrifice to right scored Yerkes, and the Series was over—lost, according to the newspapers, by Fred Snodgrass. But as Snodgrass later told Ritter: "I did drop that fly ball, and that did put what turned out to be the tying run on base, but that's a long way from 'losing a World Series.'"

He refused to take the blame, and his manager was clearly on his side: After the series McGraw gave Snodgrass a $1,000 raise.

It was the second time in four years a Giant made what was turned into a Homeric blunder that cost the team a shot at the title.

Snodgrass saw both of them. He broke into baseball in 1908, the year teammate Fred Merkle committed the infamous Merkle's Boner. That happened September 23 against the Chicago Cubs, in the midst of a tight, three-way race for the National League pennant. A rookie substitute, Merkle was a runner on first when a two-out single drove in the apparent winning run in the bottom of the ninth inning. But as Moose McCormick crossed the plate with the game-winner, Merkle, like the Giants fans, celebrated too soon. He ran to the clubhouse, neglecting to touch second. Second baseman Johnny Evers of the Cubs caught the miscue, and so did the umps.

In his interview with Lawrence Ritter, Snodgrass remembered the play well. As he described it, when Merkle saw the ball roll toward the centerfield fence, he just naturally headed for home and, just as naturally, headed to the clubhouse to celebrate winning the pennant.

He just didn't touch second.

The crowd, anxious to celebrate the pennant win, rushed onto the field. Even umpire Hand O'Day left the plate, and Bob Emsley, the second base umpire, figured the game was over. O'Day headed toward the umpires' dressing room, behind the press box.

Chicago's legendary infield of Tinker, Evers and Chance knew better.

"Evers began to call to the center fielder [Wildfire] Schulte to go and get the ball," said Snodgrass, "and Schulte hadn't even chased the ball because the game was over as far as he was concerned."

Evers finally got Schulte to fetch the ball and toss it in. It was intercepted by (Giant) Joe McGinnity, who promptly threw it in the leftfield stands.

So as thousands of fans covered the field, the umpires were told to gather with the managers to sort the whole thing out. The first thought was to bring Merkle back out to have him touch second base. That didn't fly with Chicago, of course.

Frank Chance pulled the umpires out of their dressing room to what had become a field of screams. Pandemonium was what they called it, and the umps wanted no part of pooping on the party, at least not in person.

The league president, the umps figured, makes the big bucks for these decisions. Let the president decide how this mess ends up—from his secure downtown office.

In effect the league president called for a do-over, a decision no better— nor worse—than one made every day by kids playing stickball.

The Giants eventually lost the game. The pennant race was tied again, and the Giants went on to lose to the Cubs in a playoff. As he would do for Snodgrass four years later, McGraw gave Merkle a raise, but the play would dog Merkle the rest of his life.

Merkle, Snodgrass lamented in the Ritter interview, was blamed for the boner and for blowing a pennant. But Snodgrass, with rare experience in such situations, noted that one play doesn't make or break a pennant win. Every play brings you to the next pitch, the next at bat. Every play brings a team closer to glorious victory, or devastating defeat.

Inexperience and bad luck are cruel partners.

As for Fred Snodgrass, a few facts are clear: He played on one of the greatest teams in some of the greatest seasons and hit and fielded against legends who have since taken up immortal residence in Cooperstown. During that era, he once, albeit for just a few months, led the majors in hitting ahead of a guy named Ty Cobb. Snodgrass was named to the all-time New York Giants team. His uniform is part of a permanent display in the Hall of Fame.

One week during the battle he waged with Cobb and future Hall of Famer (and .338 lifetime hitter) Nap Lajoie of Cleveland, Snodgrass hit .522. But the hitting title and the automobile that went with it belonged, perhaps even by destiny, to Cobb.

After baseball, Snodgrass launched a successful second career selling home appliances. He was even elected mayor of a town in California. He married, raised two daughters and enjoyed five grandchildren. He had a good baseball career—a fine career—and a full life.

Yet the *New York Times*, in Snodgrass' obituary of April 7, 1974, summed up his life as narrowly, as tersely, as mercilessly as a fan in a bar bet. A two-line headline, showing us all the fickleness of destiny and the strength of legend, state:

> Fred Snodgrass, 86, Dead;
> Ball Player Muffed 1912 Fly

Nippy Jones

Nippy Jones could be credited with winning a World Series on one pitch without ever swinging a bat, using his feet without ever leaving the batter's box. As amazing as that sounds, Vernal "Nippy" Jones managed to do something even more astounding, in fact almost unparalleled, in the 10th inning of Game Four of the 1957 World Series.

Nippy Jones got an umpire to change his mind.

For a player who seemed destined first for greatness, then obscurity, Jones earned his place in baseball history not for a swing of the bat but for the shine on his shoes.

A Los Angeles native who got his nickname from his father "Nip," Jones was edged out in 1946 by Jackie Robinson for the International League batting title. A late-season call-up by the St. Louis Cardinals that year, Jones hit .333 in three games at second base and had one at-bat in the World Series, which the Cards won four games to three over the Red Sox.

In 1947, with Robinson gone to the Brooklyn Dodgers, Jones owned the International League. Playing for the Rochester Red Wings, he hit .337 with 10 home runs and 81 RBIs, while playing second, third, and outfield. But the Cardinals, who called him up again in 1947, planned to install Jones at yet another position, first base, so Stan Musial could return to the outfield.

In 1948, Jones played 128 of his 132 games at first, hitting .254 and again 10 home runs and 81 RBIs. The following season was just as solid: .300 average with 8 home runs and 62 RBIs in 110 games. The 6-foot-1, 185-pound righty platoon player, who turned 24 just before the 1949 All-Star break, was a staple in the Cardinals lineup, batting cleanup between Hall of Famers Musial and "Country" Enos Slaughter. It was turning into a great season.

Then came the play, a stupid play, a routine play: Jones was a runner on first against the Dodgers when a pickoff toss came over. He slid back into the bag, feet first. The pain seared the length of his back. He was carried off on a stretcher.

"It was a herniated disk," Jones said. "They had to operate." He missed all but 13 games in 1950 and played in just 80 in 1951. The following season he moved to the Phillies but hit only .167 in eight games. Jones was exiled to the minors, where he remained for the better part of five seasons. His major league career seemed a distant memory.

But in June of 1957, the Milwaukee Braves were suddenly in dire need of a first baseman after slugger Joe Adcock broke his leg. At the age of 32, Jones was getting one more shot.

Jones performed well down the stretch, hitting .266 in 30 games. One of his two home runs for the season was an 11th-inning blast on July 26 off Stu Miller that beat the New York Giants. It was a dramatic moment, but it pales compared to what was to come.

The Braves coasted down the stretch and finished the year 95-59 under skipper Fred Haney, eight games ahead of the Cardinals. Led by right-fielder Hank Aaron, third baseman Eddie Mathews, and pitchers Warren Spahn and Lew Burdette, the Braves were formidable, but a distinct underdog going into the World Series against the New York Yankees, 98-56 that year under Casey Stengel and winners of 7 of the previous 10 Series.

The Braves, playing in their first Series since moving to Milwaukee from Boston, earned a split in the first two games in New York. But the homecoming at County Stadium was a disaster, as the Yankees crushed the Braves, 12–3, in Game Three. With the fourth game a must, Warren Spahn was sent to the mound.

After eight, the Braves were cruising 4–1, and some of the crowd gleefully headed to the exits. Then in the ninth, Yogi Berra singled, followed by another single by Gil McDougald. Haney went out to the mound but left Spahn in the game, confident he could get the final out against Elston Howard. Spahn ran the count to 3-and-2, but came in to Howard's wheelhouse. Gone. One swing, tie game.

The Braves could not score in the bottom of the ninth, and when the Yankees tacked on another run in the 10th to go up 5–4, the game and the Series seemed lost. "It would be hard to describe the thickness of the pall that hung over County Stadium and the grief-stricken congregation," Bob Considine of the International News Service would write.

An exhausted Spahn was scheduled to lead off the bottom of the 10th, when No. 25, Nippy Jones, was called out to pinch-hit. The righty dug in. He had one job: get on base, any way he could.

Tommy Byrne, a 6-foot-1, left-handed reliever, went into his windup and delivered: low and inside. The pitch bounded away from catcher Berra.

Jones squealed in pain, hopped on one foot, and started off for first. Umpire Augie Donatelli wasn't buying it.

"No!" he shouted. "The ball didn't hit you. Ball one." Then he motioned Jones back to the batter's box.

Nippy wasn't giving up easily. An argument ensued.

Chuck Bossfield, the Braves' 17-year-old ball boy, would normally retrieve balls that would skip all the way to the back stop. "But I heard them arguing about it, so I let it roll."

Good move. The ball caromed back toward the plate.

"Just then I seen the ball," Jones said years later. "It had rolled back to the backstop and was bouncing back toward home plate, and I went and picked it up. And there was this spot ..."

A smudge. Shoe polish. Black shoe polish. Most teams used saddle soap. Not Milwaukee. "We use polish," clubhouse manager Joe Taylor said after the game. "It gives us class."

It may have also given the Braves a world title.

Jones, holding the ball gingerly in his right hand as if it were an egg, showed it to Donatelli. Donatelli took off his mask and looked. "OK," Donatelli said. "Take your base."

After the game Donatelli said he had declared Jones hit by the pitch from the beginning. That account was contradicted by Jones, Byrne, Berra, and Bossfield. Regardless, Jones had made his point.

"So I ran down to first real happy, let me tell you, and the Yankees started yelling," Jones said. "Yogi Berra was the catcher, and he was jumping up and down having a fit. Then the Yankee manager [Stengel] came out. And he had a big argument, but it didn't matter. The shoe polish was there."

A strange tenet of baseball: when a lead-off batter gets on base, especially by means other than a hit, he is usually going to score. But Jones wasn't going to get a chance to touch home; he was immediately replaced by pinch-runner Felix Mantilla. Then shortstop Johnny Logan doubled Mantilla home, and Mathews promptly tagged a game-winning homer off of Bob Grim, giving the Braves a 7–5 win and knotting the Series at two.

"It's a funny thing," Jones said in a 1991 interview. "Nobody remembers Mathews' home run to win the game. But they remember me getting hit on the foot."

The at-bat would swing the game, and the Series. After Game Four, baseball writers crowded around Jones, Mathews, and other stars of the game—including the clubhouse boys who shined the shoes.

"That shoe polish turned it around," Jones said. "No question about it."

Lew Burdette won three games that Series against the Yankees, and Aaron belted three home runs and hit .393, but it is Jones, who did not get a hit in the Series, who is best remembered for leading the Braves to the world title in seven games. Jones would get one more at-bat against the Yankees, grounding out against Whitey Ford. It would be his last major league plate appearance. After bouncing around the minors for the next three seasons—as well as promoting a shoe polish—Jones retired. "I didn't want to hang around too long, like some players," Jones said. "I had enough."

Enough amounted to an 8-year career spanning 12 years but only 412 games. Jones went on to work as a fishing guide and in promotions and insurance before dying of a heart attack in 1995 at age 70.

As noted earlier, Jones' feat is almost unparalleled, but unbelievably, the scene would repeat itself just 12 years later, again involving a batter named Jones.

In the 1969 World Series, the New York Mets led the Baltimore Orioles three games to one but trailed the Birds 3–0 going into the last half of the sixth. In the bottom half of the inning, a Dave McNally curve in the dirt had Met left-fielder Cleon Jones skipping out of the way. The ball caromed into the New York dugout; umpire Lou DiMuro called it a ball.

Cleon Jones immediately argued he had been hit by the pitch. Manager Gil Hodges then produced the ball, which was smudged by shoe polish. DiMuro waved Jones on to first, Donn Clendenon then homered, and the Mets were on their way to a 5–3 win and the most improbable of Series crowns.

Besides the Jones' surname, there is another link between the '57 and '69 shoe polish incidents: Stengel. By then manager emeritus of the Mets, Stengel mischievously said his Amazin's learned a lesson from Nippy Jones and that game he had lost 12 years before as the Yankees' skipper:

"We always keep three or four balls smudged with shoe polish in the dugout."

BRIAN DOYLE

For every kid who endlessly bounces a ball against a wall to practice one-hops, for every teen who dreams of getting the call to win the World Series, for every adult who believes in himself despite long odds and scant reason, there is Brian Doyle.

Doyle scraped together a 110-game career over four major league seasons. He was one of those kids who played and replayed the Big Game alone during hours of practice in sandlots on the edge of town and in private wishes on the edge of sleep. For him, the diamonds were in plowed Kentucky tobacco fields and empty bush league parks. And, like all of us playing the game with more imagination than perspiration, he always came out a winner, a hero.

But unlike almost every one of the millions who dreamed these glories, Doyle went on to play them out in the real world, where the dreams of youth are most often batted down by a hard reality, and a hard slider. We all wish we had just one shot—that one shot to talk about and relive over a lifetime.

Doyle did, and made it count.

It was 1978. Doyle, a rookie infielder, had played 39 regular-season games for the New York Yankees, mostly at second base spelling mainstay Willie Randolph. When Doyle entered a game, everyone knew it wasn't to pinch-hit for Reggie Jackson. Doyle was put in the game for one reason: his glove. In limited duty at the plate that season, he scratched out just 10 hits, all singles, for a paltry .192.

But the 23-year-old from Cave City, Kentucky and Horse Cave High School felt something weird arrive in New York with autumn's cool. He felt he could hit. He knew he could hit. His chance to prove it came on October 3, 1978, in the first game of the American League Championship Series against the Kansas City Royals.

Just a few hours before game time Doyle wasn't even on the postseason roster. He hadn't even been in Bronx Bomber pinstripes that spring. He was in Tacoma, Washington, fighting for a starting job in Triple-A.

Yet there he was, in the tight first American League Championship Series game in Kansas City. The Yankees knew they would have to nurse their 2–0 lead against the Royals' ace, 21-game winner Dennis Leonard. So the New York fans were reintroduced to Brian Reed Doyle, second base, throws right and hits—rarely—left.

"My first at-bat against the Royals I told myself I'd hit a line drive down the third-base line, the opposite field," Doyle remembered almost 18 years later. "George Brett was playing for a bunt. I hit right to him and he caught it, but it was a pea. After that I said to myself, 'You're there.' That first at-bat really got me in the tunnel, 'The Zone' you call it today—I don't know what the Zone is, but I was in it."

Rarely has a player been so happy about an out that did not plate a run or move a runner over. It took little time for Doyle to roll those positive vibes into an earthquake.

In the fifth, with the Yankees still up 2–0, Lou Piniella opened with a single to right. That brought Royals manager Whitey Herzog out of the dugout, signaling for left-handed reliever Steve Mingori to replace the righty Leonard. Herzog wanted Mingori to pitch to the Yankees string of left-handed hitters.

Good strategy, bad results.

On a 3–2 pitch, Reggie Jackson walked. Graig Nettles then hit into a force. Runners on corners, one out. Chris Chambliss singles to right, Piniella scores from third, 3–0. Roy White, a switch-hitter, pops up. Two outs.

Brian Doyle steps into the box and digs in. Single to right. Another run in. The rout is on. The Yankees go on to win, 7–1, with Doyle going 2-for-5.

Behind 16 hits at home in Game Two, the Royals mowed through three Yankee pitchers for a 10–4 win.

The Yanks returned to New York and their winning ways in Game Three, despite Brett's three homers, to win 6–5. Home runs by Jackson and Thurman Munson, each with a runner on base, brought the Yankees back from behind and earned New York a 2–1 edge in the series.

In the next game, Yankee ace Ron Guidry went eight solid innings, and Roy White's tie-breaking homer in the sixth set the Yankees on course for a 2–1 victory and their third playoff series win over the Royals in three years.

Doyle, who split time at second base in the four-game series with Fred Stanley (normally a shortstop) and Paul Blair (outfielder), went 2-for-7 in the series, a solid .286 average.

The Yankees' 3–1 series win was the same margin by which the Los Angeles Dodgers defeated the Philadelphia Phillies in the National League Championship Series. A rematch of the 1977 World Series won by New York was on.

Randolph, an all-star, had started 134 games in the 1978 campaign, hitting his usual .279 while scoring 87 runs and swiping 36 bases. But toward the end of the season, Randolph severely pulled a hamstring as the Yankees battled back from a cavernous 14½-game deficit against the Red Sox to tie Boston on the last day before winning a one-game playoff.

Although Bucky Dent was the hero of the Boston playoff with a spectacularly timely home run in the 5–4 win, the right side of the Yankee infield now had a huge hole. Who would get the nod?

The Yankees, laden with the likes of Jackson, Munson, Nettles, Chambliss, Guidry, Hunter, Gossage, Piniella, and White, turned to Doyle.

Doyle wrote in a first-person piece for the *New York Times* in October 1992: "There was even more uncertainty for me at the end of the season, when Willie Randolph was injured."

> I did not know until the first day of the [World] Series that I had been granted permission to play. But as soon as I got word of my eligibility, much of the pressure of the season was lifted from my shoulders, and that fact had a lot to do with what I went on to accomplish.
>
> I knew that my wife would be with me for at least the next 10 days, that financial matters would be cleared up with World Series money. Even with only a quarter share, I would make more than I had made in baseball in the previous two years combined. I also knew that some of the game's greatest players had never had the chance I was getting.
>
> With those concerns off my mind, only three tasks remained. First, to thank the Lord for the opportunity of a lifetime. Second, to focus on the task at hand. Third, to have fun.

Doyle had something going for him in the post-season that the stars of the Yankees didn't: the element of surprise. A big surprise.

"They didn't know who I was. So I tried to get them to pitch to me the way I wanted to be pitched. By that I mean my best pitch was always high and inside. So I concentrated on trying to hit the other way at first, so when they saw that, they pitched the opposite way—to my strength."

The 5-foot-10, 160-pound infielder was the Yankees' strength that World Series. He provided the team seven hits, four runs, two RBIs, a .438 average to lead all hitters, six errorless games, and, to a great extent, a world championship.

In Game One in Los Angeles, the Dodgers slammed four of the Yankees pitchers for 15 hits. Dave Lopes had two homers and Dusty Baker another, against Reggie Jackson's solo shot. Final score: 11–5, L.A.

Game Two was closer. Dodgers Ron Cey drove in all of Los Angeles' runs with a three-run homer and a single off Jim "Catfish" Hunter. A strikeout of Jackson in the ninth sealed the Dodgers second win, 4–3.

Then the Series came to New York.

Guidry controlled the critical Game Three in a complete game that included a solo homer by Roy White, who would hit .333 this Series. Third baseman Nettles made four great stabs to help Guidry take the game, and the momentum, from the Dodgers. Final score: 5–1.

Game Four in New York went 10 frenetic innings. With two outs, Piniella hit a single that drove home White. Game: 4–3, New York. Series: 2–2.

The fifth game of the Series was the last to be played in Yankee Stadium, and the 1978 Yankees made a lot of the ghosts there very happy. Mickey Rivers, Bucky Dent, and a guy named Doyle each had three-hit nights for the Yankees. In a blowout, the Yankees won 12–8 behind 18 hits.

And it just wouldn't stop. Game Six seemed easy, as Dent and Doyle, the D and D Brothers to some New York writers, again collected three hits each. Catfish Hunter and Goose Gossage pitched a seven-hitter as the Yankees rolled to the storied club's 22nd world championship in style, 7–2, behind yet another Jackson homer.

Doyle, who couldn't get a line in that season's Yankees media guide, had overnight become All That Is Good in Baseball. Everyone wrote about him. Everyone talked about him.

Here's what the Associated Press told a nation:

"Doyle, the Cave City Clouter, led the Bronx Bombers in hitting, with Dent right behind at .417 and seven RBI in the six-game triumph that made the Yankees the first team ever to win four straight World Series games after dropping the first two."

It was easy, especially when Doyle made believers of everyone during the pivotal Game Five, the Sunday he beat up Los Angeles for three hits. In the second inning, he ignited a Yankees onslaught by driving in the first run in the second off Don Sutton. The RBI came on a double—his first major league hit for extra bases and only his second run batted in.

Bucky Dent and Brian Doyle became inextricably linked in this Series. Some sportswriters, as is a common trait among the species, tried to make a D-and-D gimmick stick—like Mantle and Maris and, later, Munson and Murcer were the M-and-M Boys—but it didn't really take. Neither did "Cave City Clouter," a short-lived moniker based more in alliteration than statistics.

Dent, whose belly button was well on its way to fame in cut-off T-shirt posters, was named series MVP. At shortstop he made only one error over the six games while robbing several Dodgers hits. He got ten hits along with three runs scored and seven RBIs to go along with his .417 average, which was only behind Doyle and Dodgers shortstop Bill Russell (.423) among Series regulars.

While Dent was a solid choice for MVP, especially coming off his heroics against Boston, he made sure writers did not forget Doyle's contribution, even as he collected his trophy.

"Winning the MVP was obviously my biggest thrill," Dent said after the game. "I feel I did not contribute to the ballclub because I was hurt for much of the season, so coming back and winning the MVP award was a thrill."

But Dent quickly added: "Brian Doyle is a tremendous competitor. He was put in a very tough situation and he came through for us against Boston and in the playoffs and he did a great job in the series."

That job included three hits in each of the last two games and driving home a pair of runs in the finale.

"When I think back to the 1978 World Series," Doyle wrote in his *Times* article, "my first memory is not of coming close to breaking the series record for consecutive hits, but rather of the 9-year-old boy sitting on the cardboard second base in a plowed-under tobacco field. That boy lives that dream in my memory every day."

Assuming no pink slips to his soul changed hands, fans are left to wonder just how it all happened.

Doyle, who with his brothers Denny (also a second baseman who had an eight-year major league career) and Blake teaches thousands of kids to play the game at the Doyle Baseball School in Winter Haven, Florida, thinks he has an answer.

"I didn't have much talent. The big thing was working to a goal, and not just working hard, but working smart," Doyle says today. "We can all go out and bust it and bust it, but you have to realize the only way you get better is to get smarter."

For him, that meant taking at least 100 grounders, every day.

It meant making sure that he practiced the best form because he knew hard work with the wrong mechanics wouldn't pay off. It meant studying pitchers, catchers, and, more than most other hitters, umpires. He learned tendencies, tip-offs, and strike zones. He also learned how various pitchers, catchers, and umpires could change those tendencies as game conditions evolved.

Doyle was lucky. He realized he needed to become a student of the game and that if he seized the opportunity, he had a front-row desk at the feet of many of the best teachers of any era, as he noted:

> I looked at the best and really studied the best. I realized the common denominator was strength ... so what I did was concentrate on guys who were consistent and tried to copy that. I couldn't rely on my talent, so I relied on being smart.
>
> You know, baseball is still the sport where the little guy can compete with the big guys. ... I knew I was not going to be an everyday player in the major leagues, but I wanted to be. I knew my role and my role was to always be prepared.

In four major league seasons, three campaigns with the Yankees and one final year in 1981 with the Oakland A's, Doyle was never able to climb over .200, and he finished with a .161 career average in 199 at-bats. But when he needed it most, when the pressure was the most numbing, he pulled something out of a mix of talent, smarts, and luck.

In 1982, Doyle told *Daily News* columnist Mike Lupica:

It seems like an eternity ago. Sometimes, I think of it as something I'd like to forget. It was great at the moment, don't get me wrong, but it's kind of been tough for me since, you know? Brian Doyle, former World Series hero and all that. Ever since that time, I've been up and down and hurt and haven't been able to get 100 at-bats in a row. It's been four years of utility status for a guy—me—who thinks he can still play up the middle.

By 1996, Brian Doyle the player had fully accepted the challenge of being Brian Doyle the teacher. In an interview, he made it clear he had turned his World Series experience into useful knowledge to be passed on to the next generation.

"When I talk to a kid I say everyone talks about pressure," Doyle said. "Well, I think we all need to practice pressure and you do that through preparation. If you are confident in your preparation and the pressure comes, you're there. If you're just confident in your talent—then I think that's a big gap."

In October of 1978, the philosophy paid off. "I was confident in my preparation ... and I just had a lot of fun."

AL WEIS

Baltimore Oriole slugger Frank Robinson, surrounded by celebrating teammates after the Birds had crushed the Minnesota Twins in the first-ever American League Championship Series, stepped on top of a chair to be heard.

"Ron Gasper has just said on television that the Mets will sweep us in four games," Robinson yelled. "Bring on Gasper, whoever the hell he is."

Robinson was soon corrected, but remained undaunted.

"Quiet! I've just been told that his name is Rod Gaspar, whoever the hell he is."

Rodney Earl Gaspar was a utility outfielder who hit .228 with one home run in limited action in that 1969 season for the New York Mets. While Robinson couldn't be blamed for not knowing Gaspar, there is a good chance he knew his name from the start. Robinson for sure knew he was sending a message: *We are the Orioles, most dominant team in baseball, winners of 109 games. We are the ordained. Who are you guys?*

After the Series began in that magical October, Robinson and his teammates would sound like *Butch Cassidy and the Sundance Kid: Who are these guys?* Sure, the Mets had Tom Seaver and Jerry Koosman, and Cleon Jones had a hell of a year, but who is Ed Charles? Gary Gentry? Ron Taylor? Ron Swoboda?

And who the hell is Al Weis?

Al Weis was the Baltimore Orioles' worst nightmare.

"I had a mediocre career in baseball," Weis said. "But I happened to have two good weeks in baseball. And it happened to be in a World Series."

In 1969, on a team that defied logic on its way to the most impossible of titles, it all made sense.

Al Weis was born on April 2, 1938, in the Long Island town of Franklin Square. Raised in the nearby Bethpage, Weis was a star for Farmingdale High School on a team that also included future major league pitcher Jack Lamabe.

Although he was named to a sectional all-star team, Weis wasn't drafted by a major league club, so in 1956 he and a few buddies enlisted in the navy. There the aviation structural mechanic played on the camp team in Norfolk and eventually earned notice from several major league teams. The Los Angeles Dodgers offered a tryout, while the Chicago White Sox came with a contract. Weis went to Chicago.

After a relatively short three-year apprenticeship in the minors, Weis was called up in September of 1962. "I could hit pretty good," he said, "but my strong points were speed and defense."

Weis was good, but not good enough to unseat either of a pair of all-time greats at second and short, Nellie Fox and Luis Aparicio. But a switch-hitter who could play second, short, third, and, in an emergency, the outfield was a value to any team — at least coming off the bench.

In his 10-year major-league career, Weis played more than 103 games in only two years, in 1964 and 1966 for Chicago. In 1966 he managed to hit only .155, with no home runs and only 9 RBIs. Primarily a defensive replacement, Weis never managed more than 328 at-bats in a season.

For his career spanning 800 games, Weis hit 11 home runs in 1,578 at-bats, or one for every 144 at-bats. Seven of the 11 dingers came in 1964–65.

This was no Rogers Hornsby at second.

A hard slide into second base by Frank Robinson tore Weis' knee ligaments, knocking him out for the 1967 season. Surgery cost Weis a step or two of speed, and Chicago was skeptical he would be able to return to normal.

On December 15, 1967, the White Sox traded Weis and Tommie Agee to the New York Mets for a basketful of players: Tommy Davis, Jack Fisher, Billy Wynne, and Buddy Booker.

Davis, his stellar years with the Dodgers a memory, would be gone from Chicago by 1969.

Fisher, who in 1965 and again in 1967 led the National League in losses (not an improbable feat with those Mets), went 8-13 in 1968 before being shipped to Cincinnati for his final season.

Wynne won eight games for Chicago over three years, while Booker managed five at-bats in 1968 and was gone for good from the majors.

With the trade Weis was given a chance to go home (although today he makes his home outside of Chicago, working in the shipping and receiving department for a furniture company). But the return was bittersweet: he was coming to a bad baseball team.

"All the years I played with the White Sox we were pennant contenders. When you are so close to a World Series, then in 1968 getting traded to the Mets, I thought, 'Well, there goes your chances of ever playing in the World Series.'"

Meanwhile, Agee had been the American League Rookie of the Year for the White Sox in 1966, when he hit .273 with 22 home runs and 86 RBIs. His numbers fell off dramatically in 1967 and remained pitiful after he joined the Mets in 1968 (.217, 5 HR, 17 RBI). Agee found his stroke again in 1969, however, hitting 26 homers to go along with 76 RBIs and a .217 average. He would remain a fixture in center at Shea Stadium through the 1972 season.

For a franchise that for years traditionally got burned on trades — Nolan Ryan for Jim Fregosi? Amos Otis (and Bob Johnson) for Joe Foy? Rusty

Staub for a washed-up Mickey Lolich?—this was one trade that could be directly credited with a championship.

In 1969 the two leagues expanded to 12 teams and split into two divisions, and a best three-out-of-five league championship series format was introduced. The Mets, whose best finish ever was ninth in 1966 and 1968, were finally destined to at least move up to sixth place that year.

It was a year in which the unimaginable was becoming reality in all walks of life. Man landed on the moon. Almost a half-million people gathered in upstate New York for a concert called Woodstock. Demonstrations raged in the streets against the war in Vietnam. Even in sports, the natural balance of things seemed askew: that January the New York Jets, the biggest underdogs in Super Bowl history, shocked the Baltimore Colts.

The 1969 baseball season started normally enough, with the Mets losing just as a 100-to-1 title contender was expected to do. But this was not a normal year. An example: Al Weis hit two home runs that year. Both runs beat the Cubs. They were on back-to-back days, July 15 and 16.

Consider these other oddities:

• The Mets ranked eighth in the league in batting, home runs, and stolen bases, and ninth in runs scored and eleventh in slugging—and won 100 games.

• In a September 12 doubleheader against the Pirates, the Mets won both ends of the twinbill, 1–0. Both runs were driven in by the pitchers, Jerry Koosman and Don Cardwell.

• Twenty different Mets had game-winning RBIs, including three by Seaver.

• The Mets were 9½ games out of first on July 31 and 5½ games behind Chicago as of September 2, when the Cubs were riding a five-game winning streak.

• The Mets finished eight games ahead of the Cubs, after concluding the season with a 38-11 run.

"You have to have things like that in order to win," Weis said. "It seems strange when things like that happened. But we had a good team. We played well as a unit."

The Orioles of 1969 rank with the 1954 Cleveland Indians as one of the greatest teams not to win the World Series. Baltimore was blessed with power (Frank Robinson, Boog Powell, Brooks Robinson, and Paul Blair); amazing defense—in the field Brooks Robinson at third and Mark Belanger at shortstop were maybe the best left-side infield tandems ever—and the best rotation in the American League, led by Mike Cuellar (23-11, 2.38 ERA, co–Cy Young winner), Dave McNally (20-7) and Jim Palmer (16-4).

The Twins-Orioles series matched the league's best hitting team against the best pitching team. The cliché proved out, as pitching won: in three games the Twins were held to five runs in 4–3, 1–0 and 11–2 losses.

Meanwhile, the Mets were sweeping the Atlanta Braves. Hank Aaron hit home runs in all three games and drove in seven runs while hitting .357, but it was not enough for Atlanta, 93-69 that year, which was outhit by New York .327 to .255.

Weis went only 1-for-3 that series, in which the Mets won 9–5 and 11–6 games in Atlanta and the 7–4 finale in New York. Jones hit .429 that series, but the real hero was Weis' counterpart in a second-base platoon, Ken Boswell.

Boswell had hit .407 after August 23, raising his average from .236 to .279. His hot hitting continued into the playoffs: in 12 at-bats he hit .333, with two home runs, four runs, five RBIs, and a pair of walks.

Come World Series time, he and Weis would reverse roles; against the Orioles, Boswell went 1-for-3.

The fact that the Mets were a collection of interchangeable parts—only Jones and Agee had more than 400 official at-bats that season—and their sorry history made them dismissible. All which made them more dangerous, as Weis has noted:

> We were a good ballclub. The only superstars we had were Tom Seaver [25-7 in his 1969 Cy Young season] and Jones— and Donn Clendenon maybe. But we played good baseball.
>
> That whole season we used a platoon system. I was switch-ing with Ken Boswell. Ed Kranepool was switching with Clen-denon [at first, after Clendenon was acquired in a June 15 trade with the Montreal Expos]. Ed Charles was switching with Wayne Garrett at third. Ron Swoboda was switching with Art Shamsky [in right]. That way you knew when you were going to play.
>
> We were pretty much rested. Come September we were ready.

Baseball still wasn't buying the Mets success. "I don't believe them," Braves manager Lum Harris said after the NLCS. "I don't know how they do it."

Neither did the Vegas oddsmakers, who made the Orioles an 8–5 favorite in the World Series. History was on the house's side: up to that point, no ninth-place team ever won the World Series the following year.

"We were not supposed to win that series," Weis said almost 27 years later. "If you go down the stat sheet, Baltimore had us beat at every posi-tion, or almost every position. But in a short series, anything could happen.

"We got great pitching, timely hitting and great defense," he continued. Then he adds: "We shouldn't have won."

Just in case the New Yorkers didn't get the message, Oriole left-fielder

Don Buford emphasized the point in Game One by taking Seaver deep to right on the second pitch of the home first. Baltimore, behind Cuellar, cruised to a 4–1 win. The lone Mets run came on a sacrifice fly by Weis, but not much was made of it at the time. Even Baltimore's fans were confident in the inevitable: neither Game One nor Two at Memorial Stadium would be a sell-out. The rout was apparently on.

"Bring on Ron Gasper," Frank Robinson howled again in what was becoming a battle cry.

But Baltimore's bats went silent in Game Two against Koosman, who took a no-hitter into the seventh, as he combined with Taylor on a two-hitter. The Mets first run had come in the fourth on a Clendenon home run, but Baltimore tied it in the seventh by bunching its two hits together. Into the ninth the game went tied.

With two outs, Ed Charles singled, and he went to third on a hit-and-run single to left by catcher Jerry Grote. With runners on the corners, it seemed a logical spot for Mets manager Gil Hodges to pinch-hit for Weis. But the 6-foot, 160-pound right-hander approached the plate.

"He gave me a lot of confidence in myself," Weis said of the late Hodges. "In a way I wasn't looking for a pinch-hitter—he had gone with me a lot of times during the regular season.

"The guys loved to play for him," Weis said. "In my career, I played for three managers: Al Lopez, Eddie Stanky and Gil Hodges. I know if Al Lopez or Eddie Stanky were managing the '69 Mets, I would not have hit in a lot of situations in that '69 series."

McNally got a first-pitch slider high up in the plate, and Weis spanked the ball into left, driving in Charles and giving the Mets a 2–1 lead.

"It was either a high fastball or a high slider," Weis said. "I was more of a high-ball hitter. It was a solid single to left."

Taylor got Brooks Robinson to ground out with two on and two out in the ninth to preserve the win. The Series now moved to New York, where the only empty seats were where fans had jumped out of them.

Shea Stadium was packed-in pandemonium for Game Three, which was won by the Mets, 5–0. Agee hit a lead-off home run and made two historic catches, one in left center and one in right center, that alone prevented five runs from scoring. Gary Gentry got the win, with a save recorded by a 22-year-old fireballer named Nolan Ryan.

The Orioles mystique was gone, lost in the screams in Flushing. In Game Four, Clendenon homered again, in the second, to give the Mets a 1–0 lead, a margin Seaver carried into the ninth. But Powell and Frank Robinson singled, and Brooks Robinson's sinking liner to right looked as if it would scoot past a diving Swoboda to clear the bases. But Swoboda somehow snared the ball in his webbing and held on as his face smashed into the turf, limiting Robinson to a RBI sac fly. The game remained tied through the ninth and into the bottom of the tenth.

Grote led off the tenth with a cheap double that Buford lost in the sun. He was then replaced by a pinch runner. Al Weis stepped to the plate, but now the Orioles realized the second baseman had transformed himself into Bill Mazeroski: The lifetime .219 hitter was intentionally walked, setting up the first of the two most controversial plays of the Series.

Backup catcher J. C. Martin, in a pinch-hitting role, laid a bunt down the first base line. Catcher Elrod Hendricks called for the ball, but pitcher Pete Richert either didn't hear him or ignored him. He picked the ball up and fired to first, plunking Martin on the wrist. Orioles would later charge that Martin was out of the basepath and should have been called out for interference.

No call was made, and the ball bounded toward second. Grote's pinch-runner raced around third and scored the winning run.

His name? Rod Gaspar.

In Game Five, McNally hit what was to that point the Series' most improbable home run in the third inning off Koosman, followed by a blast by Frank Robinson. Baltimore's 3–0 lead carried into the sixth.

Cleon Jones, who hit .340 that year but only .158 in the Series, danced out of the way of a low curveball from McNally. After the ball skittered into the New York dugout, he protested to homeplate umpire Lou DiMuro that he had been hit by the pitch. DiMuro called ball one.

Hodges emerged from the dugout with the ball. In a scene eerily reminiscent of the 1957 Nippy Jones incident, Hodges showed the ump the black shoe polish; DiMuro awarded the Met first base.

Clendenon then homered to cut the deficit to one. Koosman held the Orioles scoreless in the seventh. In the bottom half of the inning, McNally toed the rubber to face the first batter of the inning, Weis. The 6-foot, 160-pound second baseman was going after the first pitch that looked good.

"I didn't want to put myself into too much of a hole," he said. "The eighth-place hitter does get some good pitches to hit. But sometimes it's the opposite; sometimes they want to get to the pitcher."

Not with no outs and no one on. McNally was going after Weis. The utility man dug in his small frame. McNally, who had given up one of Weis' eight American League career home runs, delivered high heat.

"When I hit the ball I kind of knew I hit it pretty well," Weis recalled. "You look up and I see Don Buford take two or three steps in. And then he started going back." Weis was hoping the ball would carry enough for a double.

It carried all right, over the 371-foot sign in left center for a home run. As the 57,397 fans in Shea went nuts, Weis practically sprinted around the bases.

"I didn't have a home run trot," he explained.

His father, Albert, had been buying beers at the time and missed the blast, but mom Madeline, a Brooklyn Dodgers fan who converted to the Mets even before her son was traded there, was among the frenzied.

Before Game Five, Weis' wife, Barbara, was driving to the ballpark with Sharon Grote, Jerry Grote's wife. In the backseat was the Weis' son, Daniel. That day, October 16, was his sixth birthday.

"My dad is going to hit a home run for my birthday," Daniel said told the bemused women.

Dad didn't find out until later, after his blast. "What were the odds of that?"

If ever a hit that tied a game could be called a game-winning hit, it was Weis'. It was almost expected when the Mets scored twice in the eighth on a pair of doubles and an error to go up 5–3. When Cleon Jones fell to one knee in left after catching Davey Johnson's soft fly ball with two outs in the ninth, the Mets were world champions.

In the Series, Weis—who would be released by the Mets in 1971—went 5-for-11, a torrid .455 clip, with three RBIs.

"If this guy isn't the Most Valuable Player," said Cardwell, picking up the pint-sized Weis, "the sportswriters are drunk."

Clendenon would win the series MVP for hitting .357 with three homers and four RBIs.

In the madhouse that was the Mets locker room, Rod Gaspar got in the last word:

"Bring on Frank Robinson, whoever he is."

Gaspar, and the Baltimore Orioles, already knew who Al Weis was.

BILL "WAMBY" WAMBSGANSS

Bill Wambsganss took a couple of steps back to play deep at second base against Clarence Mitchell. Wambsganss' Cleveland Indians already had a 7–0 lead over the Brooklyn Dodgers in the fifth inning of Game Five of the 1920 World Series, but the Dodgers were rallying with two on and none out. Playing on the grass took away any chance the second baseman had for a double play, but that's OK. All Wamby wanted was the out. One out.

Cleveland's ace Jim Bagby went into his windup and delivered. Mitchell, Brooklyn's pitcher, stroked a line drive over second. It should have been a hit, would have been a hit, if Wambsganss wasn't playing so deep. Wamby ran over and leaped, making the catch. He had his one out.

Then he looked around the infield. Bill Wambsganss was staring at immortality. The play, a matter of seconds, would define his 91 years.

"You'd think I was born the day before," he said years later, "and died the day after."

After making the catch, Wamby—as he was named by Cleveland scoreboard chief Charlie Bang and best known because the shortened name fit in a box score—let his momentum take him toward second base. The whole time he was watching Pete Kilduff, the Dodger who was on second, still running toward third. "Figured he was a cinch," Wamby said. He stepped on second for the unexpected double play. Then he turned to his left.

There was Otto Miller. The runner from first. Two feet away.

"He just stood there," Wambsganss said in an interview on file with the Hall of Fame. "He came to a full stop, right there. Well, I just took one step and touched him lightly on the shoulder, and that was it."

There was a surprising lull in the crowd, as if the fans were collectively doing the math in their heads. "It happened so quickly it was some time before the crowd realized what had happened," Cleveland third baseman Larry Gardner said.

Said Wambsganss: "Then, of course, it dawned on them and you could hear the cheers getting louder and louder. They all threw their straw hats right onto the playing field."

Count 'em. Three outs. Bill Wambsganss, in the same game that also saw the first grand slam as well as the first home run by a pitcher in World

Series play, had just pulled off the first and only unassisted triple play in post-season history.

Cleveland native and Indiana-raised William Wambsganss was destined for the Lutheran ministry, just like his father. But Wamby had a problem: public speaking. Playing ball in front of 30,000 was no problem, but speaking in a room full of people was too much. Plus, he wasn't sure he heard the calling.

In 1912 he saw his first major league game: Cleveland was playing in a exhibition game in Fort Wayne, Indiana, where he was going to Concordia College. There, at that game, he heard it. His calling.

He had to give baseball a shot. On break from college in 1913, he played Class D ball at Cedar Rapids. After the season Wamby wrote his father, confessing he wanted to be a ball player. His father consented, and a temporary respite from the ministry became permanent when Wamby joined Cleveland in 1914.

The team was still commonly called the Naps, after their star player, Nap Lajoie. (The name Indians wouldn't be adopted until the following year.) But the Hall of Famer was well past his prime, and Wambsganss was brought in to shore up the infield. Playing mostly shortstop, Wambsganss hit .217 in 43 games that year on a team that lost 102 games.

Wamby won and held onto the starting second base job in 1915, while playing 35 games at third, despite only hitting .195 for the year. In 1916, back again at short, his average jumped to .246. He had one of his best years in 1919, hitting .278 with 60 RBIs.

As Wambsganss improved, so did the Indians. In 1915, Lajoie departed, and the following year Tris Speaker arrived in a pilfering of a trade with the Red Sox. (The two players the Sox got in return, Sad Sam Jones and Fred Thomas, never produced.) The Tribe bamboozled the Red Sox by keeping some of their better players, including Wamby, on the bench in spring training while the trade was being considered. After the Red Sox made their offer, Wambsganss was back on the field.

With Speaker on the team—the Grey Eagle became manager three years later—as well as pitchers Stan Covaleski and Bagby and shortstop Ray Chapman, Cleveland was no longer the laughing stock of the American League.

From 1915 to 1919, Cleveland's win totals rose from 57 to 84. In 1920 the Tribe went over the top, going 98-56 and winning the American League by two games over the Chicago White Sox.

But the season was marred by tragedy when star shortstop Chapman was beaned by a pitch from the Yankees Carl Mays and died the next day. The team faltered at first and looked as if it might fall out of the race. Then the Tribe discovered a rookie replacement: Joe Sewell. Sewell hit .329 in 22 games that year and .312 for his 14-year, Hall of Fame career.

Bill Wambsganss' triple play (courtesy of Baseball Hall of Fame Library, Cooperstown, New York).

The Indians were facing a tough team in the Dodgers in a best-of-nine World Series, the format from 1919 to 1921. Managed by Wilbert Robinson and featuring stars like future Hall of Famers Zack Wheat (.328 avg.) and Burleigh Grimes (23-11, 2.22 ERA), Brooklyn was hoping to ride its home-field advantage to its first title.

After Cleveland took Game One on the road, 3–1, the Dodgers took the next two at Ebbets Field before the Series shifted to League Park in Cleveland. Game Four belonged to Cleveland, 5–1, as Speaker and Wambsganss each had two hits and scored two runs. It was the best game for Wamby, who would hit only .154 with four hits for the Series.

His best game, but not his most memorable. Game Five of the Series is remembered as the "Game of Records." In addition to Wambsganss' triple play, Elmer Smith hit the first-ever Series grand slam; it would be 33 years before Mickey Mantle duplicated the feat. In the fourth, Bagby hit the first-ever series homer by a pitcher. And there was one more record, set by Mitchell, the Dodgers pitcher. In his next at-bat after the triple play, he hit another screamer, this time on the ground but again to Wambsganss. He turned the double play. Mitchell thus set the record for being responsible for the most outs in back-to-back at-bats: five.

After the 8–1 loss, the Dodgers were done; they did not score another run in dropping the last two games.

Wamby, who hit .244 in 1920, broke his arm in spring training in 1921 but still had three more strong seasons with Cleveland, including a .290 campaign in 1923. The following year he was part of a seven-player trade and was sent to the Red Sox. After two seasons he was sold to the Philadelphia Athletics, where he played only 54 games but hit .352 before being released. He was a lifetime .259 hitter over his 13 big league seasons with the Naps/Indians, Red Sox, and Athletics.

Wambsganss played seven more years in the minors, managing his last two years in Springfield and Fort Wayne. While at Springfield, one of his players was Elmer Smith, the man who hit the historic grand slam in Wamby's triple-play game 11 years before.

But Wambsganss wasn't cut out to be a baseball manager. He returned to Ohio, where he coached sandlot baseball and was manager of the order department for a screw products company. He also battled depression in his post-baseball years. Wambsganss, who was briefly hospitalized for the condition, was able to overcome the malady and live well into old age.

Bill Wambsganss died in 1985, and newspapers across the country ran his obituary. Almost all had "triple play" in the headline.

The 1920 World Series, and especially Game Five, was long remembered, if not just for its excitement but also for its weirdness.

"And, funny thing," Cleveland's Gardner said, "of all the plays people still talk about, [Wamby's] was the most unexciting."

Or as spectator and National League president John Heydler put it: "How could he miss? The ball was hit right into his hands."

Regardless, columnist Joe Williams called it "baseball's most historic play" in 1951, albeit five months before Bobby Thomson's "Shot Heard 'Round the World."

With a catch, a toe, and a tag, a man whose full name was unknown to many fans of his day has secured a spot in sports legend, one he thought would only grow if his feat was ever equaled.

"People who never heard of me," Wambsganss said in 1977, "will hear of me when somebody makes the second unassisted triple play in World Series history."

It may be a long time before those people hear the name Bill Wambsganss.

DON LARSEN

More than 50 pitchers are in the Hall of Fame.

More than 60 pitchers have won Cy Young awards.

More than 200 pitchers have thrown no-hitters.

But only one pitcher was perfect when it counted most. That pitcher was Don Larsen, who on October 8, 1956, emerged from being a thoroughly ordinary player to becoming an extraordinary figure in sports history.

When that day was over, Larsen would be the toast of the country and enter sports legend, while his New York Yankees would pull off a world championship after dropping the first two games to the Brooklyn Dodgers. The game would also make relative unknowns like Dale Mitchell, the last man to face Larsen that day, the answers to bar bets almost a half century later.

But perhaps the most enduring, the most precious legacy of that most perfect pitching performance was The Catch.

Not Mickey Mantle's, although it was astounding; not Gil McDougald's, although it was improbable; and not Andy Carey's, although it was unbelievable, literally. No, the catch that is most remembered, most rewound in sports reels, is the catch by Larsen—of Yogi Berra.

You've seen it, a shadowy gray clip of Yogi Berra running out to the mound, arms pinwheeling as he leaps up to Larsen's chest like a kid into Dad's arms after a long business trip. If anything could eclipse what Larsen had just accomplished, it might be that scene of unbridled joy, when the definition of sport as men playing a boys' game was boldfaced and underscored; when all of what is best in sport was framed in three seconds.

Too often, perhaps, the superlatives of winning moments in sport are just silly in retrospect—like the high school football team that pokes index fingers in the air amid chants of "We're Number One!" that belies the team's .500 record.

Other times superlatives are dead on.

October 8, 1956, in Yankees Stadium was such a time.

The event was witnessed by 64,519 fans who packed the stands and aisles of the Stadium, as well as tens of thousands more who skipped school or work to catch its broadcast. It was a game worth a dock in pay or a month's detention.

193

The Subway Series was the seventh and final between the Yankees and Dodgers between 1941 and 1956. Six of the Series were won by the Yankees; four went a full seven games.

The Yankees had dropped the first two games of the Series, 6–3 and 13–8. After Brooklyn mowed through seven Yankee pitchers in Game Two, the Bombers appeared well on their way to repeating the agonizing loss of the previous year to the team across town. The Yankees took the next two to knot the Series: like any post-season matchup, Game Five was pivotal.

Enter Don James Larsen, 27, with his 11-5 record that season and 3.26 ERA. He had been a Yankee just two years, part of a November 18, 1954, deal with Baltimore after a season in which Larsen was the losingest pitcher in the American League: 3-21. The trade sent him and two other Orioles—pitcher Bob Turley and shortstop Billy Hunter—to New York for six men, including Gene Woodling, as one phase of a wild 18-player trade.

In 1956, Larsen was fourth in wins in his own rotation, behind Whitey Ford (19-6), Johnny Kucks (18-9), and Tom Sturdivant (16-8). Fans looked with dismay at Larsen's name as the starter in their program. They knew he had been knocked out of Game Two in the second. They knew he struggled in 1953 and 1954 with a 10-33 record for St. Louis and Baltimore. They saw that he had changed his pitching motion to a no-windup delivery after he was shelled by Boston just a month before the World Series.

They considered all this and began to map out new routes to school and work to avoid Dodgers fans, who had a tendency to gloat after winning, especially after their one World Series win the year before. It seemed more than possible another was coming.

After all, Larsen was known for his marathon happy hours, too often punctuated by his favorite line, "Let the good times roll, baby doll!"—not exactly reassuring. His reputation as a first-string partier on a team with Mantle, Billy Martin, and Ford meant he was in the barroom big leagues and, by most accounts, Larsen proved his membership in a late night before the game that would define him.

Someone in a position to know was the late Mick. Writer Mark Shaw, author of several baseball books, including *The Perfect Yankee*, replayed the saga in a 1996 edition of the *National Pastime* magazine. He used a passage from Mantle's *My Favorite Summer: 1956*.

> I've heard and read a lot of stories about how Don Larsen was out all night drinking and partying the night before he pitched Game Five of the 1956 World Series. But I'm here to tell you that it's just not true. I know because I spent part of the night with him.
>
> I'm not going to tell you Gooney Bird [Larsen's Yankees nickname because he tried, unsuccessfully, to give others the

nickname] was a Goody Two-Shoes. He loved to party and he could do it with the best of them. He liked to drink and he was a champion in that league, too. But he also was one of the best competitors I have known. He liked his fun, but on the mound he was all business. There might have been times when he stayed up all night, drinking and partying, and pitched the next day, but he never would do that for such an important game as a World Series game. He just wouldn't let his teammates, and himself, down like that. Larsen told me he was going to have dinner with some friends, then go over to Bill Taylor's saloon on West Fifty-Seventh Street, across from the Henry Hudson Hotel, where Gooney was living at the time. He asked me to join them there, and I did.

I caught up with Larsen and his friends about nine o'clock and I stayed there about an hour and a half. In that time, I didn't see Gooney Bird have one drink. He was drinking ginger ale. And he was cold, stone sober.

I left ... about ten-thirty and went back to the St. Moritz. Later, I found out that Larsen left a few minutes after I did. He stopped for a pizza and took it back to his room at the Henry Hudson. One of Don's friends told me later that he saw Gooney go upstairs to his room with his pizza. He was sober at the time and that's how he spent the night, unless he got smashed in his room, which I doubt. But of course it makes a better story to say Larsen was out all night the night before he pitched, partying and drinking and falling-down drunk. And because of his reputation, it was easy to believe those stories. It almost seemed that people wanted to believe them, as if that made what he did even more remarkable and dramatic.

Larsen did not know he was starting until he arrived at the clubhouse. In the *National Pastime* article, he said getting the nod for that game "made my heart stop."

"I couldn't believe I was going to be the starting pitcher for the Yankees in that pivotal fifth game of the series," Larsen said. "I had a lot going on in my mind as I began to undress and get ready for my second chance at the Brooklyn Dodgers. After I put on my treasured New York Yankee uniform with the number 18 on the back, I headed for the ballfield. It was a bright, beautiful October day and I was ready to go. I knew I had to do better than the last time, keep it close, and give our club a chance to win."

Not everyone agrees with Mantle's version of the night before the game. Some even say that either in spite of—or some say, because of—any hangover,

Don Larsen (courtesy of Baseball Hall of Fame Library, Cooperstown, New York).

Larsen managed to bear down better than ever. He seemed to find the groove in his new, unorthodox motion that often takes time to take hold.

Whatever the reason, he made dem Bums—many of whom had already earned their tickets to Cooperstown—feel like, well, bums. Most swings produced only pop-ups, dribblers to Yankee cowhide, or a breeze. Larsen's no-wind-up delivery gave him such control over his 97 fastballs, sliders, and slow curves that only once did he run the count to three balls, and that was to Pee Wee Reese in the first. He then struck him out, one of seven Dodgers that day.

Twenty-seven up. Twenty-seven down. Perfect.

The result: a 2–0 win for the Yankees and a path well blazed to another World Championship.

"He was great," beamed Yogi Berra, who had caught and directed two other no-hitters by then. "In fact, I've never caught a greater pitcher than Don was today."

But as Larsen has always been quick to note, his perfect game wouldn't have happened without the Bronx Bombers—at bat and in the field—giving their best all-around showing of the Series to that point.

Mantle blasted a solo home run in the fourth—his third in the Series. In the sixth, Andy Carey lined a single up the middle. A man on. And a tough decision for manager Casey Stengel.

The next batter was Larsen, a good hitter for a pitcher. But .241 is .241, and Stengel had to weigh the possible perfect game against the game. He went with Larsen. Larsen laid down a sacrifice, and Carey moved to second. Perfect. Hank Bauer then knocked a single into the outfield, driving in the second and last score of the game.

A business-as-usual day for New York Yankees, Inc., it seems, a formula that worked 97 times that season. Pitch, field, hit, score.

The Dodgers had chances. They came as early as the second inning, when Jackie Robinson axed a grounder so hard it flew off sure-handed Carey's glove at third. As the ball ricocheted toward possible extra bases, shortstop Gil McDougald popped into view, pocketed the ball, and gunned Robinson at first.

Three innings later Gil Hodges shot a mortar toward deep center field, a ball gone in most outfields, except the one roamed by Mantle. The Mick's speed through the pain of hobbled knees made the baseball, and time, stand still. Some say the catch was more astounding than the far more famous over-the-shoulder grab by Willie Mays two years earlier.

But no time for back slaps. The next pitch also took off like a streak, this time along the right-field line beyond which not even Mickey could suspend space and time. Sandy Amoros' smash was going, going and—just foul.

There was one more gasp, in the eighth. Hodges, still seething at the double that wasn't in the fifth, teed off again. He screamed a low, hard liner between third and short. Carey dived. The ball whistled toward left field—caught. So close was the hard-to-believe play that Carey rifled the ball to first, just to be sure. Hodges shook his head and wondered just how hard he had to smack a ball to get a hit on this afternoon.

He had plenty of company, including battery mate Sal Maglie. All the 39-year-old comeback kid and winner of Game One did was pitch perfectly, too, for 3⅔ innings. He ended the game giving up just five hits against the lineup that usually got that many before most fans' first hot dog.

Sports page accounts of that last inning still give a tingle of the tension shared by thousands 40-plus years ago:

Up 2–0 against a team that could close that margin in a couple of at-bats, Larsen took the mound weary after eight hard, pressure-wracked innings in which he had retired 24 batters in a row. Worse, he had just realized he was three outs from history.

First up: Dodger outfielder Carl Furillo, a .299 lifetime hitter. He gets wood on four pitches. Each flies foul. Another crack, the ball blasts beyond the infield, but is caught in right. One out.

Next up: Roy Campanella, a double threat as a solid hitter who studies pitching as only a catcher does. He nails a drive that fades just foul. He chops another to Billy Martin at second. Martin takes an extra moment to cradle the crucial ball and fires to Joe Collins at first. Two outs.

Who's next? Manager Walter Alston was certain to replace Maglie with a pinch hitter. Dale Mitchell, a longtime .300 hitter, steps to the plate. The Dodgers bought the left-handed slugger from Cleveland in late July for just such an occasion. Hitless in four at-bats this series, he was overdue.

"I was so weak in the knees out there in the ninth inning," Larsen was quoted in *The Game & the Glory* by Joseph Reichler, "I thought I was going to faint. When Mitchell came up I was so nervous, I almost fell down. My legs were rubbery, and my fingers didn't feel like they were on my hand. I said to myself, 'Please help me out, somebody.'"

The first pitch shows it. Ball, outside. But it sets up the slider. Strike. Which sets up the fastball. Larsen's tired right arm tenses for one more. Mitchell coils, swings, misses. One-and-two. Mitchell won't expect another, not now, not after more than 90 pitches when so much is on the line and Larsen is so ahead in the count. Fastball. Mitchell rears back, swings, smack! Foul into the stands.

Each pitch brings a renewed roar from the rowdy crowd.

Everything was riding on this. The perfect game, maybe the game, maybe the Series. Larsen says a quick prayer. Mitchell watches the no-wind-up pitcher—but something's wrong. Larsen winds up. The fastball rockets in. Mitchell starts to lean into a deep cut, then holds back as the pitch tails away.

Strike.

When it was over, Larsen had pitched the first perfect game in three decades and the first perfect game in a World Series. It was just the fifth perfect game of the century. After the game, Larsen told reporters:

> I didn't start thinking about it until the seventh. Naturally, nobody on the bench mentioned it. Casey didn't even look at me. In fact, the first word spoken to me was by Yogi when he hugged me after I struck out Mitchell. Yogi rattled off something like, "Oh, you something or other."
>
> Even though I pitched a no-hitter and retired 27 men in a row, I hardly can believe it. Of course I've dreamed of it—the no-hitter, but, Oh Lord, never the perfect game.

He achieved what even he didn't dare dream of, and that's why a couple hours that occurred 40-plus years ago are still talked about today, with just as much amazement.

"It means so much because it was the only one," said Dan Bennett, a research associate at the National Baseball Library and Archive in Cooperstown, New York. "A perfect game is one of the rarest performances in baseball at any time in the season, but when it happens in a World Series it will be remembered forever."

World Series hero. It's hard to imagine a whole lot of better titles. The thrill of the feat was shared by the nation—and perhaps even by a few other worldly types, as Dave McEnery imagined in the last verse of his 1956 poem, "The Ballad of Don Larsen" on file at the National Baseball Hall of Fame.

> *Way high above the bleachers in the "Gallery in the Blue,"*
> *There was Ruth and "Mighty Matty" and the "Big Train" watching, too.*
> *And I know that they were pulling for that kid upon the mound—*
> *The day that young Don Larsen pitched the 27 down.*

Corny, but quite a tribute.

"Don Larsen was kind of an average player, at best," Bennett said. "Maybe people could look at him and see something familiar, somebody they could relate to better…. Here was a guy who had never been in the spotlight before doing something that had never been done before or since—and may never be done again."

Larsen never came close again. After an off-season as a television guest star on the "Bob Hope Show" and many other shows, supermarket ribbon-cuttings at $2,500 a snip, and life as a magazine cover boy that more than doubled his baseball salary, he became Clark Kent again.

A year after he was perfect, he led the American League in beaned batters, with 12. In all, he spent another three years with the Yankees, turning out records of 10-4, 9-6 and 4-7 with an ERA that crept from 3.26 to 4.33.

He would play another seven seasons, bouncing from Kansas City to San Francisco and Chicago (he hit .311 in the 1961 for the Giants and White Sox) to Houston, Baltimore, and the Cubs. He even played a couple games in the outfield along the way. He finished with a lifetime 81-91 record over 14 years and a 3.78 ERA.

His best performances, however, may be his World Series appearances, and not just that game in '56. In five World Series, all but one with the Yankees, he notched a 4-2 record with a 2.75 ERA.

He set World Series marks for fewest hits allowed in a game (zero, of course, in 1956), most consecutive hitless innings (11.1 over two appearances in the '56 and '57 Series), and most consecutive innings in which a runner never reached first base in a Series (9 in '56).

In 1981, a Yankees-Dodgers old-timers game was held in New York in Larsen's honor. The *New York Times* reported Larsen drew crowds at his locker that rivaled those for Mantle and DiMaggio.

A day after that perfect day four decades ago, *Times* sportswriter Arthur Daley put it this way:

"There is a sign behind the Stadium bleachers that offers a substantial threat. It says: 'Anyone interfering with play subject to arrest.' The joint was alive with cops, but none put the arm on Larsen. He interfered with Dodger play in the most blatant fashion imaginable."

STEVE BLASS

For six years, Steve Blass of the Pittsburgh Pirates was a steady major league pitcher, with flashes of brilliance. For two years, he fanned those flashes. For one World Series, he was on fire. Yet when his career is discussed, his name most often is followed by a question mark.

What happened to Steve Blass?

The numbers reveal only more questions.

Steve Blass 1971 World Series: two wins, no losses; two complete games; thirteen strikeouts; ERA: 1.00.

Steve Blass in 1972 National League Championship Series: one win, one loss, 1.72 ERA. In a total of 15.2 innings over two games, he gave up just six walks and had five strikeouts.

In the next two seasons he would go 3-9, and average more than one earned run each inning. In those two years combined, he pitched fewer games, 24, than in any of his previous eight seasons except his rookie year, in which he also pitched two dozen.

In those two years, 1973–74, Blass walked an average of nearly one batter an inning. In the previous eight years, he walked an average of one batter every three innings.

Before the 1975 baseball season began, it was all over for 31-year-old Blass. Baseball writer Roger Angell wrote in 1975:

> Of all the mysteries that surround the Steve Blass story, perhaps the most mysterious is the fact that his collapse is unique. There is no other player in recent baseball history—at least none with Blass' record and credentials—who has lost his form in such a sudden and devastating fashion and been totally unable to recover. … Blass, once his difficulties commenced, was helpless. Finally, of course, one must accept the possibility that a great many players may have suffered exactly the same sort of falling off as Blass for exactly the same reasons (whatever they may be) but were able to solve the problem and continue their athletic careers. Sudden and terrible batting and pitching slumps are mysterious while they last; the moment they end, they tend to be forgotten.
>
> What happened to Steve Blass? Nobody knows …

What the hell *did* happen to Steve Blass?

"I never found the answer. When I look back on it now it comes down to the fact that I had 10 years in the big leagues and that's all the pitching there was in my arm," Blass told the *New York Post* a decade after he retired.

Others had their theories, including poor adjustment to the white-hot fame he earned in the 1971 World Series, a slump he couldn't dig out of, his eyesight (he had to wear glasses for everything from driving to watching TV but refused to do so on the mound), teammate Roberto Clemente's death in a plane crash during a humanitarian relief effort, fear of injuring someone or being injured, problems with his health or with the Pittsburgh Pirates, or at home. None of it, Blass has said, was true.

Whatever.

What is known about Steve Blass began in a small town in Connecticut in Little League, where he was taught that baseball is, above all else, a game to be enjoyed, to be savored.

"I think most progress in baseball comes from enjoying it and then wanting to extend yourself a little, wanting it to become more. There should be a feeling of 'Let's go! Let's keep on this!'" Blass once said.

As a youth he nurtured that love of the game by pitching and fielding countless complete games against an old barn roof and wall in Falls Village, Connecticut. as he relates:

> I had all kinds of games, with different, very complicated rules, I'd throw the ball up, and then be diving into the weeds for pop-ups or running back and calling for the long fly balls and all. I'd always play a full game—a made-up game, with two big-league teams—and I'd write down the line score as I went along, and keep the results. One of the teams always had to be the Indians. I was a total Indians fan. ... I guess Herb Score was my real hero—I actually pitched against him once in Indianapolis in '63, when he was trying to make a comeback.

Ironic. Score, of course, was the great Cleveland pitcher who was felled by a line drive and would forever be dogged to some degree by his potential left unmatched.

Blass said the thrill he learned through the big league play of players like Score never left him. Even as a major leaguer on the mound in a World Series game, he had once stepped away from the rubber for a moment just to soak it all in.

No such moment was richer than the fan's dream that Blass lived out: Bottom of the ninth, seventh game of the World Series, and the ball was in his glove.

The year was 1971. The Baltimore Orioles were a powerhouse. Manager

Earl Weaver took a roster full of stars peppered with sure-bet Hall-of-Famers like Frank Robinson, Brooks Robinson, and Jim Palmer and won 101 games that year, 10 more than second-place Detroit.

In the American League Championship Series, the Orioles swept the Oakland A's in three games, 5–3, 5–1 and 5–3. Boog Powell was in his powerful form and hit two homers in Game Two. Brooks Robinson added another. As a team Baltimore hit .274, and the pitching staff toted an ERA of 2.33.

Few picked the Pirates to even meet this crew, let alone beat them.

After dropping the first game in the National League Championship Series against the San Francisco Giants in Pittsburgh, the Pirates—97-65 that year—won the next three games and the pennant. Steve Blass went five innings in that first game and pitched two more innings of middle relief in Game Four. In seven total innings his ERA was 11.57, worst on the staff, as he was wracked for 14 hits in seven innings.

But if you looked closely, you saw something very, very encouraging in Blass' performance that series. In that pressure cooker he gave up only two walks and logged 11 strikeouts. The man who battled for control most of his career, who even had thrown balls behind hitters, showed he had control now.

He needed it.

The World Series began in Baltimore October 9, 1971. The Pirates lost 5–3 to the Orioles in a game in which the Bucs were out-hit 10 to 3, and gave up three homers. Baltimore dominated on the mound as well, as Dave McNally threw a three-hit complete game, allowing no hits after the third inning.

Game Two was even uglier. Baltimore nailed the Pirates for 14 hits, all of them singles, in an 11–3 win. Brooks Robinson tied a World Series mark by reaching base five times with three hits and a pair of walks.

In Pittsburgh, the next day, October 12, Blass had to derail the Baltimore express that had screamed into town. And more than 50,000 fans filled Three Rivers Stadium to see him do it.

Like few have before or since, Blass came through.

That day the Orioles were only able to scatter three hits over nine innings in the biggest game Blass had ever seen, bigger than most he even dreamed of at that boyhood diamond against the New England barn. Only one Baltimore run scored, a solo home run by Frank Robinson. In a game that shifted the tide of the series, Blass got eight strikeouts. Flustered, the Baltimore team that was so sure-handed in the field recorded three errors.

Pittsburgh 5, Baltimore 1.

The Pirates were alive, and so was Pittsburgh. The next night, in Game Four—the first-ever World Series night game—Baltimore came on with a vengeance. The Orioles knocked Pittsburgh's Luke Walker (10-8, 3.54 ERA) off the mound in the first inning, shelling him for three hits, a walk, and three runs.

Thanks to outstanding performances by rookie pitcher Bruce Kison (6-5, 3.41 ERA) in a one-hit, six-inning stint, followed by closer Dave Giusti (5-6, 2.93 ERA) in two innings of work, the Pirates came back for a 4–3 win. It was good enough to tie the Series.

Pittsburgh blanked Baltimore 4–0 in Game Five behind the surprising pitching of Nellie Briles (8-4, 3.04 ERA). He allowed only two hits in his fifth complete game in 1971. At the plate the Pirates used nine hits to bang around the Orioles' pitchers, including ace McNally, who was rattled off the mound after four innings.

Now a game up in the Series after the rarest of comebacks from two games down, the Pirates went to Baltimore and lost Game Six, 3–2, in an electric tenth inning. After McNally redeemed himself by pitching in relief out of a bases-loaded mess handed to him in the top of the tenth, Brooks Robinson's sacrifice fly scored the game winner.

Enter Game Seven, and all the boyhood dreams and adult fears and pressure that came with it.

In a game that pitch-for-pitch was as close as any in a World Series, Blass faced all-star after all-star and came out on top. The only Baltimore hits going into the final innings were a single by Don Buford in the third and a double by Elrod Hendricks in the fifth. Neither scored; Buford never got past first base (he was picked off).

All was quiet from the frustrated Orioles bats on that cool, cloudy Sunday afternoon, until the eighth inning.

The lead-off hitter, Hendricks, singles between third and second, snaking the ball to an opening in a severe defensive shift.

Mark Belanger follows with a slow, arching single to center.

Two on. No outs. Pitcher up.

That means Mike Cuellar. He has gone eight tight innings against the Pirates, including the retirement of the first 11 Bucs in a row. Only two balls he pitched left the infield, but they resulted in two Pirates runs. One of them was a Roberto Clemente solo homer in the fourth. Regardless of the solid performance, the Orioles are now behind by two runs late in a World Series game, so Cuellar is yanked for pinch-hitter Tom Shopay, who had hit .284 that season.

Weaver, who always maintained baseball games are won with three-run homers, goes against his grain and has Shopay sacrifice the runners to second and third.

Buford then grounds out, but it scores Hendricks. Belanger, and a tie ball game, stand at third.

Then comes Davey Johnson, who had come up with a clutch single in Game Six to tie the score. He swings hard, connects, but grounds out to third.

Exit inning 8, with the Pirates still on top 2–1.

In the ninth, the Pirates knock out two singles and threaten to buy some insurance despite two outs. McNally is called in for another relief appearance and gets Willie Stargell to ground out.

The prize in sight now, Blass strides from the Pirate clubhouse where he watched the top of the inning and tries to calm his nerves.

It wouldn't be an easy final chapter.

First up was Boog Powell. The lifetime .266 hitter with 339 homers hit 22 dingers that year with a .256 average. Worse, he was fresh off an LCS in which he batted .300 with two homers in three games.

Powell grounds out to second.

One out.

Next is Frank Robinson. The odds-on Hall of Famer who hit .281 with 28 homers during the season swings, connects, and pops up to shortstop.

Two away.

Next is Merv Rettenmund. The .318 hitter who came through with a clutch single in Game Six digs in. He cracks one hard—right to shortstop.

The Pirates—and Steve Blass—do the near impossible. Like only five other teams in major league history, they came from a two-game-to-none deficit to win the championship of the world.

Clemente, of course, was the Series MVP. Hard not to give it to a guy who batted .414 with two clutch home runs.

Most ballots had Steve Blass a close second. Even Earl Weaver said after the seventh game that *he* would be drinking champagne if it wasn't for Blass.

Steve Blass really was a hero, of course. They marched in parades in his honor back in Connecticut and in Pittsburgh big things were expected of him. For a year, he delivered. He put in his best performance in 1972, going 19-8 with a 2.48 ERA. It was his best year since 1968, when he went 18-6 with a 2.13 ERA.

In the '72 LCS, which Pittsburgh lost three games to two to Cincinnati, Blass picked up a win and five strikeouts in 15 innings, along the way recording a tiny 1.72 ERA.

Then it happened.

Seven months later he would begin a major league season that would be his worst, with an earned-run average that would be the worst in the National League, at 9.81. He went 3-9 that year. In 1974 he had trouble even against minor league hitters, going 2-8 with a .9.74 ERA at Charlotte. On March 25, 1975, in an exhibition game against the Chicago White Sox, Blass pitched well for three innings. Then in the fourth he walked five runs home. They were among his eight walks that inning.

Two days later Pirates General Manager Joe L. Brown fought tears to announce that Stephen Robert Blass, who helped give so much that is priceless to a ball club and a city, was being released after 10 years.

"Steve has been so much an integral part of the team for so long that it is a sad day in the history of the Pittsburgh Pirates. ... It's very hard to make any statement at this time. ... I've had a very close relationship with Steve ever since he joined the organization. Players of his caliber are hard to replace."

Blass took the news with great strength of character.

"I think I've achieved everything I ever thought I could, even more than I thought I could," Blass said at the announcement. "I have a great amount of pride in what I've done."

"This is not a happy situation, but it's not the end of the world," he said hours after learning the life he had led for 14 of his 32 years was over. "I have no regrets."

A decade later the boy who would be World Series hero remained. Blass went on to selling class rings for a local company that also minted World Series rings; later he called Pirates games on radio. He has survived and thrived, untainted by the bitterness over missing million-dollar salaries and fame lost that eats at so many ballplayers retired against their will. As he told baseball writer Roger Angell:

> You know, this thing that's happened has been painted so bad, so tragic. Well, I don't go along with that. I know what I've done in baseball, and I give myself all the credit in the world for it. I'm not bitter about this. I've had the greatest moments a person could ever want. When I was a boy, I used to make up those fictitious games where I was always pitching in the bottom of the ninth in the World Series. Well, I really did it.
>
> It went on and happened to me. Nobody's ever enjoyed winning a big league game more than I have. All I've ever wanted to do since I was six years old was to keep playing baseball. It didn't even have to be major league ball. I've never been a goal planner—I've never said I'm going to do this or that. With me, everything was just a continuation of what had come before. I think that's why I enjoyed it so much when it did come along, when the good things did happen.

BERNIE CARBO

Some of the brightest novas in sports last but a season, one magical year in which everything comes together and all the breaks are good, all the close calls go your way.

Sometimes the accolades last a single World Series—maybe even just a game—in which every pitch arrives as if you called it and every swing feels dead solid perfect.

For Bernie Carbo, a former Rookie of the Year turned role player, his moment in the sun was as bright as any in baseball fact or fancy when he hit one of the most clutch home runs in a generation. But his moment was just that. A home run to remember was virtually forgotten barely four innings later.

It's a crisp night, this October 21, 1975, at Fenway Park. After eight years, the Fall Classic had finally returned to the classic Boston bandbox. That alone was enough to give any fan the itch, the tingle, the feeling that something very special was bound to happen.

Those feelings had proved true in past Octobers. Mickey Mantle. Bill Mazeroski. Bob Gibson. Great talents before and since provided timeless fall memories, but rarely for the Red Sox: even immortal Ted Williams hit only .200 in his only Series. Still, any team, any game, could provide history.

In 1975 the Red Sox were such a team, and Game Six was such a game.

Down three games to two to Cincinnati's Big Red Machine, the Red Sox were poised to add another chapter to the Curse of the Babe hexed 56 years before.

Boston breaks out in front 3–0 in the first on a Fred Lynn home run, but is blanked over the next six innings. The Reds, winners of 108 games that year, tie the game in a three-run fifth inning, score twice more in the seventh, and add an apparently superfluous insurance run in the top of the eighth.

Going into the bottom of the eighth, Cincinnati is in front 6–3. A victory celebration awaits the visiting clubhouse.

The Red Sox, 95-65 that year, get two on in the eighth, but with two out are just four outs from extinction. Boston manager Darrell Johnson looks to the bench for help and eyes Carbo. Johnson knows Carbo has the hit in him, partly because he turned his only other pinch-hitting appearance into a Game

Three homer and partly because the skipper received a memo a week earlier saying Carbo should be in the lineup. The memo was from Carbo.

So Carbo, who would have been the designated team flake if not for His Royal Flakiness, Bill "Spaceman" Lee, emerges from the dugout to hit for reliever Roger Moret. The Red Sox need one swing to stave off, and possibly rewrite, their October history. Reds reliever Rawly Eastwick, throwing heat on his way to a 3–0 post-season, was waiting. Carbo had never faced him before.

It showed.

Carbo, who did not play at all in the American League Championship Series against the Oakland A's, had always relied on his study of a pitcher's strengths and weaknesses and, especially, their tendencies. Without that, he had to guess, and he was guessing all wrong with Eastwick.

Now, with a full count, bad guessing can be fatal, or at least embarrassing. So Carbo forgets the pitcher and considers the guy calling the pitches from behind the plate. Him he knows.

Carbo broke in with the Reds organization as a 17-year-old in 1965 with a young backstop named Johnny Bench. Through the years Carbo would remind Bench that he was drafted before the catcher and received six times the signing bonus.

So Carbo, with a game and a World Series on the line, decides to play his hunch about Bench. Figuring the catcher likes to call for heat in the clutch, Carbo guesses fastball all the way.

He is very wrong.

Bench calls for a slider. Carbo sees it late as it drops through the strike zone. Caught halfway between glory and goat, Carbo twists through a swing he can't stop and executes possibly the worst cut in the history of major league baseball—no, make that all of baseball—but nicks enough to stay alive.

It's hard to recover from that swing, a kind of pants-fly-open-in-front-of-the-class sort of experience. But Carbo, a six-year veteran, knows about making adjustments. He digs in again—and again guesses fastball.

Prays fastball.

It is a fastball.

The swing from the 5-foot-11, 173-pounder is sweet, the sound of the ball off the bat even sweeter. The ball arches into the lights, disappearing in the deep center-field seats.

"I knew pretty much what Johnny Bench was doing—mostly fastballs—and he fooled me once with the worst swing in baseball," Carbo said. "But the next pitch was a fastball, and I got it."

The famed ballpark had rarely, if ever, erupted louder, but not too loud for a conversation on the field.

"Isn't this fun?" Pete Rose yelled to Carbo. "This is what the game is all about!"

Carbo's three-run homer tied the game at six. The Sox loaded the bases in the ninth but failed to score, and the game stayed tied through the tenth and eleventh.

Bottom of the twelfth. Carlton Fisk steps up to the plate. Score's knotted. Stomachs knotted. A nation watches.

Pudge swings, and the fly heads toward the Green Monster in left. Fisk makes a two-armed, diagonal chopping motion: Stay fair! Stay fair! He talks the ball out of a long-strike, as it smacks off the foul pole.

Fair. Fisk takes off toward first, hopping like a Little Leaguer.

One of the defining moments of sports ends one of baseball's greatest games. The image of Fisk swinging, chopping, hoping and hopping, will be replayed as long as there are fans.

No one at the moment shouted that ball fair any louder than Carbo, the Man of the Hour—the man of the hour just passed.

The fond memory is diminished only by the result of that Series, which Boston lost in a 4–3 seventh game. Fisk would later say people in Boston still think the Sox won that Series, three games to four.

Carbo is not a star who tires of soaking up the stardom or returning to his greatest moment. He was among friends on both sides of the scorecard that Series, having broken into the majors with the Reds and skipper Sparky Anderson. The reunion was made sweeter when Carbo took a chance to end the long-simmering feud with Anderson, his one-time mentor, sage, and drill sergeant, that began over a salary dispute shortly after his rookie season. After that they drifted apart. Carbo was traded to St. Louis during the 1972 season.

But the rift with such a monumental figure in his life would continue no longer. Carbo told Sparky: "You were like a father to me." Carbo apologized and thanked the skipper for all he had done for him. Anderson would later write that Carbo was one of the few players he considered a close personal friend.

The perpetually up-and-down Carbo finally had his house in order. Now he could concentrate on baseball.

Part of why he was sync in the 1975 Series, Carbo believes, is because he wasn't in the 1970 Series. It was the outfielder's rookie year, a year he hit .310, tied for ninth in the league, with 21 homers and 63 RBIs. The *Sporting News* named Carbo Rookie of the Year.

The regular season is not the post-season. In the series against the Baltimore Orioles, Carbo went hitless and the Birds beat the Reds in five games. In fact, in 14 post-season at-bats, Carbo failed to get a hit. He was involved in a controversial play at home in Game One of the Series, called out after O's catcher Elrod Hendricks tagged him with his glove—while his bare hand clutched the ball. The umpire, Ken Burkhart, knocked out of position by Hendricks as the backstop jumped out to field a high chopper in front of the plate by Ty Cline, didn't see the miscue—or Carbo miss home. The play was viewed by some as a turning point in the Series.

Given a second chance, Carbo just knew he would be better. He was in the best shape of his life in 1975 and made a pact with himself to go with his first instinct on every play, every pitch. This, he swore, would be his redemption.

It worked. He guessed right on both pitches he hit for home runs. For the series he hit .429, with two homers, four RBIs, and four runs scored.

But in Game Seven, in his last World Series at-bat, he let himself down. He swung to ensure he wouldn't take a third strike, popping out to second.

Carbo is a devout Christian today, preaching baseball and God's way to at-risk youths. He wasn't always.

For years the alcohol and pills and cocaine and crack were catching up on Carbo. All told he spent much of 28 years drunk or high, or scamming how to become either or both. He took uppers because he was down, he took downers because he was too up to sleep.

The World Series quasi-hero turned into the .235 journeyman. After Boston there was Milwaukee in 1976, then Boston again, then Cleveland, then a second tour in St. Louis, then Pittsburgh.

Then, after baseball, the streets. He was out of baseball by 1980. He was 33 with a life of uncertainty ahead.

He went from high to high, wanting to commit suicide in between. His dad died, then his divorce was final. With nowhere to turn, the instinct he once trusted told him to call Bill Lee. Lee directed him to Ferguson Jenkins and Joe Garagiola, and BAT. Baseball Assistance Team helps ex-players in need, financially and otherwise.

For Carbo, otherwise meant rehab. He was in a hospital, painfully confronting the life he had tried to run away from with lots of substance and lots of abuse. It was 2 A.M., and he was given sleeping pills to come down. Didn't work. For four hours he kept rolling over the television's remote control, flashing the screen on and off, driving himself crazy, unable to control even this one thing in his life. He thought he must be nuts.

Rehab did more than leave Carbo clean and sober and on a path to a religious awakening. It left him diagnosed.

He found he is bipolar or manic-depressive, a condition that can make the sufferer depressed for two or three months at a time, or much of a baseball season.

The kind of manic phase he experienced during the World Series can give higher highs than street drugs, giving the sufferer the energy, clarity, and and drive to write books, develop theorems, even become a World Series hero and then drop to the depths of misery.

Therapy and medication has led Carbo to his new life, but it was a painful therapy that forced the Detroit native to confront sexual abuse by a distant relative he had undergone as a child, an incident he was warned as a kid never to talk about.

Today some might think it is better not to discuss such painful memories, but not if they talked to him.

Carbo runs Diamond Club Ministries, teaching lessons in baseball and life to those with few prospects in either. His mission has taken him throughout the United States, to Canada, to Cuba, to prisons. The lessons are as hard as a short-hop, but the lectures on the evils of drink and drugs come from a man who has stared them both down.

Today, living on a small player's pension and on the road with his family much of the year, Carbo is satisfied with life, satisfied with his past. Life is good, really for the first time, except for that October of 1975.

Carbo is going around a hard path in life today, but a good one. And this time it's not Pete Rose shouting about how much fun the game is, that this is what it's all about.

Around the Horn

DISCO DEMOLITION NIGHT

From bat day to giving away used cars between innings to Fat Fan Day, baseball has made some of its most memorable hits through promotions aimed at filling seats with, well, fans' seats.

But with the hits come some misses, and perhaps the worst of these was in Chicago on the night of July 12, 1979.

For 98 cents—the same numbers as a local rock radio station's channel—fans could attend a doubleheader between the White Sox and the Detroit Tigers. The gimmick? Bring a disco record and watch it burn with thousands of others in a center-field pyre between games.

Rock and roll vs. disco. It was a clash of the time worse than striped shirts and polka-dot ties. Student bodies were split like political parties in 1930s Germany. Rock and roll was the soundtrack of rebellion, of causes, and disco was about not letting lyrics get in the way of a monotonous beat. Disco music, however, was winning, taking over the movies and bars, and rock and rollers—who may not have known who their congressman was—were mounting a fervid backlash.

So Comiskey Park was rocking with a festival atmosphere, less baseball perhaps than summer rock concert. Marijuana smoke swirled in the venerable park and players complained of rowdiness in the stands that made them nervous. Detroit center-fielder Ron LeFlore said a golf ball skittered between his legs while he was trying to make a putout; many players kept one eye on play and another on the black discs of K.C. & the Sunshine Band and the Village People slicing through the hot summer night air.

Tiger pitcher Aurelio Lopez and catcher Ed Putman dodged Unidentified Frisbee Objects during warmups before the eighth, wondering if they somehow ended up at a riot-prone South American soccer game.

Then it got worse.

The White Sox lost the frequently interrupted first game, 4–1. But as it drew to a close tension was mounting amid the 50,000-plus unusually unruly fans not so much out of fear for another "L" in the column the next day for a line in the police blotter or obits.

Chicago disc jockey Steve Dahl and Loreli, whose credentials for co-hosting appeared to hinge less on a resume than on a centerfold photo, took to the field to touch off the disco inferno.

Fifteen minutes of diatribe over the evils of the shallow, synthesized dance music with a beat and not much more helped whip into a frenzy a crowd that needed little assistance. Vinyl records, in those pre–compact-disc days, curled and burned as bluish-black smoke wafted to the upper decks. The d.j. and his research assistant left the lectern, in a hurry.

But this was a case when showmanship probably shouldn't have left the audience wanting more.

It began at the box seats. A couple frenzied rockers jumped the low gate. Then came their disciples. Reporters estimated that in two or three minutes as many as 7,000 people crowded onto the field where in 15 minutes major league baseball was supposed to be played.

The growing mob cared little, having been swept into the moment they came to celebrate. Some obscene banners like "Disco Sucks!" and other slogans that almost rhymed with that were thrust into the air and rippled in the wake of running youths. Television news cameras the next day and rock and roll documentaries two decades later replayed the scene of hairy, sweaty youths in T-shirts and bell-bottomed jeans running amid the foggy layers of smoke. The footage looked more Middle East than Midwest.

Perhaps one of the very few surprises of the promotion was that at the center was Bill Veeck, baseball's master showman who in order to sell tickets would stoop lower than the midget he once sent to the plate.

He was helped by the young turks of promotion with which he surrounded himself, including his son, Mike, who is credited with masterminding this stunt, his first. They knew music and the growing backlash against disco; Bill Veeck knew the value of a good promotion. None of them, apparently, knew enough about what a hot night, youth, and rock and roll indignation could add up to.

Bill Veeck tried to calm the scene, to little avail. "Please clear the field!" pleaded the old man over and over for a half-hour as history added to his already checkered chapter in baseball annals.

Harry "Take Me Out to the Ballgame" Caray also tried to take the protesting mob out of the ballpark, but with little success.

The field cleared only after outrage waned, and the mounted Chicago police force grew. A lingering thousand were scooted away, some in handcuffs, some at the invitation of swinging billy clubs (this was, after all, Chicago and young protesters).

But men who stared down 90 mph fastballs weren't anxious to play a game after all that, with so many of them still in the stands, some with radios, and the Bee Gees still getting so much air play.

There was some torn-up turf in front of the mound and an infield spot or two looked like Pete Rose had given sliding lessons, but groundskeepers quickly padded and pounded the problems.

Veeck, who so appropriately titled his autobiography *Veeck—As in Wreck*, was clearly shaken, but not stirred enough to give up a game through forfeit as Detroit manager Sparky Anderson demanded.

"I am amazed, shocked and chagrined," Veeck told reporters. "I think the grounds for forfeiting are specious at best. There was nobody on the field during the playing of the [first] game. It's true there was some sod missing. Otherwise nothing was wrong. We made no further repairs the next day, and the field was ruled playable. I'm terribly upset. I can only make apologies to the fans and my players for what turned out to be an ill-advised promotion."

American League president Lee MacPhail ruled the following day that the White Sox had to forfeit the second game, rather than replaying it as Veeck had hoped after umpire-in-chief Dave Phillips called it off.

MacPhail's order was simple: "It was the judgment of the umpire that it was not possible to start the second game because of inadequate crowd control and damage to the playing field, both of which are the responsibility of the home team."

The game disco ducked was just the fourth forfeit in league history up to that time, all of which, oddly, happened in the 1970s. The Washington Senators gave a game to the Yankees in 1971 because fans ran onto the field. Toronto got a free one from Baltimore in 1977 because of a squabble over a tarp on the mound in the bullpen, and the Cleveland Indians lost an uncontested contest to the Texas Rangers in 1974 on a special night for baseball fans. It wasn't a holiday or the thick of a pennant race. It was Beer Night.

Enough beefy midwesterners bellied up to the bars and beer vendors that night to cause enough unrest in the stands to give the players a rest.

Ten-ounce beers were sold for a dime to the 65,000 in attendance. Nice idea, but the execs should have been reading the sports pages as closely as the accounting ledgers. They might have rethought Beer Night, coming as it did a week after a fight broke out between the teams in Texas and an Indian was doused by a fan's beer.

By the time the game in Cleveland was over, an umpire would narrowly evade a kiss from a woman fan at the plate and Ranger outfielder Jeff Burroughs would be attacked by a half-dozen Cleveland fans.

Just another promotion gone terribly stupid. Sometimes, as in Chicago and Cleveland on those nights, promotions end in tatters, a mistake by front-office types blinded by the bottom line. Most of the time, though, they aren't tragic or regrettable, just silly.

The National Baseball Hall of Fame Library in Cooperstown, New York, keeps no fewer than three overflowing files on baseball promotions and a small shelf for Veeck alone. A quick perusal can leave you shaking your head, wondering why it isn't enough just to offer a baseball game:

In 1971 the Cleveland Indians won the "Maybe It's Not the Thought That

Counts Gift Award" by offering a can of deodorant to each mother as part of a Mother's Day promotion.

In 1976 the Tacoma Twins gave away 14 used cars between innings of a doubleheader with Sacramento. A record crowd of 11,721 showed up. The same promotion was done two decades later by the Buffalo Bisons Triple A team in Western New York, until a "prize" car almost exploded at ignition and had to be pushed from the field.

Pick any decade in any venue from an Oklahoma bush league to the modern majors and you find a cow-milking contest, like the one the Kansas City Royals had in 1970 during Farmer Night. That memorable evening also included greased pig tackling and the giveaway of four 72-ounce steaks. Yes, 72 ounces.

About that time the Tarboro minor league club in Ayden, North Carolina, was weighing the benefits of Fat Fan Day. The club decided it wasn't such a thin premise for a promotion and beefed it up with free admission for every man and woman over 200 pounds as well as a fattest fan contest for a season's pass to the Coastal Plain League games in Ayden.

Years later in the 1980s the Triple A Rochester, New York, Red Wings mined a similar vein when they flew in an Englishman known for his gluttony. The 6-foot-1, 240-pounder downed a 64-ounce beer pitcher in six seconds and another one in nine seconds—while being held upside down. Later he ate a light bulb.

A nearly memorable moment almost happened in Charleston, South Carolina, when the River Dogs planned a Father's Day promotion that included a free vasectomy. The local Roman Catholic Diocese, led by the bishop (a season ticket holder), helped scrub that 1997 event before it happened.

And the St. Paul Saints in Minnesota offers massages to fans by masseuses in nuns' habits and re-creation of plays by mimes in Mime-O-Vision. (Fans, rightfully of course, showered the mimes with hot dogs and sent them back to their glass boxes.)

It's trendy to call baseball boring. Maybe that's what's behind promotions like Disco Demolition Night. Maybe baseball is just too much of a business, with too much emphasis on filling every possible seat, regardless of how it affects or distorts the game.

But maybe it's something closer to what Veeck always said. Maybe we have to remember baseball is, after all, a game. So maybe a little sideshow isn't so bad. At least, maybe not now that disco really is dead.

THE BLACK CAT OF FLUSHING

Baseball has had a dog that made a minor-league box score for running the bases with a player, several donkeys as mascots, and, of course, of course, the talking horse: Mr. Ed who slid into home and scared the bejeezus out of Johnny Roseboro.

But no animal ever helped a team win a most improbable of championships like the Black Cat of Flushing.

Granted, you have to be a little superstitious and a believer of omens to buy the significance of the Black Cat of Flushing. Still, it becomes easier as you grope for answers as to how the long-lowly New York Mets could become world champions.

After all, as God in the form of George Burns once said, "My last miracle was the '69 Mets."

The Black Cat of Flushing didn't really have a name; in fact, no one could be sure if they had ever seen her before, or again. But on a September night in 1969, at Shea Stadium, the cat made a memorable debut in a game between the Chicago Cubs and the Mets, emerging seemingly out of nowhere onto the field.

Then it gave the Cubs the whammy. And Chicago was finished.

The Cubs, managed by Leo Durocher, were threatening to end a 24-year post-season drought, holding a comfortable lead in the National League East in the first year the leagues were split into two divisions. Chicago's offense featured five players with 20 or more home runs, paced by third baseman Ron Santo's 29, as well as a pair of 100-RBI men in Santo and Ernie Banks. Meanwhile, the pitching staff had five hurlers with at least 10 wins, and a pair of 20-game winners: Ferguson Jenkins (21-15, 3.21 ERA) and Bill Hands (20-14, 2.49 ERA).

In July the Mets had taken three of four at Shea against the Cubs, a series that included two signature moments of the season: Tom Seaver losing a perfect game with one out in the ninth on a single by Jimmy Qualls, and Santo clicking his heels after the Cubs beat the Mets in the third game. Still, by the end of the month the Mets were languishing in third place.

The Cubs lead over the Mets entering August was 9½ games. New York cut the gap, but on September 2, Chicago won its fifth straight and still held a 5½-game lead. By the time the Cubs arrived at Shea for a two-game series six days later, the lead had dwindled to 2½, the result of Chicago going 11-13 over a 24-game stretch, while the Mets went 18-6. Still, with the Mets' history of futility, the division still seemed to be in the bag for the Cubs—until a cat jumped out.

In game one on September 8, the first pitch of the home first from Hands was aimed at Tommie Agee's head. The intimidation tactic backfired. New York became charged, Agee homered in the at-bat after he got dusted, and the Mets won, 3–2. A Chicago win in game two could still stifle the Mets' juggernaut, so Durocher decided to go with his ace, Jenkins.

Shea Stadium was electrified for the series finale: fans out in left set fire to a Cubs pennant, while others sang choruses of "Goodbye, Leo" to Durocher. The skepticism of those who weren't believers in portents must have at least been shaken in the top of the first.

As Cubs second baseman Glenn Beckert swung a bat in the on-deck circle, a black cat emerged on the field. All of the sudden it just seemed, well, there. It crossed Beckert's path and stopped in front of the Cubs: some would say it stared right at Durocher. The cat then ran the length of the dugout, down foul territory, and disappeared under the stands in left.

"He looked in the dugout and gave them the jinx," longtime Mets head groundskeeper Pete Flynn said. "The cat came from behind home plate and went in front of the Cubs dugout. It was a bizarre moment. It just stopped for a second and stared into the dugout. It looked right at [Durocher]."

The game had barely started, but the Cubs were done. They dropped the game, 7–1, en route to losing 10 of 11 games in early September. The Mets finished the last leg of the season 38-11 to take the division by a shocking eight games. After defeating the Atlanta Braves and the Baltimore Orioles, the Mets were the unlikeliest of champions.

"Right out of central casting," outfielder Ron Swoboda told the *New York Post* in 1997. "We were neck and neck with the Cubs in the middle of a tense series and then it was like, 'Cue the cat.' I mean, reality and symbolism were merging. Everyone was laughing, saying 'The curse is on.'"

Legendary New York sportswriter Jack Lang was at the Black Cat of Flushing game. Afterward, Lang said, Durocher was convinced his team had been set up.

"Leo thought it was planned," Lang said. "[Other] people thought it was planned. I don't think it was. It wasn't a trained cat. It couldn't have been staged."

Added second baseman Al Weis years later: "As far as I know it wasn't one of our tricks."

But, c'mon: a black cat, emerging out of nowhere, running in front of the visiting team's dugout in a big pennant-drive game? *Too* coincidental. Or spooky.

Not really, Flynn said. The groundskeeper explained that Shea, and ballparks throughout baseball, are full of cats. Shea also has its share of pigeons, squirrels and, of course, mice.

"They live in the stadium," Flynn explained of the cats. "People come in and drop them off," abandoning them.

Joe Pignatano, a Mets coach at the time, dismissed any supernatural significance to the cat's appearance or any role in the team's dramatic turnaround. "It wasn't that black cat, I'll tell you that," he said. "It was the guy in left field [Cleon Jones] hitting .340 and the guy at first base [Donn Clendenon]."

Still, this cat had a better sense of timing than most actors.

And she did make it onto the field.

Happened before and since, Flynn said.

But during a key game in a pennant chase?

The raucous crowd of more than 31,000 probably had something to do with it, he replies.

"I don't know if it was the noise of the crowd that frightened her," he said. "The cat was scared."

But of all the cats that could have popped out, a black cat?

"It just happened to be a black cat," Flynn said. Then he had to laugh. "But it worked."

THE 1976 CHICAGO
WHITE SOX UNIFORMS

Major league baseball as fashion show has included over-the-knee socks that looked more like fish-net stockings, shirts without sleeves, caps with stiff sides and a flat top, V-necks, and laced-up collars. The runway has even included those god-awful Tequila Sunrise outfits of the 1970s Astros that looked more at home in a local beer league, made opposing pitcher Steve Stone physically ill, and kept fans adjusting the hue on their TV sets. But the worst sartorial blunder of all may have been when the Chicago White Sox donned shorts.

That's right, shorts.

It was 1976, and America was in the midst of a spree of fashion felonies, from polyester shirts to printed bell bottoms to shoes with heels thicker than lighted dance floors. Not even baseball was to survive the decade's assault on outerwear, Chicago White Sox owner Bill Veeck decided, so he came up with a uniform that broke the mold—and thank goodness for that. No patent was necessary because no imitation was threatened.

Picture this: black shoes, white socks just under the knees with stripes ringing the calf like some CYO basketball uniform, dark blue Bermuda shorts, a loose, double-knit pajama top not to be tucked into the pants, wide and flying black collars like a leisure suit imploding on its wearer, white T-shirt, and black cap with "SOX" that on first glance looked like S.O.S. After a second glance, the S.O.S. actually seemed appropriate.

Even the color changed, from red trim on white to a dark or navy blue. The tome *Baseball Uniforms of the 20th Century: The Official Major League Baseball Guide* by Marc Okkonen, identified as the authority on the subject, called the Sox shorts "the most innovative idea in baseball uniforms since the sleeveless vest." But while the sleeveless vest, perhaps best remembered for being used by the Pittsburgh Pirates (1950s) and later by the Kansas City A's (1963) and Oakland A's (1970s), prompted comments and some support, the shorts of Chicago incurred immediate wrath from most fans.

"I don't think there's ever been anything quite like it," said Okkonen in 1997, who also wrote *Minor League Baseball Towns of Michigan*.

"Ever the showman," the author stated in his 1991 uniforms guide, "Veeck even presented a Bermuda shorts version briefly in 1976. When 56-year-old coach Minnie Minoso made a token game appearance in 1980, this avant garde uniform must have made him wonder if the year was truly 1980 or maybe 2080."

Newspaper and broadcast accounts of what turned out to be the brief experiment with shorts were limited. Mostly the news popped up in columns or sports page briefs (pun pretty much intended) under musings or rantings about the latest oddity perpetrated by Veeck. The style risk never seemed to make the grade for fashion magazines, either, not even *G.Q.*

Okkonen explained that shorts weren't unheard of in professional baseball by 1976, just unremembered. The Pacific Coast League's Hollywood Stars wore shorts as part of one version of their uniform for a whole season in the 1950s. And the All-America Girls Professional Baseball League, the World War II women's enterprise portrayed in the movie *A League of Their Own*, featured shorts and short skirts, Okkonen noted.

The movie, in fact, portrayed a bit of criticism about the leg exposure, which was chalked up more to promotional interests than baseball. After all, this wasn't a slow-pitch, bunt-and-jog league, it was baseball, with sliding for bases and diving for line drives.

"There must have been a ton of strawberries," Okkonen said, referring to leg bruises and scabs.

He added that Veeck's bold stroke apparently violated none of baseball's rules, only people's sensibilities.

"It wasn't a question of being illegal. I'm sure Bill Veeck was smart enough not to do anything he'd get fined for," Okkonen said. "Remember, when he put the midget up to the plate he had a contract in his back pocket."

Yes, the Eddie Gaedel incident, done by Veeck decades earlier as a promotional stunt. Just one in a series of Veeck moments that often rankled established baseball.

"I don't think the players liked the shorts at all," Okkonen said.

It is easy to imagine why. In a league with artificial turf and players wearing steel spikes, the idea of exposed legs is about as comforting as wearing Speedos in Grand Prix motorcycle racing.

"Our new uniforms," Veeck wrote in *Sports Illustrated* in the spring of 1976 upon his return to baseball, "with the old White Sox colors, the old-fashioned long lettering and the turn-of-the-century collars are perhaps my little way of hinting that strange and wondrous things are going to be happening at old Comiskey Park. Just as the three styles of pants—shorts, clam-diggers and knickers—are a way of informing our fans that we are not necessarily going to be bound by tradition."

Fortunately, the uniforms never became one.

BULLPEN CARS

By the 1960s the relief pitcher was coming into his own as a star, instead of being viewed as a has-been or never-was clinging to the big leagues. They threw nasty fastballs and nastier sliders. They intimidated. They were mean, mean and tough.

But not tough enough to walk in from the bullpen. What, an athlete walking 300 feet? That was *tooooo* much.

As America passionately pursued leisure, and choruses against the pampered athlete began to grow louder, the national pastime got cushier. A batter could always walk to first base. But by the '60s a relief pitcher could ride to the mound.

The bullpen car was born.

Throughout its history baseball has dabbled with various innovations, from the multitude of incarnations of catcher's gear (the most recent being the adoption of the hockey-style mask) to orange baseballs to A's owner Charlie Finley's mechanical rabbit that brought replacement balls to umpires. Many stuck, like the warning track, padded fences, and refinements of fielding gloves.

But baseball's on-field vehicle came and went, brought about by tinkering, brought down by bravado.

The Yankees used a pin-striped Datsun, which would drive around the warning track before depositing the pitcher as close to the mound as possible. Often the fans would have no clue who was coming into the game until the passenger door open and the reliever would pop out, jacket draped casually over his arm. (Upon appearing, ace Yankee closer Sparky Lyle would be greeted with the graduation song, "Pomp and Circumstance.")

This car would also be part of one of the great baseball quotes ever, courtesy of Oriole pitcher Mike Flanagan:

"I could never play in New York. The first time I ever came into a game there, I got into the bullpen car and they told me to lock the doors."

But most bullpen cars did not come with doors, or hoods, or windshields. Rather, they were converted golf carts featuring an oversized baseball for a canopy and capped with the team's cap. At Shea Stadium, monstrous hats were stored for every visiting team.

"They used it to save time," said former Mets coach Joe Pignatano. "Most guys on the visiting teams would run in. It was just a superstition, I guess."

Mets head groundskeeper Pete Flynn said bullpen cars—often the targets of debris when visiting pitchers were being carted in—came in around 1964 and departed in the 1980s. "I haven't see a carriage in the past 10, 15 years," he said. Why did they leave the game? No clue, he said.

The bullpen car was a passing fad, a small niche of the game lost. There was a time when players prided themselves on their ability to toss their gloves to certain spots on the field, where they would leave them while at bat. No rule per se banned it; it just sort of faded away.

The bullpen car faded as relief pitchers, as a way of loosening up and appearing menacing, began stalking their way in from the pen instead of riding in relative luxury. Once a common sight, the bullpen car died unnoticed.

COLT STADIUM

When trying today to put an accusing finger on baseball's worst ballpark ever, it is best to work backward.

There is, of course, the Metrodome, a dimly lit indoor football stadium in Minneapolis where baseball is also played that is unsuitable for either sport.

Behind that is the Kingdome in Seattle, which has all the charm of a cinder block, but has an advantage over the Metrodome in that fielders can at least see the ball.

Behind them are the three cookie-cutter stadiums: Three Rivers Stadium in Pittsburgh, Riverfront Stadium (now, ugh, Cynergy Field) in Cincinnati, and Veterans Stadium in Philadelphia. These multipurpose monstrosities are interchangeable and equally repulsive; they are truly stadiums, closer to parking garages than ballparks.

Then there is the granddaddy, the birthplace of artificial turf and domed stadiums. The Astrodome. Houston's multicolored uniforms in the 1970s were perfect for this field because both rejected good taste with all the fury of a Mark McGwire home run.

Taking away the uniqueness of the Astrodome when it was built, any of these alleged ballparks could be worthy of being designated the worst-ever. Some old-time parks like Sicks' Stadium in Seattle (the one-year home of the one-year Seattle Pilots), Jarry Park in Montreal (where the sun set behind third base), or the Baker Bowl in Philadelphia would also deserve consideration.

But if the Astrodome begat the awful wave of sixties/seventies stadium styles, we have to select the park that came before the Astrodome.

We present Colt Stadium, home of the Houston Colt .45s, which later became the Astros. Any park that would make the Astrodome look good has to rate at the bottom of our list.

"Colt Stadium could be a definite worst ballpark," said Bob Bluthardt, chairman of the Society for American Baseball Research's Ballpark Committee. "They had the mosquitoes the size of 747s, if you talk to some Texans. Colt Stadium would be very far down or the bottom."

To be fair, Colt Stadium was designed to be a temporary home to the National League expansion team that started in 1962 along with the New York Mets. Still, while the Mets set the all-time record for losses in a season that first year, this Texas stadium and the people who suffered through the games there may have been the real losers.

Judge Roy Hofheinz had a dream: to build an indoor sports stadium that would feature the greatest luxury a Texan could hope for on a summer day: air conditioning. This would be his "Eighth Wonder of the World" and would cost an astronomical (pun intended) $22 million. Today that would get you a number three starter for four years.

Problem: the Colt .45s were starting play in 1962, and the dream stadium would not be ready by then. Solution: slap together a temporary park until the real facility could be constructed.

Colt Stadium, billed as a permanent structure designed to hold future athletic events once the Colts moved to the then-unnamed domed stadium, cost a paltry $1.5 million to put up. Today its site, about 1,000 feet from the Astrodome, is buried beneath a parking lot.

But as workers built the Astrodome next door, major league baseball in Houston was born in this single-deck, exposed stadium which sat 32,221. It was perfectly if blandly symmetrical, and deep: 360 feet down the lines, 395 feet to the power alleys, and 420 feet to dead center.

Tal Smith, then farm director for the Colts who went on to hold top front-office positions with the Astros, said the ability of fans to watch the construction of the Astrodome a few football fields away helped them deal with their minimalist surroundings those first three years.

"It was basically scaffolding and planks and folding chairs," he said.

Inaugural season-ticket holder Stanley Cohen said Colt Stadium was not the worst he had ever seen. "It looked like a pretty good high school stadium," he said, no small accomplishment in a state that is mad with scholastic football fever.

"It was plain vanilla," Cohen continued. "They knew they were getting into another stadium. Everything was temporary."

The stadium was temporary, but the heat and the bugs will be remembered forever.

"An afternoon game in the middle of the summer was unbearable," Cohen said. "And during the night, you had the mosquitoes."

"That," says Smith, "is why Houston had the world's first domed stadium."

Houston finished eighth that first season (ahead of the Cubs and Mets) under Harry Craft, with a 64-96 record. Dick Farrell was the ace of the staff, compiling a 3.02 ERA, 11 complete games, and 203 strikeouts—to go along with a 10-20 record. The hitting star was Cuban Roman Mejias: .286, 24 home runs, 76 RBIs. It was his only notable season in a nondescript nine-year career.

In fact, the most notable person attached to the team was its public address announcer, a veritable kid, no less: Dan Rather.

Possibly because of the stadium, possibly because of the Colts' poor play, the team only drew 2.4 million fans in its three years at Colt Stadium, an average of around 10,000 a game. When the Astrodome opened in 1965, the team drew 2.15 million that year alone.

"If you talk to anybody who had an occasion to see a game at Colt Stadium, they'd say those two things: the heat and mosquitoes," Smith recalled. "It was hot. It was humid.

"But it was a fun place," he adds.

Smith, the man who helped solve the problem of the Astrodome's dying indoor grass by bringing artificial turf and its brand-name, Astroturf, to the game, talks about the awe that surrounded Houston and the country when the Astrodome was built. And while the building today seem antiquated, it truly was an architectural marvel with an influence that extended beyond sports.

But when you talk about Colt Stadium, you can hear the fondness in his voice. Sure the ballpark did not meet major league standards, but it was a start. And, as he said, fun.

"It was the flair for color and openness," he explained. "It was bright, colorful, like color in the circus. The pennants were flying all over the place, not like a car lot, tastefully done. There was a private club (needed in Texas back then to serve liquor), the Fast Draw Club. All the park attendants and ushers and ticket takers were all costumed. [The park] carried out a western theme. For three years it served the purpose quite well."

As of this writing, the Astros were looking for a new ballpark. Another Astrodome? No, says Smith.

"Baseball is played best when it's played on natural grass in the afternoon," he said.

Not another Colt Stadium? No, laughs Smith: he would like to see a retractable dome this time.

And that, in the world and especially Houston, is no wonder.

WAHCONAH PARK

Wahconah Park was erected during the Wilson administration on a Pittsfield, Massachusetts, site that has been home to baseball since 1892. Wooden and quirky, it is a shade younger than its neighbor two hours to the east, Fenway. This minor league park, unquestionably, was built to last.

It also, unquestionably, was built backward.

With the Berkshire Mountains looming over the center-field fence, Wahconah is baseball's parallel universe, where lefties are northpaws and it's the sun that sometimes can cause game delays.

Unlike almost every other park in America, it is built facing due west. As a result, it's the batters who wear sunglasses in the early innings of night games, games that can be halted early in the New York–Penn League Class A season because of the setting sun. Anybody can have a rain delay; only at Wahconah can a game be interrupted by a perfect summer evening.

"I guess back then they never thought of playing night games," Pittsfield general manager Rick Murphy said of the park constructed in 1919.

The delays are pretty rare, a handful a year, and last about 15 minutes or so. But leave your seat in the second inning for a quick bite to eat, and you could come back to a deserted ballfield.

Almost all other professional open-air ballparks are built facing east or east-northeast. (Sam Lynn Ballpark in Bakersfield, California, and Vince Genna Stadium in Bend, Oregon, are the most notable exceptions, and both have obstructions to block the setting sun. Kindrick Field in Helena, Montana, faces south-southeast, with the sun setting behind first.) This allows the sun to set behind the batter—picture the shadows creeping toward the mound of Yankee Stadium.

Because of the normal eastern configuration, lefties earned the moniker southpaws because their throws would be heading west and their arms would come around from the south side of the mound. Wahconah is the opposite: In the process the park offers vistas of a pretty mountain and prettier sunsets. It's a great view.

Unless you are a batter. Then it can get pretty ugly. Wahconah may be the only ballpark where left-handers are relieved to see a fellow southpaw, er, lefty, on the mound.

Wahconah Park. The foreground shadow at top is one of the fake owls that hang from the rafters to frighten pigeons away (courtesy of *Times Union*, Albany, New York. Copyright, 1996).

"Man, it's tough. With a righty, he's coming right out of the sun," said Tripp Keister, a member of the 1992 Pittsfield Mets. "The hardest part is when it's just starting to set. But once the sun goes down you have a good hitter's background."

But this quirky park doesn't give up hits easily. While the fences in left center (350 feet) and center (374 feet) are certainly reachable, the ball doesn't seem to carry well there, despite the thinner mountain air. And if you are a left-handed hitter who pulls to the gap, forget ever hitting a home run: the power alley in right juts out to 430 feet. If there is a consolation to a hitter battling nature and the outfield, it's that the stands are about as close to the plate as the mound, not leaving much foul ball territory.

It is unknown how much of the original ballpark remains after major renovations in 1941 and 1976; minor league baseball was absent from Pittsfield from 1930 to 1941, and during this Depression era much of the grandstand was used for kindling. But the 5,200-seat park looks much as it did when Lou Gehrig's Hartford team came to town in 1923 to play the Pittsfield Hillies. Fake owls hang from the rafters to keep pigeons away, and area residents sit on back porches to watch the games for free.

Wahconah has been the on-and-off home to five Class A and AA affiliates—the Red Sox, Rangers, Brewers, Cubs, and Mets—as well as other minor league teams such as the Pittsfield Hillies and Electrics. In addition to the visiting Gehrig, many of the game's greats played in Pittsfield on the way to the majors, including Carlton Fisk, Rafael Palmeiro, Mark Grace, and George "Boomer" Scott, who in 1965 won the Eastern League Triple Crown (.319, 25 HR, 95 RBI) for the Pittsfield Red Sox.

"I won the Triple Crown and we won the pennant," Scott said. "That's what got me to the big leagues. I often think of my time in Pittsfield."

In 1989, team officials tried to eradicate the sun delays. The first idea—stringing nylon netting between two light stanchions in center—was abandoned when an intern was blown off his feet trying to put it up. The second suggestion, installing an old drive-in movie screen, also was discarded because of the unsure footing behind the fence on the banks of the Housatonic River. The sun delay will stay, at least until Mother Nature steps in.

"This is a gorgeous park, a perfect minor league park," said team owner and president William Gladstone, a member of the National Baseball Hall of Fame and Museum's board of directors. "There isn't anything I would change."

Wahconah's 15 minutes, or 75 or so years, of fame soon may disappear in the shadows of the large oak trees stationed behind the center-field fence. As the trees along the Housatonic grow, the Wahconah Park sun delay may soon fade to black. What will be left behind is nothing more than an extremely fan-friendly park.

"It's fun to kid about," Gladstone said in the summer of 1994. "But the trees are growing. It's becoming somewhat academic."

And so will set baseball's sun delay.

INDEX